Writer's Digest Handbook of Making Money Freelance Writing

Writer's Digest Handbook of

Making Money Freelance Writing

From the editors of *Writer's Digest* magazine

Amanda L. Boyd
Thomas Clark
Peter Blocksom
Jo Gilbert

WRITER'S DIGEST BOOKS
CINCINNATI, OHIO

The Writer's Digest Handbook of Making Money Freelance Writing. Copyright © 1997 by Writer's Digest Books. Printed and bound in the United States of America. All rights reserved. No part of this book may be reproduced in any form or by any electronic or mechanical means including information storage and retrieval systems without permission in writing from the publisher, except by a reviewer, who may quote brief passages in a review. Published by Writer's Digest Books, an imprint of F&W Publications, Inc., 1507 Dana Avenue, Cincinnati, Ohio 45207. (800) 289-0963. First edition.

Every effort has been made to trace copyright holders. Writer's Digest Books would be interested in hearing from any copyright holders not here acknowledged.

This hardcover edition of *The Writer's Digest Handbook of Making Money Freelance Writing* features a "self-jacket" that eliminates the need for a separate dust jacket. It provides sturdy protection for your book while it saves paper, trees and energy.

Other fine Writer's Digest Books are available from your local bookstore or direct from the publisher.

01 00 99 98 97   5 4 3 2 1

Library of Congress Cataloging-in-Publication Data

   The writer's digest handbook of making money freelance writing / edited by Amanda L. Boyd . . . [et al.].—1st ed.
      p.   cm.
   Includes index.
   ISBN 0-89879-777-2 (alk. paper)
   1. Authorship-Marketing. 2. Freelance journalism. I. Boyd, Amanda. II. Writer's digest (Cincinnati, Ohio)
PN161.W82   1997
808'.02—dc20   96-43403
                                                                    CIP

Edited by Amanda L. Boyd
Production edited by Patrick Souhan
Interior designed by Kathleen DeZarn
Cover designed by Chad Planner

The permissions on page v constitute an extension of this copyright page.

Permissions

About the Authors

Donna Albrecht is the author of four hundred articles and three books, including *Buying a Home When You're Single* (Wiley). She also teaches university writing workshops.

Liza Galin Asher

Lawrence Block wrote about fiction writing for fourteen years in *Writer's Digest*. His columns have been collected in *Telling Lies for a Profit* and *Spider, Spin Me a Web*, both published by William Morrow.

Robert W. Bly is the author of *Direct Mail Profits: How to Get More Leads and Sales by Mail* (Asher-Gallant Press) and *Secrets of a Freelance Writer: How to Earn $85,000 a Year* (Henry Holt).

Sally-Jo Bowman is a full-time freelance writer whose work appears regularly in *Aloha, National Parks* and *Sierra* magazines. She is an adjunct professor of journalism at the University of Oregon.

Linda Brodsky is a freelance copywriter based in Lynbrook, New York.

Robyn Carr is the author of *Practical Tips for Writing Popular Fiction* (Writer's Digest Books) and the psychological thriller *Mind Tryst* (St. Martin's). Her novel *By Right of Arms* won a Romance Writers of America Golden Medallion for best historical novel.

Dana K. Cassell is a full-time writer/editor and the executive director of Cassell Network of Writers.

Larry Chambers worked for sixteen years in the investment management field before starting his writing career. He's on the advisory boards of the *Journal of Investing* and *American Entrepreneur* and is a senior editor for *The Journal of Military Special Operations*. He also has written seven books, and lives in Ojai, California.

David Francis Curran is a freelancer who has written for *Mother Earth News, Woman's Day, Writer's Yearbook* and other periodicals.

Peter H. Desmond of Cambridge, Massachusetts, is an Enrolled Agent (EA) authorized to represent taxpayers before the IRS. A member of The National Writers Union, he has sold articles to various trade magazines and is aiming for the slicks.

Leonard Felder, Ph.D., is a psychologist in Los Angeles whose books include *Making Peace With Yourself, Making Peace With Your Parents* and *The Ten Challenges*.

Russell Galen

Mark Henricks, a full-time freelancer based in New York City, has sold articles to *PC World, Venture, Texas Business, Air Cargo World* and *American City and County.*

Dennis E. Hensley, Ph.D., has been a correspondent for *Writer's Digest* for nineteen years. His twenty-eight books include *The Gift* (Harvest House) and *Writing for Profit* (Thomas Nelson Co.).

Gary A. Hensley is an independent financial consultant in Bay City, Michigan. His articles have appeared in *Shop-Talk, Ophthalmology Management* and *National Public Accountant*, among others.

Ellen Kozak, who practices copyright, publishing and entertainment law in Milwaukee, Wisconsin, is also a published novelist and freelance journalist. Her prize-winning book, *From Pen to Print: The Secrets of Getting Published Successfully*, was published by Henry Holt & Co., which will bring out the second edition of her book, *Every Writer's Guide to Copyright and Publishing Law* later this year.

Dean R. Lambe co-wrote *The Odysseus Solution*, and his short fiction has appeared in *Omni* and *Analog* magazines.

Gary Legwold is a writer living in Minneapolis. He is the author of hundreds of magazine articles on health and fitness and has written two books on Scandinavian heritage: *The Last Word on Lefse* (1992, still in print) and his new book, *The Last Word on Lutefisk* (1996).

Gregg Levoy, author of *This Business of Writing* (Writer's Digest Books) and the forthcoming book *Callings* (Random House), has written for *The New York Times Magazine, Omni, Psychology Today, Vogue, Reader's Digest* and others. He lives in Tucson, Arizona.

Sue Fagalde Lick

Sandy MacDonald is a freelance writer, editor and translator based in Cambridge, Massachusetts. She contributes regularly to *Parenting, Family Circle, Ski, Worth* and many other magazines. She was awarded an NEA Fellowship for Literary Translation in 1989.

James McKechnie has written tax and business articles for *Writer's Digest, Alaska Business Monthly*, and *Southeast Alaska Business Journal.*

Mandy Matson is a freelancer whose articles have appeared in *Reader's Digest, Parade, Health* and others. She is the author of *Using Your Camcorder* (Amphoto).

James Morgan has been editorial director of *Southern* magazine and a former articles editor for *Playboy.*

Hank Nuwer is a visiting professor of journalism at the University of Richmond.

Loriann Hoff Oberlin is the author of *Writing for Money* (Writer's Digest Books) and contributes to national magazines. She also produces newsletters and public relations materials for nonprofit and corporate clients in Pittsburgh, Pennsylvania.

Carl and **Ann Purcell,** a husband and wife team based in Virginia, have published their articles and photos in *Travel/Holiday, Chevron USA Odyssey, Parade* and elsewhere.

Tana Reiff is a writer, editor and desktop publisher in Lancaster, Pennsylvania. She is the author of more than eighty titles for adolescent and adult new readers.

Cindy Robertson

Dick Schaaf is a Minnesota-based business writer and speaker. Since co-authoring *The Service Edge* (NAL Books), he has revisited America's pacesetting service providers for a new book, *Keeping the Edge* (Dutton), chosen one of the best business books of 1995 by Soundview Executive Book Summaries and *Library Journal.* Schaaf served as special projects editor for *Training* magazine and as the Twin Cities correspondent for PBS's *The Nightly Business Report.* He speaks frequently to business and professional groups on service issues.

Norman Schreiber has written for *Smithsonian, Village Voice, Travel & Leisure* and other national publications.

Michael H. Sedge lives and writes in Naples, Italy, where he sells and resells nearly 120 articles a year to editors at Silver Kris (Singapore), R&R (Germany) and Peak (Hong Kong), among others. He's the author of *Commercialization of the Oceans* (Franklin Watts).

Art Spikol, a former *Writer's Digest* columnist, now runs Art Spikol and Associates.

Jay Stuller is intimately familiar with the audiences of dozens of national magazines, including *Smithsonian, Audubon* and *Reader's Digest.*

Paul M. Thompson is a full-time business writer for a Detroit-area marketing communications agency. He's written speeches, videos, training material, brochures and direct mail, primarily for the automotive industry.

John M. Wilson is a widely-published freelance journalist and author of *The Complete Guide to Magazine Article Writing* (Writer's Digest Books). He is also the author of Doubleday's Benjamin Justice Mystery Series.

Tom Yates has been writing for about eighteen years and currently serves as vehicle editor for *Law & Order Magazine.* His articles have also appeared in the *Detroit Free Press,* the *Detroit News* and *Popular Mechanics.*

Howard G. Zaharoff's publishing credits include articles on copyright and computer law for *The Boston Globe, Computer World* and *Software Magazine.*

Table of Contents

SECTION III:

The Freelancer's Lifestyle

Introduction

When you work for *Writer's Digest*, you answer a lot of questions. Free-lance writers of every specialization and skill level call and write to ask us for advice and referrals and information. But some of the most often asked questions have nothing to do with the craft of writing. I mean, the act of arranging words on paper. This really isn't strange. These questions deal with everything from "How do I negotiate with an editor?" (even, "*Can* I negotiate with an editor?") to "How do I break into a market I've never written for?" to "How much can I expect to make writing?" In short, these writers want to know about the *business* of freelancing.

You hold in your hands our best answers to those questions (and hundreds more).

In these pages, you won't find advice on building stronger characters or writing snappy dialogue. You *will* find the best advice *Writer's Digest* has to offer on conducting yourself as a freelancer: tips on keeping concise tax records, negotiating with editors, protecting your copyrights, researching new markets, setting up a space to write in and deciding when—or if—to quit your day job. It's valuable—even vital—information that your creative writing teacher never thought to tell you (even though it's much more important than understanding the motivation of your hero's sidekick).

To make it easy for you to find the information you need, we've separated this book into three sections: Conducting the Freelance Business, Freelance Opportunities and The Freelancer's Lifestyle. In Conducting the Freelance Business, we look at how to operate as a freelancer. To be successful, you must make freelancing your business. That means you have to think about how much you're going to charge, what receipts you need to save for tax time and how to get your money (or *more* money) from a publisher. And to protect your assets, you need to know your rights—copyrights, specifically.

In Freelance Opportunities, we turn to the business of selling what you write—the freelancer's number one objective. Smart freelancers always keep an eye out for new opportunities. But simply adding new markets to your sales list isn't your only answer. There are other free-lance services that can add to your résumé—and your bank account.

In the final section, The Freelancer's Lifestyle, are tips for dealing with freelancing's impact on your life. For most of us, this isn't a nine to five job. (Although it *can* be . . . and we explain that.) Successful freelancing means finding the time to write, a place to write and a way to get the writing done.

So many questions. If only we could get this book to answer the phone. . . .

Amanda Boyd
Assistant Editor
Writer's Digest magazine

Conducting the Freelance Business

How to Keep the Money Coming

BY TANA REIFF

Writing for money is surely at the top of the list of Unreliable Sources of Income. One day you're kissing a fat royalty check and the next you're kicking yourself for writing that "on-spec" article that got the guillotine. Yet, there are ways to overcome that problem—ways to keep the cash flowing just about as regularly as the business allows.

To keep the money coming, you must keep the *work* coming, but there's more to it than that. For example, the royalty check is a product not only of your writing success but also of your business savvy in getting involved in a project with high income potential. The dead duck you wrote on spec can be blamed at least as much on your choosing to write on speculation as on the work's quality.

Most writers operate as one-person businesses. Even so, such businesses encompass virtually all the operational elements of a large corporation. Like that of a big company, a freelance writer's income flow depends on the activity and interaction of five basic departments: Planning, Marketing, Production, Accounting and Personnel. The difference between writer and corporation lies in scale, of course, but also in the fact that the writer alone wears all the departmental hats.

To keep the freelance-writing business going, then—to keep the money coming—you as writer/president/CEO must be sure each of these five departments does its job.

THE PLANNING DEPARTMENT

Before you drift through another year, map out the exact business of your business. Examine not only the types of writing you plan to do (copywriting, fiction, magazine articles, etc.), but also the types of "income schedules" your projects will produce (one-time, quick turn-around payments; long-term payments; regular [e.g., monthly] payments; etc.). If you must, consider altering either or both to improve cash flow, in these ways:

Diversify the types of writing you do. Unless you have no commercial intentions whatsoever—bless your heart—you will probably need to leverage your talents into several specialties if you want to get paid commensurate with the time you spend writing. A discouragingly low number of people make a respectable living writing *only* novels or short stories or magazine nonfiction. So to make ends meet, a lot of writers diversify. Even F. Scott Fitzgerald branched out into screenwriting.

Diversification is not degradation if you like what you're writing. Often, lots of unknowns like me make money regularly because we're willing to expand our focus and try different writing projects.

I began as an adult basic education reading and English teacher. As part of that job, I advised the student newspaper, produced publicity brochures for the school, taught and critiqued student writing, and helped students write résumés. A few months into my teaching, I realized that absolutely no easy-reading fiction for beginning adult readers was available, so I wrote some little books myself and used them with my students.

Working with the student newspaper spurred me to apply for a federal grant project to produce a little magazine for adult basic education students. From that project, I learned so much about publications that I now write articles for national magazines, write and produce brochures and newsletters for local businesses, and continue to receive grants to produce adult basic education public relations and how-to projects. Drawn from my experiences teaching writing and grammar, I wrote a basic writing course for adults, I copyedit articles for two computer magazines, and run a résumé and letter service. By recognizing a market for low-reading-level fiction, I got seven novelettes published. Then the same publisher asked me to write eight workbooks for another project, and a second set of seven novelettes has been released. And from all the things I've mentioned, I could start another list of off-shoots.

But I don't do *everything*. I do not, for one, have the personality or inclination to write most kinds of advertising copy, so that is not on my list of specialties.

To parlay your talents into new areas, list everything you've read in the past week (newspaper articles, a brochure at the bank, instructions for your new oil lamp, *anything*), then determine what *you* could write if you had the chance. Here are some general writing categories from which you might choose your specialties according to your interests, experience and talents:

Advertising copy; annual reports; audiovisual scripts; books (fiction and nonfiction); brochures (for products or services); catalogs; children's books; columns; comedy; copyediting; educational/training materials; magazine or newspaper feature articles; fundraising solicitations; ghost-writing; greeting cards; handbooks (e.g., for specific organizations); humor; indexing; lecturing; manuals (for software, technical equipment operation, trouble-shooting, etc.); newsletters; package labels; poetry; photography (with or without your writing); press releases; proposals (for grants, business ventures, etc.); public relations materials; radio commercials; résumés; reports (e.g., for business consultants); reviews (of books, movies, plays, dance); sales letters; short stories; speeches; sports writing (e.g., as a stringer for a local newspaper); teaching creative writing (or how to sell writing), journalism, poetry, technical writing; television documentary scripts (e.g., for area PBS station); travel writing.

When you diversify, however, maintain creative balance. If you started as a poet, don't stop writing poetry. Even if you never sell a poem, you can stay in tune with your best artistry, and perhaps apply your talent for poetic prose to your paying projects. You'll be a better writer for the effort. You'll also maintain the love of writing that initiated your desire to make money at it.

Diversify the kinds of projects you write, based on how regularly, and when, payments are made (this is what I meant by "income schedule"). I like to have a combination of long-term projects, periodic commitments and short-term jobs on my desk at all times. Meshing these fills in my time—and my cash flow—quite well.

An example of a *long-term project* is my annual grant work. Grants projects assure me income for a year at a clip. Book work is another example—the payment won't be immediate, so you can consider yourself as investing in the future. If the book succeeds, the payment will be both substantial (the advance), then regular (royalties).

My *periodic (and seasonal) commitments* include editing bimonthly computer magazines, producing quarterly newsletters for two businesses, and writing spring sales letters for an amusement park.

Another periodic moneymaker is writing a column. This is not an easy sell, but if you have a specialty, you have a crack at it. I know a man who writes monthly columns on wildlife management for two state outdoors magazines, and his chances for going national are excellent.

Also, when doing public relations work, try to be placed on a retainer. A woman I know who edits a newsletter for a state legal defense agency gets a check every month even though the agency supplies her with copy irregularly.

Short-term projects include brochures, which may be spread out over a month or more, and résumés, which can be completed, from interview to printing, in a week or two.

I also like to have at least one magazine article in progress at all times, but this is too undependable a source of income to ink into the schedule. Because their value as a solid return on time investment is rather shaky, articles are practically in their own class, though you can overcome that problem by learning to squeeze the last dime out of every article you do. While you're still in the planning stages, design projects to have built-in resale value or "extension value." When I write for a regional business newspaper, I try to land assignments on topics that are general enough to resell elsewhere. I've resold articles on office condos, signs and hiring freelance advertising services. A hot topic can sell more than once, either in its original form or with a new angle for a different market. Sell only first rights to the first publisher, explore potential secondary outlets and syndicates willing to purchase reprint rights (check *Writer's Market*), then expend a minimum of time and money to revise, duplicate and mail your work. (Self-syndication is an ideal application of computer-generated form letters.)

Working a topic from several angles is genius. First, you need the right topic. I have a friend who is a lawyer by vocation and a race car driver by avocation. To promote his racing career, he writes articles for racing magazines. In the course of researching an article, he met a sports psychologist. What a great topic for multiple angles! He's starting with an article on mentally preparing for a race. After that, he'll apply mental preparation to virtually any sport he knows.

Be willing to take chances. Not *wild* chances—don't buy "futures" in someone's harebrained scheme, such as when a small publisher offers you nothing up front and 10 percent of proceeds that can't possibly add up to the time you would have to invest. But the occasional on-spec article could open up a new market. And even if you're not usually a book writer, a royalty-paying project with a reputable publisher can be worth the risk. When I wrote those seven little fiction paperbacks for an educational publisher, I never dreamed how lucrative the equivalent of two months' work could be. And my new series practically guaranteed me long-term income.

You can also extend your own skills: Learn enough about graphic design and production, printing and photography to know how to sub-contract services that augment your writing. Or offer corollary services yourself if you really develop a talent.

THE MARKETING DEPARTMENT

Now that you know what you're selling, how will you sell it?

Identify your markets: the most likely publishers, the most appropriate magazines, the businesses with whom you'd feel most comfortable working.

Space doesn't allow me to give a detailed strategy for searching out sources, but I can offer these tips:

- Look to both local and national markets.
- Ask your librarian for directories that will aid in your search, from *Writer's Market* to *The Standard Directory of Advertisers*.
- Don't overlook your local yellow pages.
- Turn to both commercial and nonprofit organizations as potential clients.
- Ask current clients for recommendations for potential clients who might need similar work.
- Be creative in your search—and consider any company, organization, magazine, shop or individual that must communicate with another segment of the world as a potential client.

Aim direct proposals at your potential markets. One of the beauties of being a writer is that you can do much of your selling *in writing.* Learn to write selling proposals—for books, articles, grants, business writing projects, whatever. Keep as many proposals as possible in circulation, and recycle the rejections right away.

Increase your general visibility, particularly among local markets. To do this:

- Advertise. Buy a yellow pages listing.
- Put your name on promotional items such as pens and calendars that you can distribute to people and get your name around. Check out an advertising specialties catalog and choose from the array of trinkets and gadgets and even *useful* items on which to have your name imprinted. The calendars I designed and which I give to anyone who walks into my office have not only brought in repeat business, such as résumé updates, but also clients' friends in need of a brochure or

newsletter. Promotional items can also advertise your services at other locations. I deliver my calendars to graphics suppliers with whom I do business: the place that makes my offset plates for printing, my typesetters, my graphic artists, my printers. Their clients, who could also be my clients, see the calendar hanging on the wall twelve months of the year.

- Be creative. One unusual way I gained visibility was to join a barter club, which has been a source of income I simply wouldn't have had otherwise. Members of the club are eager to spend their trade credits, and *must* spend them on products and services offered within the exchange. So I get requests for brochures and copyediting from a jeweler, a pharmacy and a carpet store—businesses that wouldn't even consider a writer who isn't a member. I also do the club's newsletter.

- Establish yourself as an expert in one of your writing specialties. I was writing résumés as a business before anyone else in my small city, so when the public library needed a leader for a seminar on résumés, they called me. One of the newspapers did a feature article on my seminar. The library didn't pay me, but I probably got five hundred dollars worth of business out of that one event. One woman saved the newspaper article and called me for a résumé four years later! I've since done résumé seminars for several clubs and the YWCA.

- Plan a short course or seminar related to one of your specialties. Then find an outlet—a community college, a Boys Club, the chamber of commerce, an advertising association. Even if you get paid little or nothing, there's promotional value in your effort.

- Combine these techniques. One writer friend of mine applied several brilliant marketing principles in an effort to end a mid-winter cash drought. The experience turned into an excellent example of how one thing leads to another. First, for a measly $100 he wrote a survey article on area advertising agencies for the business supplement of a daily newspaper. Researching the article brought him into contact with important people in every agency in town. The day after a brief interview, the president of one of the larger agencies called my friend to ask if he could write an annual report on short notice. When the ad agency article appeared, the publisher of a county farming newspaper called my friend and offered him the editor's job.

Maintain already-established contacts. For example, write a congratulatory letter to a one-shot client: "Your travel brochure turned out great. I hope we can work together on copy for another project in the future." If the client liked your work, chances are good that he won't turn to someone else next time he needs a writer.

THE PRODUCTION DEPARTMENT

To sell consistently and profitably, you must practice efficient production methods. Take these steps:

Take control of your "production schedule" with time management. It's always better to have a bit too much work than not enough. But if you don't properly coordinate that work, you can feel like a Rube Goldberg machine, levers and gears and moving parts flying in all directions.

Consider how you'll juggle your projects. What major projects can you plan for the next year or so? What smaller projects (résumés, sales letters, copyediting) can you fill in with? This is difficult. For instance, you could send out a number of queries in March to line up work for the summer. If you're lucky, you'll get go-aheads on everything by May. More likely, you'll get one or two assignments for the summer while the other queries get rejected and resubmitted or, worse, sit on some editor's desk with no response till September.

Though writing is a business, it's not the same as, say, the plastics industry. The plastics maker can project the number of units he can feasibly sell over the next year. The best you can do is plan larger projects in advance as specifically as foresight allows, pursue your regular specialties as you go along, then be prepared to work efficiently when new go-aheads do come through.

Begin your time-management planning by analyzing your best working times of day. I *try* to bunch small tasks in the morning, when my powers of concentration are not at their peak and when the phone interrupts most frequently. My afternoons are best for buckling down to a bigger project when I have three or four hours to devote to it. This plan runs slightly off course when a client walks in unexpectedly at three o'clock or a family member needs immediate attention, but overall it works better than just grabbing at whatever project I'm in the mood for. (I admit to succumbing to a mood compulsion now and then if I think it will benefit productivity.)

If you are a part-time writer, your day may not be as adjustable. When you hold an outside job or spend a large portion of your life with children, you're tempted to cram thirty-five words of writing into every minuscule time crevice. Let me suggest a more productive method. Use small time gaps only for the quickest phone calls, for mindless tasks such as photocopying and mailing, or for listing tasks to be worked on later. Set aside your largest available time chunks for absorbing yourself in a project. That way, you can interview a subject, organize your notes and outline your writing while aboard the same train of thought. Three or four hours of concentration in one block produces much more than five or six hours of stolen moments.

As you work, observe *how* you are working. When interviewing, for example, ask only the questions to which you need answers, and steer the person away from tangential conversation—though an occasional digression can produce some sterling quotes or lead your writing in a direction you may not have anticipated. Interviewees can be terribly interesting to chat with, but for time's sake, try to keep your conversation germane.

By observing how you work, you can take control of the time you spend on both short-term projects such as a single interview and long-term projects such as grant work. Grant application procedures require that I submit a timeline for the year, which keeps me on a schedule. I must estimate the number of hours each project will consume and budget my fee accordingly. The first few years I under- or over-estimated the time, but by keeping time logs, I can now estimate to within plus or minus five hours. That's a fairly precise tolerance on a two hundred-hour project. Then breaking down a big project into manageable steps helps me stay on track for that project while seeing where I can fill in other work.

Use efficient production tools. Anyone serious about selling writing must maximize equipment usage. For my résumé service, I store each résumé on disk. This encourages people to return for updates because it's less expensive for them and for me. And because my word processing software has a mail-merge feature, I offer my résumé clients form letter service for sending the same cover letter to a batch of employers. I don't advertise the letter service broadly because I don't want to become a secretarial service, but it's an easy money-maker and a natural extension of the résumé business.

The right equipment can also make you more accessible to your markets. When the answer's *yes*, editors and clients often use the phone to tell you so. That's one good reason that, despite its resemblance to an uninvited guest, a good telephone within arm's reach is essential. An automatic dialing feature is a time-saver, too. And break down and buy an answering machine or subscribe to voice mail through your local phone company. No legitimate business can afford to let phone calls go unanswered.

Set up an appropriate workspace. Perhaps that spare bedroom will suffice as your office. But if you meet frequently with clients, you might need an office away from home. Working under a roof other than the one under which you live can be a boon to productivity, more than compensating for the extra overhead a rented office entails. Walk-in business, which just doesn't happen at home, helps assure a steadier flow of commercial work.

No matter where you work, set aside a separate, organized, tax deductible area where paper flow, communication, storage and the level of noise are all under your control.

Maintain high product quality. The last important function of the Production Department is quality control. Efficiency can mean cutting corners, but make sure you're not cutting the *wrong* corners. People won't continue to pay for your work if it's not worth paying for. It's difficult to be your own monitor, but you must do it. To reinforce quality assurance, work out a deal with a writer friend to review each other's work.

Revise as much as necessary, but know when it's time to stop. I've found that one of the few pitfalls of a word processor is that it's so easy to keep making changes. I had to learn to recognize when a piece of work was *finished.*

Just remember at all times: *Every project that leaves your office should be the best it can be.* If it's not, you have an inferior product, and businesses that produce inferior products won't sustain steady revenues.

THE ACCOUNTING DEPARTMENT

For a person who likes to play with words, can there be a bigger anathema than number crunching? Yes, you must learn the basics of bookkeeping, billing and all the other accounting functions of business. Here's how to get your accounting department to work most efficiently for you.

Get an accountant to set up an easy general ledger system for you to manage. I let my accountant handle all tax-related matters, especially filing returns; it almost always pays off.

Set pricing policies. Standard book and magazine agreements limit your control, but here are two ways to ensure you're receiving adequate remuneration:

- Negotiate payment, reimbursement for expenses and rights being sold, which is possible more often than you may realize.
- When you've become marketable enough, stop accepting work that pays beneath your self-imposed minimum. If you seek more of a thrill than seeing your name in print, don't sell yourself short.

You have greater pricing control for your local clientele. You can estimate your total fee in advance based on your hourly rate. To figure a fair rate, estimate how much you'd be worth in a comparable salaried position (if you're a part-time writer, reduce that figure proportionately) and add at least 20 percent for benefits, another 20 to 30 percent for overhead, and perhaps yet another 5 percent for profit on capital investments in your business. Divide the total by the number of hours you can realistically work in a year. (Unless you are way above average, you will *not* be able to bill out more than twenty or thirty hours per week, and you won't work more than forty-eight or fifty full weeks.) Also consider what the market will bear in your area: If other writers in your town are working for $35 an hour and you're charging $10, you're either saying you're not worth much or you're underselling for no good reason. Then again, your local market may not bear as high a rate as you'd like to make. If that's the case, don't price yourself out of the market unless you're that much better than everyone else. Or, look for work farther from home. (For a more detailed formula, see "How to Set Your Rates" on page 91.)

Another good source to setting your rates is *The National Writer's Union Guide to Freelance Rates and Standard Practices.*

Review your pricing periodically. You'll probably not earn as much as the president of GM, but if you worked hard all year and got paid like a fast-food hamburger flipper, something's wrong. Fix it. Up your rate, cut expenses, shoot for higher paying markets, but make what you're worth.

Make sure your customers pay the bills. Send an invoice to clients you've done job work for (you can also use invoices to prod payment from slow-paying magazines). At a seminar I once attended on accounting for small businesses, the accountant in charge asked us, "When's the best time to bill?" Attendees offered several answers: "Once a week." "Once a month." "Every other Friday." I raised my hand and said, "At the time of service." "That's the best time of all . . . if you can swing it," said the accountant. For many kinds of writing, you *can* swing it. Using a professional-looking invoice form imprinted with your name, present the bill with the completed work, dated that day and, if possible, receive payment on the spot. However, in many circles, "net thirty days" remains standard, though in reality that often means thrity-five days or forty-three days or sometimes much longer. When writing for magazines, you encounter two main choices, neither of which is yours: payment on acceptance, which often means several months after you've mailed the manuscript, or payment on publication, which can drag out long after the piece has been accepted. The latter may be worth avoiding altogether.

If you don't receive payment according to the agreed upon terms, don't be shy about taking action. On day thirty-one of a net thirty days invoice it's time for a reminder. This can be merely a copy of the bill with a note on it. And if the policy is stated on the invoice, you can attach a service charge for overdue bills (check your state's usury laws for the maximum charge, and make sure you state this policy on the invoice). If you don't get paid after sixty days, your client deserves a dunning notice, something along the lines of "Your account is delinquent. Please pay immediately to avoid collection efforts." If you *still* don't get paid, the dunning message would say, "Must this account be turned over to my attorney? Immediate payment is requested within ten days." Then follow through on your threat. If an assertive phone call doesn't produce results, file a suit in small claims court, for which you don't need an attorney. If you win—and the law is almost certainly on your side—your client will be liable for the full amount owed plus court costs.

You won't collect on every account, but there's no question that persistence can make the difference between collection and nonpayment. The same publication owed another freelancer and me each six hundred dollars. I pursued the matter; the other writer did not. The ordeal cost me at least six hundred dollars worth of sanity, but after six months I did get paid. The other writer never did. When it comes to accounts payable, there are too many folks for whom the saying "ignore it and it will go away" is a motto. As the payee, don't stay out of sight or you'll surely end up out of mind—theirs and yours—*and* out of your money.

THE PERSONNEL DEPARTMENT

A big obstacle to a decent, reliable writing income is that you are the sole staff. If me, myself and I don't show up for work, or aren't feeling well, or are emotionally fried, none of us gets paid. As head of the

Personnel Department, you must work to maintain a healthy, rested, no-excuses work force.

But that's not enough. Your staff doesn't press out a product from a mold; rather, the bulk of the work must be constantly invented. To get the refueling creativity demands, your staff needs continuing contact with the rest of the world. To grow professionally, get some in-service training: socialize, go on trips, stay in touch with the humanity that exists beyond your office door. And always stay on top of the ever-changing markets for your work. Attend conferences related to your specialty areas, too.

But you may have to expand more than yourself—you may have to expand the staff size. When you get involved with work other than straight writing, your business may need to work with subcontractors, collaborators or even employees. I subcontract a graphic artist and typesetter when a writing project calls for design. I mark up the cost of these services (that is, I charge my client for actual cost plus a percentage) to compensate for my time in dealing with them. Whatever you do, don't *lose* money on subcontractors. You're offering more than writing services and should be paid more.

Working with a collaborator can be a wonderfully synergistic relationship. By writing money articles with a financial planner, my research is done for me and I'm selling articles on subjects I could never write by myself. And she's always ready with a new idea because she observes common problems among her clients—typical financial problems that people all over the country share.

I hired a part-time assistant when I realized I was overworked with the kinds of tasks that someone with less experience could be doing. (When is it time to hire someone? For me, that realization came with the help of a free business counselor from SCORE, the Service Corps of Retired Executives, who asked me the core question, "What would *you* be doing while your assistant does what you used to do?") When I have an assistant, which isn't always, that person types, runs errands and even does some everyday writing and editing for me. This frees me to work on the more substantial, better paying projects. And, because I bill out her time at a higher rate than I pay her, I am compensated for the space in which she works, the equipment I purchased for her use, and the time it takes to manage an employee. What's more, if I have to be out of the office, my business is still generating income. Yes, having an employee can complicate matters, but it can also result in fewer interruptions and ready help when needed. My accountant handles the payroll tax returns that are due every quarter.

INTERDEPARTMENTAL RELATIONS

Now and then, there will still be a blank day on your calendar, but when all the departments are in gear, you won't just give up and go fishing. Slow times are marketing times: Get a query in the mail, court a new client, analyze your general ledger to determine your most profitable sources of income. If the Planning Department has planned, if the Marketing Department has sold, and if the Personnel Department has provided a sharp staff, the Production Department will be back in full swing in no time—and the Accounting Department will be busily processing a flowing stream of receivables. Even the company president will be pleased.

FOUR TIPS FOR BEGINNING FREELANCERS

BY LIZA GALIN ASHER

It's inevitable. As a beginning freelancer, you're going to make errors. But remembering these tips will keep you moving in the right direction.

- *Writing is a business.* Freelancers are salespeople; ideas are their products. Creativity and talent do count, but if you're timid about promoting yourself, your prose will remain unprinted. You may even find that you expend more time and energy on brainstorming, researching ideas and preparing queries than writing articles themselves. But as you become a more proficient salesperson and writer, you'll need to do less selling.

- *Think small and local.* Your goal is to get published, not to write a cover story for *Vanity Fair*. Neighborhood newspapers are good training grounds, as are trade newspapers and magazines. Go ahead and pursue those ideas that you believe are perfect for the nationals, but know you'll probably have to work your way up.

- *Get the most out of what you write.* You can often generate more than one article from an idea. The information for an article I wrote about alternative cancer treatment centers also spawned a profile of one of the center's physicians. Rework old pieces by updating them or taking a new angle. Submit rejected manuscripts to other publications.

- *Your first big sale is a significant event,* but it's not a signal to quit your day job. There can be quite a bit of lag time between the first and second sale. A good time to consider going full-time is when your freelancing income equals at least 50 percent of your day job's salary.

Stalking the
Business Client

BY PAUL M. THOMPSON

To be a successful writer, you must be a successful business-person yourself, and that means being able to find and develop customers. Indeed, writing may be the easiest part of your job. Finding customers who are able and willing to give you steady business isn't easy, but once you have a base of clients, you have what it takes to build a business.

There are two common sources of business writing clients: direct contact and agency referral. Direct clients are those you pursue and work with on your own. Usually, these are smaller businesses that don't have in-house writers or in-house advertising agencies. They are probably the most likely market for writers who don't live in metropolitan areas. However, there are small businesses in big cities, too, and you can approach these clients directly.

The other primary source of business writing assignments is an agency that might specialize in advertising, public relations, communications or marketing services. Although these organizations usually have staff writers, they often supplement their in-house efforts with freelancers. They may, for example, have specialized assignments that can't be handled by staff writers, or (more often) they may face a workload that the in-house people can't handle. Yet the agency might not have enough additional work to justify hiring a full-time writer. Because of this, agencies find it cost-effective to hire freelancers for short-term assignments.

THE KEY TO FINDING CLIENTS
Finding writing clients is no different from finding any kind of business customer. You must be an aggressive and persistent salesperson, working constantly to get your name (and your reputation as a writer) in front of the widest possible audience. The key to success is *net-*

working. Consider your friends, co-workers, neighbors and civic contacts for a start. Make sure these people know you're a writer looking for assignments. Who's to say your Uncle Harry doesn't work with a small-business owner who needs some help with his advertising? Keep your name (as a writer) in front of as many people as possible.

Of course, Uncle Harry can only take you so far. You'll have more success if you target the people in your own areas of expertise. That means becoming involved with professional and trade groups, and staying current with local and national trade publications. The more personal contacts you can develop in your area of business, the more success you'll have. So, if you want to write for the computer industry, for example, find local user groups who will appreciate your knowledge.

LOOK PROFESSIONAL

If you're serious about writing for businesses, you must look professional. That means business cards and stationery. No one will take you seriously unless you take yourself seriously. Often, the first contact you make will be through the mail, so your letterhead *is* your first impression. The cost of a supply of stationery and business cards is a small price to pay to get your foot in the door.

PERSONAL CONTACT

Though mail may be the only way to open some doors, you should do all you can to make in-person contact with potential clients. People tend to remember faces, not phone calls or mail, and letters all too often end up buried in forgotten file folders. An in-person meeting, whether with a client or agency creative director, gives you a chance to make a personal impression and *sell* yourself.

Getting that in-person meeting won't always be easy, especially if you're making a cold call on someone who has no idea who you are. In that case, your first step should be a letter—no more than one page, and (of course) written as well as you can write it. Just as a query letter to a magazine editor requires some advance research (the magazine's audience, the kinds of articles recently run, etc.), this introductory letter should also target its recipient. It should:

- Establish your writing credentials.
- Show how you can meet a particular need of the client/agency.
- Describe your previous work in this field (possibly with samples).

- Mention references (if appropriate).
- Ask for an in-person meeting.
- Indicate when you'll follow up with a telephone call.

Of course, no one is going to hire you based on such a letter, but it may help you to get your foot in the door.

You're not likely to get an assignment based on one meeting, either, so follow-up is important. Make regular phone calls to stay in touch (but *don't* be obnoxious or pestering—call no more than once a month, or make a judgment based on the client's receptiveness). If you can't find a suitable rationale for a follow-up letter, use your imagination. Last Thanksgiving I got a card from a writer with a turkey on the front saying "gobble, gobble, gobble, etc." I opened the card and it said "I wrote that!" The card didn't bring that writer an assignment, but it did help me keep his name in mind.

BUILDING A CLIENT BASE

One of the fundamental principles of business is that it's easier to get business from customers you already have than to find new customers. Once you have a stable of clients, it pays to develop as much business as you can from them. Look for ways to create follow-up assignments— things your client may not think of. For example, perhaps you've written a customer brochure for a new product. Are retail salespeople familiar with the product? Will they need an introductory piece? Perhaps they'd profit from full-scale training with a booklet and video. Is a news release appropriate for the product? Direct mail? A technician repair manual? Is a stockholder communication appropriate?

You can also use your success with one client to find additional customers. The best reference you can have is a satisfied customer. Ask your clients if you can use their names as references. You might even ask them to spread your name around (they'll usually agree). Show finished samples of your work to other potential customers (providing you don't disclose any proprietary information—you must protect paying clients). If a project worked well for one business, chances are you can find competing clients who have similar needs.

You'll have to decide, however, whether you can ethically work for your clients' competitors. If your client demands exclusivity, agree *only* if he or she can offer sufficient business to keep you from needing to go elsewhere.

A DOZEN TIPS FOR FINDING CLIENTS

Volunteer to write a civic/charity newsletter. Many organizations have newsletters, and many that don't would like to. If you're a beginner, writing a newsletter offers you portfolio material, valuable experience and excellent contacts. Most civic organizations have influential executives on their boards, and these people are often businesspeople with writing needs, people you can impress by producing an organization newsletter. Some such organizations may even be able to pay you for writing/editing a newsletter, allowing you to increase your income and your list of potential clients.

Introduce yourself to a business printer. Small businesses with publication needs usually work with local printers. Such a printer will know not only who needs to print what, but which businesses need writers. Taking a printer to lunch could be one of the best investments you make. It may give you personal entrée to several potential clients, and it can do so through personal introduction, eliminating the dreaded cold call.

Having a relationship with a printer makes good business sense from other angles, as well. You may get clients who want you to be their one-stop source for writing, editing and printing. Knowing you can trust a printer to handle your deadlines gives you the ability to sell yourself as an all-around communications resource.

Take a potential client to lunch. Even better than a one-on-one interview is a lunch. Any client will appreciate the gesture. Plus, a luncheon meeting gives you a chance to show your personality and develop a real relationship. Lunch, dinner, drinks or even a social event can be used to cement a relationship. Most businesspeople entertain clients—why shouldn't you? And doing so is usually tax deductible.

Send relevant industry information to clients. Look for any excuse to stay in touch with a client. If you find an article that refers to something the client is working on, send it along with an "FYI" note. This keeps your name in front of the client and shows you're thinking of his or her interests. Such information doesn't even have to be business-related; maybe it deals with your client's hobby. Whatever it is, it shows you understand your client.

Look for bad writing. This can be especially productive in smaller markets, where clients often do their own writing. If you see a poorly written newspaper advertisement, or a brochure or mailing that isn't put together as well as it could be, look at it as an opportunity for you to help. Don't, however, just show the client how you can improve the communication—show how the improvement will boost sales, improve productivity, or otherwise positively influence the bottom line. Be sure, too, that you're diplomatic in your approach. After all, the client may have written it, and may consider himself or herself the next Hemingway!

List yourself in the yellow pages. How do *you* find a service when you don't know where else to look? Small businesses may start with the yellow pages, too. A display ad will be most effective, but these are usually expensive. Even a simple listing will get you noticed. In smaller markets, you may be the *only* writer listed. You might consider placing a listing under more than one heading depending on your specialty (such as "Writers," "Communications Consultants," "Brochures," etc.).

Join a business communications organization. Besides becoming involved in civic groups and trade organizations, consider joining an organization for business communicators. Most large cities have one or more groups catering to people in marketing communications. These organizations provide fertile grounds for meaningful networking. The Public Relations Society of America (3rd Floor, 33 Irving Place, New York, NY 10003) and the International Association of Business Communicators (Suite 600, One Hallidie Plaza, San Francisco, CA 94102) are two of the best known business communications organizations. Local groups may also exist in your city.

Focus on company departments that need writing. In most corporations virtually all writing needs are centered in a handful of departments. Public Relations (or Corporate Communications) needs writers for internal and external audiences and, like outside agencies, they may have more writing than the staff can handle. The Personnel Department (Human Resources) also needs training material. This can include print, audio, video or a combination of the three.

Establish contact with the local media. Radio, television and newspapers deal with advertisers and advertising agencies, and if you develop contacts with the media, you may be able to use these to establish secondary contacts with potential clients. An ad salesperson for a local radio station occasionally may have to write copy for small businesses. That salesperson may know who most needs writing help and would be willing to pay for your services.

Establish contact with your local chamber of commerce. The chamber of commerce is probably the best single means of getting your name in front of businesspeople. By becoming involved in chamber activities, you can get to know the movers and shakers in your business community. The chamber is a prime field for serious networking.

Put an ad in a trade publication. Every industry has its "bible," a magazine or newsletter that *everyone* in the business reads. What better way could there be to reach your target audience? Display ads can be expensive, but most of these publications have very reasonable classified sections. If it's a regional publication, so much the better.

Teach a writing course. Most community colleges or night schools offer (or would like to offer) courses for people who want to either improve their writing or work on a specific kind of writing (such as business writing). It usually doesn't take extensive credentials to teach such courses once or twice a week for a few months. Doing so will give you an additional source of income, provide excellent credentials for your portfolio *and* give you one more set of contacts for new business.

Finding business writing clients is the same as finding any kind of customers. You must have a *marketable service* (good writing *and* a knowledge of the client's business), you've got to be good at *selling yourself*, you must be *persistent* and you can't be discouraged by the word *no*.

The Care and Feeding of Clients

BY PAUL M. THOMPSON

Writing for a client is tougher than writing for an editor. While editors want to sell magazines or books, a client might have any number of motivations: He might need to advertise a product, publicize a service, train employees, sell directly to the public or accomplish any of the other goals that can be served by good writing.

There's another crucial difference between editors and clients: While editors make their living using the written word, writing is often far down the list of a client's talents. And though some clients may see themselves as great writers (especially when they edit *your* copy), few really understand the writing process.

And that's good, because it creates a demand for freelance writers like you. The following tips can help you increase your market value to clients, and thus bring you more assignments.

Be a consultant first, a writer second. If all you do is put your customer's words into literate prose, you're not giving that client much value. However, if you really understand his or her business and can help it achieve its goals through effective communication, then you're really part of the client's team.

Get to know as much as you can about your customer's business. You should know how the industry works, what your client sells, who buys it, who the competition is and what the latest trends are. If your client is in the computer business, for example, you should strive to know almost as much about that business as he or she knows.

That knowledge will make your writing topical and informative to a sophisticated audience. But it will also help you understand what your client *really* needs, which won't always be exactly what you're asked to provide. A strategic approach to your client's business will help that client reach long-term goals. Best of all, you'll be around, and remembered, when those goals are achieved.

Developing a strong relationship with a client is probably more important than what you actually write. This doesn't mean you can get by with mediocre writing. To build a strong relationship, you must prove you can write well. However, once clients appreciate your knowledge and experience, your work will be greatly simplified because they won't be as critical of your writing.

Find out who the real client is. This isn't as easy as it sounds. Although your principal contact might be one individual, that person's boss (or boss's boss) may be the ultimate judge of your work.

If at all possible, try to get a face-to-face session with this ultimate client. Your contact person may think he or she knows what the big boss wants, but if you can hear those signals firsthand, you'll usually reduce the number of rewrites.

Unfortunately, this isn't possible in many large corporations. Egos tend to get in the way, and upper management usually doesn't get interested in a project until the last minute. The vice president may not have time to meet with the writer a month before a presentation is due; then, three days before deadline, that VP might demand innumerable changes. Until you develop a relationship with senior executives, you'll probably have to write and rewrite for the corporate underling, and then do it all over when the big boss arrives.

Forget you ever had an ego. If you write for a client, get used to having your best copy butchered. Clients routinely tear great copy to pieces with all the delicacy of Attila the Hun, and they often don't stop at the fifth or sixth draft.

This problem can increase with high visibility projects where several clients get involved. (Do you remember that the camel is a horse created by a committee?) You can defend your copy (diplomatically, of course), but you should also get used to changing it, even when the revisions don't improve it.

If you have a problem with this, you have two choices: Change your attitude or find another outlet for your writing.

You can write only as well as you listen. Your first meetings with a client are critical. Listen carefully to what is said, and don't be afraid to ask questions. After all, your ultimate audience may need the same explanation you're searching for.

Notice, also, what is *not* said. Body language, facial expressions, tone of voice and other between-the-lines signals can often provide important insight into political or other considerations that should shape your writing.

Get to the first draft as soon as possible. Most clients, even those with years of experience, often don't really know what they want until they see what they *don't* want. They'll give you more precise guidance once they see something on paper.

Therefore, the sooner you can get to a first draft, the sooner you'll know what the client *really* wants. You still need to proofread and double-check that draft, and you may want to spend a little extra time if it's for a client you've never worked with. However, agonizing over minor details in the first draft is usually counterproductive. The second draft is the key document because it will better reflect the client's real needs.

Deadlines are important, but not as important as quality. Deadlines often make a professional writer's life miserable. They mean lost weekends and burned midnight oil, and they are usually caused by last-minute changes by the client.

However, you *must* be able to meet unrealistic deadlines. Business moves on a schedule, and that crucial advertising kick-off or conference isn't going to be moved back to give you an extra day to polish your script.

But you must also live with the final version of your work. If there are any mistakes in the brochure that goes out to customers, you'll be held accountable by clients who have remarkably long memories. Therefore, don't let the client move deadlines if, by doing so, he or she will compromise the quality of what you do.

This is a tough one because you also want to fulfill the client's wishes. It's not easy to stand up and tell the senior vice president that it's too late to make changes to tomorrow afternoon's conference. But it's easier than trying to explain afterward why his slides were wrong.

Remember your audience—even if your client doesn't. The needs of your audience should be established very clearly during your first input session. That shouldn't be difficult. What *is* often tough is to keep those needs in perspective while the document winds its way through the approval process.

Your writing may fit your audience to a tee *until* the document comes back from the engineering, legal and marketing departments stuffed full of corporate doublespeak. As the professional writer, you must keep everyone focused on the original purpose your writing is to serve.

Documents tend to expand during the approval process. Assignment length can also be a problem. A fifteen-minute speech becomes twenty-two minutes when all the comments get baked in; a four-page brochure becomes six pages, or requires a typeface readable only with a microscope.

Again, you're the professional writer and you need to keep everyone on track. If you agreed to a fifteen-minute speech in the first session, there was probably a good reason for it, and you must help your client edit the final product to the most effective length.

This can become a little tricky when your client (or you) must tell a superior that his or her comments aren't going to make the final draft. It helps to be a diplomat, as well as a writer.

Watch for the point of diminishing returns. This is especially important if you're a freelancer working on a fixed fee. At some point in the development of the finished product, changes usually become nit-picking. A word here, a sentence there, a caption for a photo. When this starts happening over and over again, the changes are usually more trouble than they're worth.

This is when you need to be honest with your client, and explain that it may be counterproductive for you to continue to be involved. In most cases, the client's word processing department can make these changes more easily (and more cheaply) than you. Drawing the line on your investment of time isn't always easy. But if you want to make a decent living in this business, it's essential.

Diplomacy also becomes critical when you must ask the client for more money, based on changes to the original project. There is no easy formula, and this isn't an easy request to make because clients usually don't get promoted for increasing the size of their budgets.

However, if major changes of direction are required in the middle of a project, and if these changes require you to significantly increase the amount of time you spend writing, then you deserve more money. If the client disagrees, you should finish the project, but think twice about working with that client again. If you're in doubt, especially if you're working with a new client, you're probably better off biting the bullet. But remember, you're in a business. Your time is your livelihood.

Writing for clients isn't easy. Last minute changes, unrealistic deadlines and corporate politics can all be extremely frustrating. But the work is steady, it can be quite rewarding from a creative standpoint and it's very lucrative!

The Service Edge

BY DICK SCHAAF

I became a freelancer on the seventh (and last) day of my first job out of college. In a few short minutes, I went from being the managing editor of a small trade magazine to wondering how I was going to pay the rent. If I were going to survive as a writer and editor (which was the point of college), I would have to make it on work I could find, do, deliver and be paid for.

In short, I had to become a business.

If you're writing to make money, you must become a business, too. It isn't hard. But it is work. The rules are the same for freelancers as for Marriott Hotels, FedEx or L.L. Bean: Take care of your customers and they'll take care of you. After all, running a business is little more than the act and art of having customers—people who pay you money for the goods you produce or the services you render. Satisfied customers control the frequency with which you'll be able to write three of the most exciting words in the English language—*For Deposit Only.*

But make no mistake: Readers are *not* your customers. Editors are. (Readers are *their* customers.) Whether you're writing for magazines, book publishers, corporations or advertising and PR agencies, your ability to make money is going to be determined not only by your basic skills as a writer, but also—and perhaps even more so—by your ability to satisfy your editors in a business relationship.

And there's no better competitive edge these days than superior customer service.

GETTING INTO SERVICE

Look at the writing market from an editor's vantage point. Competence is a given: There's no shortage of writers ready and willing to take on assignments. Most of them can research, spell, punctuate and write their names on the back of a check. The writer who is easy to do business with will have the inside track.

To freelancers wrapped up in their muses, this may smack of heresy. After all, we've schooled ourselves to think of writing as art, not commerce. Editors search for, develop and value writers as resources: the more consistent, dependable, reliable—and businesslike—the better.

The ability to write effectively and entertainingly is the bedrock on which successful businesses can be built and managed. But there's a lot of bedrock out there. Until you build something on it, all you have is a flat, vacant spot. Service is the tool you need to begin building.

Good service won't overcome bad writing, of course. But in a marketplace where competent prose is a given, good service separates the superior professionals from the average ones. As someone in the business of writing, you win or lose based on your ability to play by the rules of the marketplace. And most of those rules, you'll find, do not involve the product—the written material—you produce. They involve the value-added service you deliver. Nine times out of ten, the difference between a healthy, well-fed muse and a struggling, anorexic one is going to depend on how well or how poorly you support her with editor-pleasing service.

Think of it as a modern Golden Rule: Those with the gold make the rules. In the freelance relationship, editors have the gold. If they want service—and they do—service is what you must deliver.

So what exactly is service? And how do you deliver it? In *The Service Edge: 101 Companies That Profit From Customer Care*, management consultant Ron Zemke and I profiled businesses that make money on the quality of the service they deliver. Most of those firms, we found, focus their efforts on three areas:

- differentiating between the needs and the expectations of their customers;
- adopting both short-term and long-term perspectives on their relationships with those customers;
- organizing themselves around five basic operating principles that help focus the business on customer satisfaction.

MEETING NEEDS VS. EXPECTATIONS

When editors decide (or when, through a query, you convince them to decide) they *need* an article on the general irrelevance of the Dow

Jones Industrial Average or the nutritional insanity of no-cholesterol potato chips, your natural tendency will be to focus exclusively on satisfying that need with the story you write.

But editors also have *expectations* of how their needs will be satisfied. And satisfying those expectations generally will involve far more than writing and delivering the actual story.

Think about what happens when you take your car in for a tune-up. You need a service performed, but you won't be in the shop when the work is being done, any more than the editor will be there to look over your shoulder as you interview sources and pound away at the keyboard. What will make that tune-up good or bad in your judgment will be how well the shop meets your expectations in the transaction.

For example, you may expect your car will be ready by five, the job will be done for $49.95, and your car will be returned to you without grease on the seats or the radio turned to a station you find obnoxious. None of these has anything to do with the actual tune-up work, but all of them will play a role in how you feel about the job when it's done.

If you walk through the door at 4:55 P.M. and the car is still up on the hoist, it doesn't matter to you that the people working underneath may moonlight for Bobby Unser or have found something potentially life-threateningly wrong with your front end. You know it's going to be a long time before you get out of there. You have a pretty strong hunch it's going to cost a whole lot more than $49.95. And you're dissatisfied. Next time you may well go somewhere else because your expectations were not met, even though your need was.

Editors work the same way. Basic editor expectations can include:

- a manuscript that's typed, double-spaced, on one side of sheets of clean, white, nonerasable bond paper—or one that arrives on computer disk or via modem;
- words spelled correctly, especially such important words as the names of sources;
- a manuscript that runs the expected length, not half or double the words assigned;
- a story that arrives on time—or a timely request for a deadline extension, if one becomes necessary;
- a story that quotes sources the editor suggested or supplied to the writer;
- a timely bill for expenses that satisfies accounting requirements and doesn't approximate the cost of a new computer;

- a progress report, if one was discussed or requested;
- a phone number at which you, an answering machine or someone who knows you, can be reached if the editor needs to get in touch with you;
- anything else the editor decides to expect (this falls under the new Golden Rule).

It is possible—in fact, it's almost normal—for a writer to satisfy the need part of the equation, but stumble on the expectations side of the ledger. And the result can be a constant quest for new editors to do business with. You typically don't get a second chance with dissatisfied customers, regardless of the cause of their dissatisfaction.

When I freelanced in the late seventies, magazines were my meal ticket. Deadlines were my Achilles' heel. I wrote well. But I delivered late. As a result, my experience fell into two categories. There were editors for whom I wrote once or twice, but never again—not because my stories didn't fulfill the assigned need, but because there were plenty of writers who could satisfy needs on or about the expected due date. There were also, thankfully, editors I wrote for on a regular basis because they liked my work enough to overlook my periodic deadline failures.

Years later when I became an editor, a colleague I'd once written for confided that she had two deadlines for writers like me: the real one and the one she put on assignment contracts. As an editor, I have writers for whom I'll do the same. But not many.

SHORT-TERM VS. LONG-TERM RELATIONSHIPS
Everything counts for the customer, from the visual appearance of your manuscript to its timely appearance at the editor's office. If you're thinking about writing only one story for a given editor, you don't have to worry about the supporting details. If you're seeing the editor as a market with long-term potential, you must.

In financial terms, the latter is the way to go. Research shows it costs five times as much to attract a new customer as it does to keep one you already have. The first time you write for someone, you probably won't break even on your time if you consider not only what it took to complete the assignment, but also what it took you to land the assignment in the first place. The payoff comes from the second assignment, and the tenth—from working for people you already know well how to satisfy, and who are satisfied enough to come back to you with more work.

In recent years there's been a major change in the theory of selling. The sales cycle used to be likened to a one-night stand. You wooed. You won. You consummated. Then you started looking for a new conquest. Today, the operative metaphor is a marriage: a long-term relationship in which both parties have a stake. Here's another area where the writing trade mimics other kinds of business. Customers will stick with a proven performer rather than experiment constantly with new ones because it's easier for them, less hassle for them, less risky for them. Editors are no exception.

For a writer, marketing time—time spent querying, making presentations, developing contacts and otherwise drumming up new business—provides a very low return on investment. The highest return comes from doing what you get paid to do: writing. Developing long-term relationships with editors will provide a much better long-term payoff than would a succession of one-assignment stands.

When I started freelancing, I made a point of meeting the editors I wanted to work for whenever and as often as I could. I wanted to be more than a name on a query letter or file card. I didn't know it at the time, but that made perfect sense from the standpoint of marketing psychology. People like to buy from those they know and trust. They're reluctant to buy from strangers.

I saw its effectiveness demonstrated when I was delivering a manuscript, in person, to an editor at an inflight magazine. While in the building, I stopped by the office of another editor I'd written for a couple of months before. He looked up, recognized me, said hello— then cast a calculating eye at the four-inch stack of queries in his in-basket. He was supposed to spend his afternoon sifting queries, he told me. But if he assigned something to me, he could rationalize putting the job off for another day or two. I walked out with a five hundred dollar assignment and a renewed understanding that cultivating editors makes good, long-term business sense.

OPERATING LIKE A BUSINESS

In analyzing the companies profiled in *The Service Edge*, Ron Zemke identified five basic operating principles that consistently underlie the activities of highly successful service providers. Even if your "organization" only consists of who you see in the mirror every morning, you can adapt these principles to the way you do business.

Listen, understand and respond to the customer. Nothing is more important to good service than knowing and delivering what the customer wants from you. Assuming that you can write competently, your success as a business has much to do with the relationships you develop with the editors who buy and publish your work.

What do editors want? Ask them. They'll tell you. In many cases, they'll make it easy for you: writer's guidelines (which are usually available for a business-size, self-addressed, stamped envelope), listings in *Writer's Market*, market updates in *Writer's Digest* and other writing magazines, and correspondence and telephone conversations. Any time you talk to targeted editors, read their publications or have a chance to find out more about their competitive marketplace, take notes. In any long-term relationship, experience is the best teacher. Pay attention.

Define superior service and establish a service strategy. If you're listening to your editorial customers, defining *superior service* will be a lot simpler. For the most part, your customers tell you what you must (and can) do to compete effectively. That's your service strategy.

Your service strategy may involve defining one or several niches for yourself. If you want to write about health care, for example, and the editors buying stories about health care value expertise, you must have—or demonstrate your ability and willingness to acquire—health-care expertise. The same will be true if your intended niche is computers, or sports or travel or anything else.

Of course, your strategy must have value in the customer's eyes. Your expertise in health care is irrelevant to the editor of a travel magazine—unless you can show how the editor's readers will benefit from a story on finding emergency medical services overseas. The more you know about your editorial customers, the better able you'll be to develop and constantly fine-tune a profitable service strategy.

Set standards and measure performance. Most businesses don't really know what their *customers* need and expect of them. Consequently, their service strategies typically have more to do with internal convenience than customer priorities. When it comes time to measure performance, they concentrate on financial, quantifiable and "countable" elements that may have little or nothing to do with service success.

Quantity and quality are two different things, so *what* you measure is as important as *that* you measure. A 1,200-word story is neither better nor worse than a 2,000-word story. The true measure of customer satisfaction is how well or how poorly the article meets the editor's needs and expectations. That's what will determine whether you'll have a chance to write for that market again. And each editor is entitled to define satisfaction in his or her own unique and peculiar way.

The solution? Set standards that have value to your customers—you can begin with the list of editors' expectations I gave earlier. Then determine how well you meet those standards. Follow up on your work. Have you satisfied the editor's expectations on the assignment? Did you deliver on time? Was your work on target? Did you get your facts straight? Did your lines rhyme?

At the publishing company I worked for, we filled out report cards for each story we edited. The overall grade reflected both style and substance considerations: when the story arrived, what we paid the writer, how much editing time it required, whether the facts were checked and the sources were properly identified, and any comments we had about doing business with the writer. When we had assignments to make, we would often go through those report cards to find writers with the subject-matter expertise and the work habits that suggested they could do what we needed done.

Many writers knew we had this system. None of them ever asked me what kind of grades they received. Or why.

Select, train and empower employees to work for the customer. This applies to writers in a figurative sense. Once you accept the idea that an editor is a customer with both needs and expectations that must be satisfied, you'll begin to see how much impact the way you do business has on how often you have a chance to open an envelope with a check in it. As you identify editor-pleasing behaviors, you must commit yourself to repeating them on a regular basis.

Training deserves special consideration. The best advice I ever received on doing things in general came from a handyman uncle. Don't skimp on tools, he said. The better your tools, the better the quality of what you make with them. If you're working with tools that frustrate you, you won't enjoy what you're doing nearly as much.

Training is a tool you use to develop and extend your abilities. It may mean learning to use a computer or an online information service. It may mean subscribing to magazines that broaden your horizons or deepen your knowledge of a given field. It may mean joining—or starting—groups that support your interests. It may mean all of the above and more.

Like a professional athlete, you're in a competitive business. No matter how long you've been doing what you're doing, there's always someone coming along with new skills and the energy to put them to work. When you stop growing as a writer, you find yourself being typecast by editors as someone who can deliver only within a narrow spectrum. The good assignments, the exciting and challenging ones that stretch you, go somewhere else. Just like an athlete, you must keep training to keep yourself in playing condition.

Recognize and reward accomplishments. It's easy to get so caught up in the day-to-day grind of whatever it is you're doing that achievements slide by almost unnoticed. Along that path lies burnout. Good service should have payoffs. Make sure it does. The same basic tactics used in businesses' incentive and recognition systems to reward sales performance can be employed to help you achieve your service goals as a writer.

For example, when—but only when—you hit a deadline or have an article accepted by a new publication, celebrate. Buy a book. See a movie. Take a long lunch with a friend. Earmark a percentage of the money you're paid on assignments from previous customers for something you want: upgraded software for your computer, a really nice briefcase or travel set, a computer game the kids'll never see.

The first $500 I made as a freelancer back in 1975 went for an electric typewriter with a carbon ribbon, an investment in a good tool that made my work look better and made me feel good every time I switched it on. Twenty-some years later, I took my first substantial speaking fee down to the computer store and turned it into a laptop so I could write on the road.

SHARPENING YOUR EDGE

These principles do not constitute a quick, easy, mindless five-step plan that automatically and forever will make everything wonderful for you. Good service involves work, and it's a job that's never done. No matter what the game, they reset the scoreboard to zero every time it's played.

We now live and work in a service economy. Nearly 75 percent of our nation's Gross National Product derives not from the production of goods, but from the performance of services. And performance is a good word to finish with. Each encounter you have with an editor is a performance that is reviewed by an audience. If the review is favorable, you may get an encore or return engagement. If your audience gives thumbs down, you'll have to take your act someplace else.

To be successful as a writing business, you must demonstrate to editors—one by one, and over and over again—that you can deliver what they need the way they want it. The words you write are only the beginning. Service is your marketing edge.

Making a Full-Time Impression as a Part-Time Writer

BY DONNA ALBRECHT

How many times have you heard the phrase "Appearances are everything"? While not absolutely true (after all, stylish letterhead won't make up for lousy writing), the professional image you project as a writer will definitely affect the way editors and interview subjects react to you and your work.

You already know what makes people appear professional. Among other qualities, they know their stuff, communicate clearly in all correspondence, are available by phone, and are able to meet at a mutually agreeable time and place when necessary.

But what if you're writing part time around another job or family responsibilities? Are there techniques you can use to project that professional image? Yes.

The three areas you must focus on require some thought (and some equipment), as well as cooperation from family members. When you handle these three areas competently, however, there's no reason why anyone you deal with in your writing has to know you do it less than full time.

THE WRITE IMAGE

As a writer, your first contact with an editor will usually be a letter. It can be very tempting to think that the fanciest, most elaborate letterhead will get the best response. Your neighborhood print shop may encourage that belief.

But fancy logos and foil accents don't sell articles. Your excellent writing skills do. All you really need on your letterhead is your name, address and daytime phone number (and fax number, if you have one).

If your budget is tight, consider creating letterhead on your computer. Set your name and address in a larger and more dramatic typeface than the one you normally type with, and you'll have a template ready to write all your letters on.

Or, you can have your print shop create a simple letterhead with black ink on white, beige or gray paper. Resist the urge to choose vivid or unusual paper colors. These colors may be fun, but aren't likely to convey the professional image you're trying to cultivate.

Whatever you do, keep your letterhead simple. That way, you'll hold down your costs *and* keep the editor focused on your sterling prose, not the paper it was written on. And for the most professional look, use the same layout on the return address section of your envelopes and business cards as you do on your letterhead.

If you use an ink jet or laser printer, ask for a few sample sheets of the paper to run through your machine before you invest a lot of money on paper and envelopes. Some higher-priced papers have a texture that doesn't print as attractively as smoother papers. And if you're printing your own letterhead, check with your stationery store for sheets of business card stock that you can print up.

One note about your business cards: If you have another job, the last thing you want to do is hand out those cards when you're dealing with writing contacts. It would be like advertising that you're not really a professional writer. If economy dictates that you can have only one card, keep it extremely simple. My friend Shari, who's successful as both a writer and a real estate professional, has a card that gives just her name, address and phone number. People remember her in the context of the role she was in when they got the card.

One mistake some writers make on their cards is to list their specialties, such as *article writing, speech writing, technical writing, humor,* etc. The problem is this can eliminate you from consideration for other work, which you might be perfectly qualified to do.

I've found that by simply putting *Writer* on my card (at the top, in large print so it's Rolodex-effective), people will often assume that I do whatever kind of writing they need. Then, as we talk, I focus the conversation on projects similar to theirs that I've done previously.

PLAYING TELEPHONE TAG

When you write part time, it's a sure bet that you won't be sitting by the phone waiting for it to ring. If you have another job, your employer will probably not look kindly on you tying up his phone to further your writing career. If you're a homemaker, you're dealing with a whole different set of challenges.

If you work days, you should give your home number to editors, sources, etc. Be sure to have an answering machine on that line, preferably the kind that allows you to pick up your messages from other locations. That way, you can handle any necessary calls on your lunch or coffee breaks.

Many answering machines also have the ability to record both sides of a conversation. This can be a very useful feature if you do interviews by phone. Just be sure to let the other person know, while the tape is running, that you're taping. Most people won't mind being recorded if you say it will help ensure accurate quotes.

Before you start using the machine, however, you must record your outgoing message. These words will play a critical role in shaping the caller's perception of you, so keep it professional, brief and to the point. Unless you write humor, don't try to be cute.

My husband's business contacts sometimes call him at home, so our message has to sound professional for both of us: "You have reached the Albrechts' voice mail. No one is available to take your call right now. Please leave your name and number at the tone."

Speak clearly, and be absolutely sure there are no household background noises, as they'll make you sound amateurish. (The same advice holds true when you're interviewing sources from your home phone.)

Speaking of family, you'll have to either get their cooperation in how the phone is answered, or get a second phone line for writing only.

Once your children start using the phone, you may need to set up some house rules, especially during business hours. One way to handle incoming calls is to get the automated message center, available from your phone company, that picks up if your line is busy. If you prefer call waiting, make sure your children agree to hang up on their calls immediately if a second one comes in.

Since you'll have limited time to do your phone work, you may want to set aside the same hour each day, perhaps during your lunch break. If you do call from your outside office, however, be sure to get a calling card from your long-distance service and use it. (This also gives you a record of your calls for tax purposes.) Otherwise, find a quiet phone booth somewhere near work and make that your lunchtime office.

Take advantage of time zone differences whenever possible, both for convenience and to save on your phone bill. For instance, writers on the East Coast can make calls to the Midwest and West Coast after

5 P.M. West Coast writers often make calls to the East before their workday.

If you're having trouble reaching someone and can't get through the impersonal web of the automated phone system, try these techniques:

• If you're already in the system, hit "0" for operator, and you'll usually get a real, live person.

• Pretend you don't have a touch-tone phone. Most systems will shunt you to the operator if you just wait a moment after the first set of instructions.

MEETINGS AND INTERVIEWS

Although you can write any hour of the day (or night), and return phone calls at odd moments, you'll have to be more flexible and creative when it comes to scheduling meetings and interviews. These can be a real test of the professional image you're working to project.

When you need to meet face-to-face with an editor or source, consider scheduling a breakfast meeting at a coffee shop convenient to both of you. Or, arrange a weekend meeting when you're both free from workday stresses. When necessary, consider taking a day of your vacation time to invest in your writing career.

Dress appropriately. The image of a writer taking artistic license for how he or she looks works best in the movies.

All in all, it's quite possible to convey a professional impression, regardless of how many hours a week you write. And when your professionalism comes across through the way you sound, dress, act and send correspondence, you make it easier for editors and others to see you as a professional writer and to focus their attention on your wonderful work.

Playing
"The Contacts Game"

BY GREGG LEVOY

When I was a toddler, I am told, I regularly held my breath until I turned blue and passed out.

This was usually in response to something my twin brother got that I didn't.

Because of the attention this fearsome little tactic attracted, however, my brother soon adopted it himself. For awhile, we were dropping at the slightest hint of sibling inequity.

Children are geniuses at self-promotion, and none more so than twins (as each has a need to distinguish him- or herself from the other that takes on Darwinian urgency). My childhood was, in retrospect, good practice for being a self-employed writer.

There are, of course, more elegant approaches to publicizing yourself than feigning suffocation. Still, the principle remains the same: You don't get attention if nobody knows you exist.

Writers are not "discovered" as quarks and cave paintings are discovered. You must go *get* discovered. Success may be as much a function of what others can do for you as what you can do for yourself, but you must know how to encourage others to "do" for you.

Enter "the contacts game."

To a lot of writers, unfortunately, the contacts game is a contemptuous enterprise, a smarmy con game based on the belief that success solely depends on "who you know." The implication is that people are elevated not by virtue of their art, but by their artifice, an oily talent for flattery and a certain facility with small talk.

But those who complain most bitterly are usually those having the most difficulty breaking in, and who are angry with themselves for not having the courage to get to know people who could help them.

To the degree that making contacts involves exposing yourself, this practice does demand courage. Self-promotion becomes particularly intimidating when it involves making direct contact with people. Doing so forces you to confront both how you feel about putting yourself out there, and what you feel your writing is worth.

The process might seem less fearsome if you keep in mind that valuable contacts aren't necessarily the people writers most often think of: editors, producers, agents, writing instructors, colleagues. Contacts can also include friends and acquaintances, even strangers. Therefore, as you go about your writing career, remember that playing the contacts game to win means, above all, being willing to simply relate to people, tell them what you do and ask them what they do.

Here are some examples from my own files:

• Several authors whose books I read, and with whom I struck up correspondences (beginning with simple fan letters), later recommended my book to their college writing students.

• A colleague once said, "Call this editor, tell him I sent you and mail him some of your stuff." That editor ended up sending me to the Pacific Northwest for two weeks on assignment.

• An editor of mine who quit to become a freelance writer provided me with invaluable insight into negotiating with editors—information he was not so free to divulge while an editor.

• A woman who attended one of my lectures invited me to be an instructor at a large writers' conference she went on to chair some years later.

The contacts game starts when you begin drawing on the strengths of the people closest to you, people with whom you have the greatest chance to succeed: friends who run their own businesses, consultants whose mistakes you can profit from, old college professors and former bosses who might have leads for you, a family member who's an accountant, fellow freelancers whose brains you can pick, anyone who has faith in you.

Businesses with large "founder teams" typically fare better than those with smaller ones, or those with only one person at the helm. So don't rely too heavily on your rugged individualism. There will be plenty of opportunity for that in the day-to-day labor of keeping the wheels turning. Plug in regularly to a community of people who are both realistic and optimistic, and who are busy with passions of their own. Says poet Nikki Giovanni, "Do not surround yourself with people who do not have dreams."

SEVEN WAYS TO MAKE CONTACTS

1. **Tell everybody.** Word of mouth starts with yours. Don't miss an opportunity to tell people that you're a writer and you're for hire. I've heard of people using their answering machines to let anyone calling know they're looking for writing jobs.

Go through your address books. Send postcards to your acquaintances asking them if they know anyone who'd be interested in your services. Use recommendations to build an active mailing list. You'll be glad you did, especially if you hope to publish a book, teach or start your own freelance business.

2. **Keep a press box.** Be ready to send out information about yourself to anyone your contacts refer you to, or refer to you. Develop a file that includes your résumé, published clips, letters of recommendation, reviews, photo, book dust jackets, business card, brochure, or whatever you have available that shows you off and is relevant to the kind of writing you do. Don't be shy about sending out this material. Remember what Will Rogers said: "If you done it, it ain't bragging."

3. **Sound the trumpets.** Don't just do a good job, make sure you're *noticed* doing a good job. Whenever anything of yours hits print, make clean copies of it and send them out, with the briefest cover letter, to people who might be interested: editors you work with, editors you've pitched but haven't cracked yet, colleagues, agents, hometown and alumni publications (local boy or girl makes good), and professional organization newsletters, which usually have a section for sounding off about members.

4. **Volunteer.** Don't just join those professional organizations; volunteer to serve on a committee, put together a conference, edit a newsletter. You'll make contacts you couldn't make in any other way and get your name on all sorts of literature.

When I first moved to San Francisco to freelance full-time, I volunteered to work every Friday afternoon at the offices of Media Alliance, a local professional organization for media-related people (I actually considered it a form of tithing at the time). I answered phones, did publicity, set up seminars, acted as class assistant to MA instructors (and thereby got free classes), had first access to the job file, wrote articles for the organization newspaper and met a *lot* of people.

Eventually I pitched that group my first class, marketing for freelance writers, and I got the go-ahead. It had everything to do with the group's familiarity with me. Media Alliance now offers several of my classes, sends me countless consultees, gives me free advertising and exposure, invites me to teach at conferences and provides me with priceless contacts.

5. **Apprentice.** Another of the most effective ways of trading labor for learning—and getting contacts, visibility and an inside track that few freelancers possess—is the Renaissance tradition of apprenticing. The primary qualification is eagerness.

As an apprentice (or intern), you can see what one portion of the writing field looks like from the inside out, and should you ever decide to make a run for the freelance life, the apprenticeship experience will make your outside-in perspective vastly more insightful.

As a college student I interned at *Writer's Digest.* The job paid only $20 a week at the time, but I got to see how a magazine operates, what editors do and what writers look like from the editorial viewpoint. I also got a letter of recommendation more valuable than an Ivy League diploma. And the editor who took me on, John Brady, is the same fellow who fifteen years later referred Writer's Digest Books to me when they were looking for someone to write a book about the business of writing.

There are scores of internship programs in the writing industry, part-time and full-time, that are open to college students, career changers and even those reentering the workforce. These include, but aren't limited to, advertising, television, magazines, book publishing, journalism and business writing.

6. **Teach.** If you have competence in an area and enjoy teaching, do so. It's great exposure and supplemental income, an excellent way to add to your mailing list and meet colleagues, and a terrific antidote to the isolation of writing.

Consider offering workshops and lectures to college community education departments, service clubs, trade associations, church/temple groups, high school writing or journalism classes, senior centers, cruise lines, writers' groups and conferences, or even through your own home or a rental space. Or contact the instructors of full-semester college writing courses and offer yourself as a guest lecturer.

7. **Get into the community.** As Mickey Rooney once said, put on a show. Gather friends and do an evening of erotic poetry sponsored by a local bookstore or coffeehouse. Organize a chain-story marathon as a benefit for a local charity. Host a works-in-progress presentation. And tell the media about it.

MAKING CONTACT, NOT JUST CONTACTS

The more personal you make the contacts game, the better. It isn't about cold-bloodedly "working a room." It's not even about making contacts. It's about making *contact*! We've all been hurt at some point by other people's intentions, or been uncertain why we were being befriended; it's these experiences that taint the contacts game. But when you develop real relationships, people become willing to open their address books to you.

You can't fake this, though. You either have a genuine interest in others, or you're just smiling and saying cheese. People can tell the difference.

You touch people by realizing that they want what everyone wants: recognition, respect and the feeling of importance. So show them they matter to you (and matter as more than contact). Compliment them, confide in them, tell them you value their efforts, offer your support or services, put something personal in all your correspondence, thank them for their business or their friendship.

You can touch people by giving them honest feedback, too. It's indispensable, and because it's so rare, it takes on a disproportionate weight of significance. Think of how you feel after receiving a sincere compliment.

You can also touch people by the sheer force of your own exuberance. Encountering enthusiasm gives people a "contact high." It generates energy. It tells them that whatever assistance they offer will go toward a worthy cause, and be appreciated.

The contacts game is about how you relate to virtually everybody with whom you come into contact. After one of my "How to Sell What You Write" workshops, during which I'd mentioned a New York trip I was planning to visit my editors, a student told me about her brother there who I might enjoy meeting. "You guys would probably like each other," she said. "Besides, he's an editor at *Savvy* magazine."

A contact like that—the "I have somebody you should meet" variety—only grows out of your being as authentic to yourself as possible, and remembering that what you put out is what you attract. You've probably noticed that when you leave the house in a crummy mood, the whole world tends to mirror your unhappiness: People cut you off on the road, salespeople ignore you and you end up in the longest line at the bank.

A personal referral also changes the whole balance of power when approaching an influential person. Imagine if someone called you and said that a friend or colleague of yours (or a sister!) had told them you'd be a great person to talk to. You might think twice about turning this person away cold. That recommendation makes you just a bit accountable.

Accountability is one reason I guard my own contacts jealously (as do most writers). I need to *know* someone before I turn him or her loose on my editors or other valued contacts. If someone is going to drop my name, I want to be proud of my involvement, not embarrassed by my lack of discretion.

USING YOUR CONTACTS

Making contacts is only part of the game. You must be willing to *use* them, to ask for what you want, and to follow through.

Most people don't appreciate the potential power within even a small circle of friends. This potential was clinically demonstrated some years ago by psychologist Stanley Milgram. In what he called the "Small World Experiment," he showed that almost any two strangers in the world could be connected with one another through no more than five intermediate acquaintances!

To make use of this potential, though, you must be comfortable. If you hate calling up strangers out of the blue, use the epistolary approach. If you feel more comfortable meeting people in classes and professional seminars than at parties, save yourself the sweat and hangovers. If you feel you come across terribly on TV, but have a voice like God's on the radio, don't try to get on television; go for radio. And if you find that meeting your clients face-to-face helps get your enthusiasm across, shine up your shoes.

THE VALUE OF FACE-TO-FACE CONTACT

I, for one, find that face-to-face contact with my editors not only helps get my enthusiasm across, but provides an invigorating change of pace from the monasticism of writing. It also brings the writer/editor relationship to a personal level, which is the key to winning at the contacts game.

I didn't always feel this way. The thought of meeting editors in person, even ones I'd been working with for years, once scared the daylights out of me. Nearly all of them reside in New York City, and in my imagination they held forth from offices with commanding vistas of midtown Manhattan, complete with secretaries shaped like full-backs, bad attitudes about California and hoards of would-be writers camped out on their doorsteps.

My apprehension kept me from making the trip for years—until one winter day when I got a phone call from John Brady. During our conversation he expressed surprise (with a trace of disappointment) that I hadn't made The Trip. He said that if I did so, I would probably triple my business. I was so flabbergasted at the prospect that I neglected to ask him if he meant it would triple my income or just my workload.

But I decided that, even if it only doubled my income, it would be worth the temporary discomfort. I made the decision to go.

Over the next two months, I prepared for The Trip by:

- writing brief letters to ten editors—some I had worked with for several years, some I had only written a single piece for and the one whose sister had suggested I get in touch. I told them of my upcoming trip, expressed my enthusiasm to meet them and asked if they'd like to set up lunch appointments ahead of time. (Three did. Five waited until I hit town. And two didn't have time to see me.)
- preparing several story ideas to pitch to each editor, and literally rehearsing them using 3×5 cards.
- sending reminder notes two weeks before the trip. With each note I also included a couple of my best recent clips, with mention that I was bringing a handful of story ideas they'd want to hear about.
- sending last-minute postcards telling the editors that I would give them each a call when I arrived.

With that I went to New York, met editors at some of the top magazines in the world and came home with nearly a year's worth of assignments!

Parts of the experience, however, *were* genuinely intimidating. Consider my meeting with the editor of *Glamour* magazine, who consented to a brief meeting in her office, and who was decked out in a flamboyant chartreuse and pink outfit with power-shoulders wide enough to be seen from other galaxies. The moment her secretary led me into the office and sat me down, the editor took an exaggerated glance at her watch and said, "You have twenty minutes. Go."

Forty-five minutes later, I walked out with two go-aheads.

All in all, The Trip both boosted my self-esteem and transformed my relationships with several editors. They became more friendly and less formal.

I've since discovered that such personal contacts have had a stabilizing effect on my career. In a publishing world where mega-mergers, buyouts and magazine failures are commonplace, it's better to develop relationships with people than with magazines. When someone moves, they take you with them. But when magazines die, which they do with far greater regularity than editors, they take a chunk of your income with them.

Income that only another contact can replace.

Writer Meets Editor

BY JAMES MORGAN

Believe it or not, lots of people think editors and writers are one and the same. I once presided over a chamber of commerce publication and even my boss didn't understand the difference; to him, a writer was someone he could pay peanuts whenever his services were needed, while an editor was someone he had to pay peanuts *all* the time. And for what? All he saw in the magazine was the writing.

One day I overheard him asking his henchman, "Can't we run this magazine without an editor?" To which I eventually replied, "Without *this* editor you can," and split.

No, editors and writers aren't the same. They're mutant species of the same genus, of course, and they exhibit certain vestigial similarities; but they're really two different animals. A magazine needs both kinds, and each kind needs the other. And when the relationship works the way it's supposed to, it's tremendously rewarding for both.

How, exactly, does that relationship work? Several metaphors come to mind: the editor as headquarters general (I visualize someone kind and Ike-like, though you writers are likely to conjure up Brando in *Apocalypse Now*) with the writer as frontline soldier. Or the editor as baseball manager with the writer as designated hitter. Or how about this: the editor as circus ringmaster, the writer as high-wire artist. There's something about the circus metaphor that's perversely appropriate.

But metaphors have their limits, don't they? Really, the best way to understand how editors and writers are supposed to work with one another is to follow them through the process that links them—in this case, the preparation of a magazine article. Every project is different, of course—that's part of what makes our business stimulating—and every editor-writer relationship is different, too. But the process itself is pretty much the same every time. By seeing how at least one experienced editor thinks it *ought* to go, maybe you can figure out why it sometimes doesn't go that way for you. Then next time, maybe it will.

STEP 1: THE ASSIGNMENT

It all starts with an idea. If the idea comes from the writer in the form of a query, the editor generally makes a few suggestions and then dispatches the writer to go out and seek whatever the two of them have decided they're after. But if the idea comes from the editor, the process is a little more complex.

In terms of the editor-writer relationship, the important thing is that (a) the editor choose the right writer for the job, and (b) the editor explain what the heck he wants the writer to do.

You may think I'm insulting you by offering such obvious information. The fact is, though, experienced writers know that many editors don't have any real idea of what they want until they've seen samples of what they *don't* want. Of course, because this is a partnership, it's as much the writer's fault as it is the editor's: As a writer, you shouldn't accept an assignment unless you're comfortable that you and the editor are working on the same story.

All of which is why I believe so strongly in the assignment letter: Aside from formalizing the basic information about length, fee and deadline, it gives the editor a chance to think and rethink his concept, to word it just right; it also gives the writer something to refer to from time to time when writing the piece. And finally, it provides a point of reference if there's still some disagreement over whether the finished piece accomplished what it was supposed to do.

But we're getting ahead of ourselves. The first point I mentioned in regard to the editor-writer relationship was the editor's choice of the right writer. Obviously, there's a lot of subjectivity involved in that choice, and I think that's fine: The editor has a right to pick someone he feels comfortable working with—someone he feels not only can do the job, but also can bring something special to it.

When I was at *Playboy*, we decided to assign an article on David Duke, then the young, slick, buttoned-down, silver-tongued leader of what he called a "new" Ku Klux Klan. While there are Klansmen everywhere, we felt that the piece needed a Southern writer, someone to whom Duke's boiling racist blood might at least be viscerally understandable. We didn't want someone who *agreed* with him, mind you, but someone who might bring a sense of complexity to the piece. And since the Klan isn't the same as the D.A.R., we also wanted someone who wasn't afraid to take that proverbial walk on the wild side.

Others had suggested articles on the Klan, but the writer we came up with was Harry Crews, the earthy, eloquent Georgia native who teaches English between novels and articles on such subjects as bulldog fighting, truckers and traveling carnivals—all of which sounded to us like perfect practice for this assignment.

More about that later. We gave Crews the Klan assignment because it fit his experience. But if an editor simply relies on a writer's past assignments in order to give him more of the same, then writer, editor and magazine will all get stale. One of the most inspired matchups I've ever been associated with also happened during my *Playboy* days. One of the editors had the brilliant notion of sending a New York street kid to cover the much-venerated (in the South) Alabama football coach Bear Bryant. The writer was Richard Price, who by then had written a couple of tough novels about street gangs and has since won an Oscar for his gritty screenplay for *The Color of Money*. Price wasn't interested in football particularly, and he didn't know a thing about the South; but he was interested in power and winning with all the heart a New York street kid can muster, and he came back with an irreverent yet sensitive piece on one of football's greats.

So the choice of writer is very important—but that's only the beginning of the editor's job. After he's picked the writer, and before the writer gets out on his own, the editor must do everything he can to make sure he and his writer understand each other. Virtually no law of science can ensure that two human beings will actually *communicate* effectively. And sometimes both parties let this process get complicated by the presence of a third party—the agent.

Not all writers have agents, of course, and not all writers who have agents use them for magazine pieces. But when an agent is involved, his job is primarily to make sure the writer gets as much money as possible. The agents are the bankers of this business, the scorekeepers, the bill collectors, the dealers, the readers and writers of small print. Essence and Meaning are languages they seldom speak, at least with editors. For many writers, the agent lifts the unpleasant burden of discussing money so the writer can concentrate on the sometimes unpleasant-but-preferable task of writing.

But in no case should either the editor or writer allow the agent to be the total communications conduit. Talk Money with the agent, but talk Meaning with each other. One of the joys—and ironies—of this business is that while it *is* a business, its success depends on the effectiveness of the personal, human communication. To be effective businesspeople, editors and writers must be human first, businesspeople second.

And to be human means to understand human frailty—which raises the subject of procrastination. Some editors think they're doing the writer a favor by leaving the deadline open. I think most people, editors included, work better with a definite deadline. Whose rule is that about a job expanding to fill the time available? An assignment without a deadline can become a psychological albatross for the writer: As you know, it's hard as hell to sit alone in a room and run your soul through a word processor, and there's a tendency to hold on to your soul until somebody says you have to bare it. Besides, an editor who doesn't set deadlines can't very well do the rest of his job—planning timely issues, working out a balanced mix, that sort of stuff. Chaos may be the natural order of things in this business, and you're more likely to remain sane if you realize you can't change that. But you still *try*.

STEP 2: THE WAITING GAME

Harry Crews's piece on the Klan was due, but instead of a manuscript, a short letter and a Polaroid color photograph landed in my in-box. The letter was apologetic: Crews is a proud man, and he had never missed a deadline before. But there had been a little trouble, he said, and he was laid up a bit. The attached photograph was to show me what a man's stomach looks like after it's been mauled with a spring-loaded blackjack.

When I called Crews, he apologized again for missing the deadline and asked whether I still wanted him to finish the piece. Of *course* I did, but that was beside the point: How was he? Was he taking care of himself? As it turns out he was, in his way, and we went on with the prosaic details of discussing the piece and setting a new deadline. When the article was in, Crews wrote me a note thanking me for being understanding.

Understanding is something an editor must be, especially once that assignment is made and the writer is out in the trenches. Out there any number of things can go wrong, and the editor must stand by to act as monitor, cheerleader, big brother, best friend, devil's advocate, drill sergeant, banker, marriage counselor, travel agent, coach and shrink. Any editor in his right mind would've been understanding in Crew's case, but not every situation is that clear-cut. I once called a writer for days trying to find out where her manuscript was. When I finally got through, her daughter answered the phone and said, "She can't talk right now—she's meditating." Right about then I was tempted to give her a new mantra: *unemployed*. But her copy arrived the next day, and it was brilliant, as usual. (You writers should bear this in mind: If you insist on being pains in the ass, you better make sure you're worth it.)

I could go on for pages about the various cases in which editors are called on to be understanding about the situations writers have put them in—or vice versa, depending on who's telling the story. The point is, being understanding is the ideal; being responsive is the absolute minimum. Once an editor gets an assignment made, he goes on to deal with other writers, other assignments, and each one has its own litany of facts, fees, logistics and nuances. The editor is a busy person, but he should never get so busy that he can't return his writers' phone calls, answer their letters, see that their expense checks are sent, that their questions are answered. There are many thrills to being an editor, but there's also a heap of drudgery, and an editor must be able to work that drudgery into his day. Mainly, he must figure out his priorities, just like any other manager must do, and that means remembering that those writers he's already assigned are more important, maybe, than the new ones he's working on. He must look to the future, but if he doesn't take care of today there won't be any future left when he gets there.

Writers are the people editors call to solve the editors' problems, so it's only fair that editors be the ones writers call to solve their problems. There's no guarantee, of course, that the editor will be of any *real* help at this stage, but sometimes that's OK. At this point, the writer who's wrestling with how to organize the piece, for example, is satisfied to hear the editor say: "Damn, I don't know. Let's talk about it." And maybe that's all it'll take—a return to that one-on-one human relationship that existed before the assignment letter went out.

Something both editors and writers should remember, though, is that each of you is well served by a writer who, having dug into the story a bit, calls the editor and says, "Hey, the story *isn't* the way you see it—it isn't the way we discussed it beforehand." I mention this because I've stressed so much the editor's responsibility to convey *his* concept, *his* feelings about the piece he's assigning. But in the end, the writer is the one on the front line, the one who senses the shape of the story first, the one who has to invest his time and energies writing the piece. If he feels that it's nowhere near the story the editor is expecting, he'd better say so, and right now.

STEP 3: THE MANUSCRIPT

I can't remember an article ever being as good in actuality as it was in my mind at the moment I assigned it.

There's a reason for that, of course: In my mind I hadn't encountered any obstacles, hadn't gone so far as to think in lines, or even paragraphs; I hadn't crafted a lead or an ending, no hard-hitting images, no drop-dead dialogue. All I had was a vague *feeling*, a sense of tone. That, coupled with my reason for assigning the piece, had made the article a great read—mentally.

But even in the magazine world, where some egos need a wide-load sign, and larger-than-life dreams career through the halls, sooner or later you must deal with reality. A manuscript *is* reality, the first recorded stage in the magazine process. Reality shrinks the farther you go toward actual publication: The writer grapples with the infinity of the initial concept, eventually pinning a slice of it to paper; the editor deals with a little less—his own earlier preconceptions and purposes balanced against what the writer finally gives him; the art director considers the editor's ideas and comes up with something he must contain on a few pages; the keyliner measures his world in picas.

As soon as the piece comes in, the editor shifts an internal gear or two and glides from his conceptualizer role to that of synthesizer. No more blue skies, no Technicolor visions. Now he must balance his expectations against the actual manuscript, mix in the fact checker's suggestions, weigh alterations asked by the legal department, occasionally even trim for the prosaic-yet-profound purpose of fitting the article into the magazine. (I sometimes think of the assignment stage as the period of promise . . . and everything afterward as the period of *com*promise.)

Now comes the critical moment. Just picture where the editor and writer are sitting in this emotion-charged game. All along, the editor has put the pressure on the writer, challenged him to perform, exhorted him, cajoled. Now it's the editor's turn to play offense, to get off the sidelines and show his stuff: his judgment, his critical acumen, his ability to focus, to select, to figure out and diplomatically convey to the writer what the hell to *do* with all those pages sitting in the editor's in-box stained with the writer's blood. It's relatively easy to have a good idea, but it's not so easy to know how to move it, through other people, from concept to printed page.

And the writer? He's tense. Writing is a potentially humiliating experience, a hero-or-goat risk venture, and the writer wants to know—at the same time that he doesn't—what the editor's verdict is.

I prefer to give a piece a couple of readings and then respond to the writer by mail. With a letter, the editor gets to think out and organize what he has to say; he gets to soften his criticisms with a few strokes; and the writer can read the letter several times, so that the editor's words have a chance to sink in, and maybe make sense, before the writer responds. I generally suggest that the writer give me a call after he's had a chance to read and think about my comments.

If a writer's smart, he'll give the editor a couple of weeks before calling to see what the editor thinks of the piece. And if the editor's smart, he won't wait for the writer to call. That's a lesson I think about every time I recall an episode I endured with a writer I'll call Ballard.

I was working late one afternoon and made the mistake of picking up an after-hours phone call. "Morgan?" said the voice. "This is Ballard. What did you think about my piece?" I had received his article the day before.

"Hey, man," I said, feeling a little like Dr. Faustus taking an unscreened call from Mephistopheles. The fact was, I *had* read his piece, and I liked it—but there was something a little off about it, something vague, possibly structural. I just hadn't set aside the time to figure out what the problem was, and I didn't want to commit to buying it just yet.

"Well?" he said. I could hear him puffing on a cigarette like a man getting ready to go to war.

"Well," I said, "I like the piece . . . but there seems to be something slightly wrong with it that I haven't been able to put my finger on. Something structural, maybe."

"You don't like it," he said, lighting up again.

"Yeah, I *do*," I said. "It's just that—"

"Well, you can just put that SOB in an envelope and ship it right back. I don't *deserve* this kind of treatment."

At which point *I* got mad and we went on from there. I apologized to him for not getting in touch within twenty-four hours (I think my sarcasm went right past him), but told him I wasn't shipping the piece back until I got around to figuring out what it needed, which I did within the next day or so. I sent him a letter with my comments and he thought they were on target; we then made the necessary corrections. Later he told me he had just gotten nervous and impatient and decided he couldn't wait any longer.

Oh, one other thing: Before calling, he had fortified himself with fourteen beers.

There's a lot about the editor-writer relationship that can drive either party to drink, and at no time does the process get more tense than at this stage, this twilight zone between the time the writer has turned in his manuscript and the editor has uttered the five words a freelancer never tires of hearing: "What's your Social Security number?" That means a check will soon be on its way.

But even after that, the road is littered with obstacles. The editor will put a pencil to the piece, of course, and will send galleys off for the writer to review. If the main revisions have already been done by this point—as they certainly should've been—there should be a few surprises. But I think a few words about this process are in order, for editors as well as writers.

Editing *isn't* rewriting. Editing *isn't* homogenizing a writer's style so that the only thing different from one article to another is the subject. Forget for a moment that the editor holds the power of the purse strings; that kind of power is weak in comparison to the power of good editing because editing is diplomacy, and diplomacy is getting what you want by convincing others that what you want is right. Diplomacy is tact, taste and timing. And compromise.

Richard Price wrote his piece on Bear Bryant about twice as long as it appeared in the magazine—which is to say, a lot longer than we asked for. He was apprehensive when his editor told him it was going to have to be cut, but he was willing to wait and see. The editor made the cuts, taking out large chunks at a time. When you cut, you usually have to rework the transitions so the paragraphs fit together again. The editor sent the revisions to Price, along with a suggestion for a new ending. Price rewrote some of the transitions and tried for another ending, which *we* then didn't like. We reorganized a paragraph or two to shape yet another ending—which Price didn't like. Finally, Price came up with still another ending that all of us could live with. Fortunately, Bear Bryant never suffered such a working over on the playing field.

It's all part of the give-and-take of the editor-writer alliance. Ours is a very personal, private work that's eventually displayed in public, and we have to be careful of—and thankful for—each other. *Playboy* couldn't really have demanded that Price accept our ending of his piece—after all, we hired him to give us his insights into Bear Bryant, and his name goes on the piece. But the magazine's name goes *over* the piece, and if we had felt, say, that the ending he wanted was somehow an embarrassment to the magazine (we didn't, by the way), we probably would've had to reject the article. Seldom does it come to that if it's gone as far as this project had, because by that time both parties have a real stake in making the thing work. The art of compromise doesn't mean simply rolling over; it means knowing how far to roll before you draw the line.

All editors have been guilty of drawing it too early. When Norman Mailer wanted more space than usual between the lines of *Playboy*'s excerpt of *The Executioner's Song*, Mailer's gripping story of Gary Gilmore, I refused; fortunately, editorial director Arthur Kretchmer decided it was worth having a look at the type before we said no, and we wound up salvaging a blockbuster.

But sometimes we don't draw the line soon enough. I once endured the ravings of a wonderful writer who, having reviewed the galleys of his article, suddenly turned into an insufferable prima donna: *We had cut some commas, and he wanted them put back.* Our copy chief had marked them to be omitted and I had approved the cuts. All professional magazines have stylebooks that cover everything from whether to spell *okay* "okay" or "OK," or what to do in the case of serial commas. It's the copyeditor's job to ride herd on style, so the editor of an individual article is usually caught between a rock (the copyeditor) and a hard place (the writer). The editor must try to please both. I do believe, however, that the editor on the piece, not the copyeditor, should have the final say on how a piece should run.

In the case of the comma prima donna, I eventually agreed to go over the galleys with him and hear the case for keeping each damn comma. It took a lot of conversations, a lot of hours, and it underscored for me what an ego-intensive business this is, what hard questions there are to answer. All the writer has is his words and how he's strung them together. I understand that. I also understand that if *every* writer went to the mat over every comma, we'd never get out a magazine.

I was going to end this piece with the preceding paragraph, but that didn't seem quite fair: The example wasn't typical, really, of the editor-writer relationship. It was just a glimpse, for the purpose of example, at how minuscule the points of discussion can be, and how vast the understanding and sensitivity each must have for the other. I'm sure writers tell just as many such stories about editors.

But editors, because they hold the purse strings, generally get the last word, and I thought I might change that here. Because a friend of mine, a writer who was once an editor, inscribed his first book to me with words that capture something basic about this marriage of talents that is the editor-writer relationship. On the surface he's talking economics, a subject editors and writers often discuss. But between the lines, there's more: a truth, maybe, about the temperaments of each side, and a hint at each one's occasional yearnings, when his own chosen pressures get too fierce, to switch places with the other:

> *Writin' ain't as bad*
> *as goin' to work.*
> *It also ain't as good*
> *as makin' a living.*

At the time, I thought he was writing about himself. Now I know he was talking about all of us.

How to Call an Editor

BY GARY LEGWOLD

F our years ago I made two telephone calls that changed my life. I was then managing editor/features of a McGraw-Hill sports medicine journal, but it was time to either give free-lancing my best shot or trash the idea for good.

I picked up the phone and called *Esquire*. Only as I was transferred to "whoever edits the Sports Clinic department" did I wonder if I weren't being a bit impulsive.

"Hello."

"Ah . . . to whom am I speaking," I asked.

Pause. (Gary, what have you *done*?) The person said he was Curtis Pesmen, chief of research and editor of the Sports Clinic (now Active Health) department. We talked. Nice guy. I made a note to send him some clips and ideas.

I hung up and called Paul Krantz, former health and education editor at *Better Homes and Gardens*. Again, we talked. Again, nice guy. He mentioned they were trying to attract young readers and had ideas for a department called Fitness Matters. Considering my background, might I be interested in that department?

Although I did end up selling articles to both magazines and have worked with both editors since, I now cringe at the mistakes I made with those calls—mistakes that new freelancers often make when they reach for the telephone. I should have known both magazines much better—and I especially should have known who Pesmen was at *Esquire*. Perhaps the only reason Pesmen and Krantz gave me the time of day was that I was an editor myself at a magazine in their area of interest.

But I should have had a story idea—a well-conceived story idea—and written it down, mailed it and waited before I called. So write first, then call.

You can't expect to start building a relationship with an editor by calling; many editors distrust what they hear from eager-beaver strangers on the phone. In fact, if you are a developing writer, the rule is write first, then write some more. You must have credibility and experience in developing and writing articles before you call and start mixing it up with an editor. Think of a phone call as an audition; if you're not prepared and not used to being "on stage," it'll show and you'll quickly hear "Don't call us, we'll call you."

I say this to discourage some writers from calling and misusing, if not abusing, the phone. But there are writers, writers with experience, talent and ideas, who can use the phone to their advantage. *If* they're the right writers calling at the right time with the right message.

A properly set-up phone conversation can demonstrate your professionalism, enthusiasm, flexibility, competence and confidence. And unlike a letter, a personal talk with an editor gives you a chance to listen, to sense openings and possibilities, and to gain insight into an editor's planning and thinking. Likewise, your call helps the editor judge *you.* Some query letters come off "pushy and disgusting," says Annette Spence, an editor I've worked with. "Sometimes after a talk you see the writer isn't such a snot."

I'm a phone fan because it adds a personal, and at times powerful, touch to my dealings with editors. The phone is a tool that has helped my sales. Follow these ten guidelines, and it can help yours, too.

Know the magazine before you call. You've heard this before. But you'll keep hearing it because it's editors' most common advice to freelancers.

Knowing a magazine is different than reading *about* the magazine in *Writer's Market.* "You can always tell the callers who are just going down a list in a writer's guide," says Christopher Koch, former executive editor at the now-defunct *Bicycle Guide.*

Write before you call. Editors don't cotton to callers who ring them up just to say: "Hey, I'm out here. What's cookin'?" Editors prefer a letter first outlining your background, with some clips and story ideas. Don't spend too much time on all the honors and glories in your background; it's helpful but it's also past tense. Editors are planning future issues and are under pressure to come up with good ideas. If you can do that now and then for a handful of editors—and follow it up with a good story—you'll seldom be out of work.

Wait before you call. Don't call right away to see if your letter was received. Give editors two or three weeks to consider ideas.

Know yourself before you call. Be honest about your abilities. Ask yourself, "How good am I on the phone?" To improve your phone skills:

- Analyze a tape of yourself. Do you sound honest, upbeat, friendly and self-assured?
- Develop a pleasing voice. Work on diction. Concentrate on consonants, which begin and end many words. Check how fast you speak. Too fast or slow and you'll lose an editor. Sales experts advise speaking at about 140 words a minute.
- Before calling, write a script. But don't read it when talking to the editor. You'll sound canned or too slick. Have the script handy so you won't waste time when covering the important points of your call.
- Call when you're up. It's hard to be upbeat when you're down.
- Call when you don't need to call. If you sound desperate for work, editors—thinking perhaps there's good reason you're desperate for work—will say, "Let's call the whole thing off."
- Stand up as you talk. It will help you think and field questions.

A word about confidence. When calling, confidence is everything. If you have it, show it; if you don't have it, develop it because editors look for it. Writers "can't fake it on the phone," says Krantz at *Better Homes and Gardens.* "They should have knowledge and a certain confidence in being a professional."

Be courteous. "At times it's almost frenzied around here, and a caller from out of the blue assumes I should talk," says Kate Delhagen, former senior editor at *Runner's World.* "It's better if you ask, 'Have you got time to talk?' "

You may have to reschedule several times before the editor has time to talk. Take this as a good sign; editors say so if they don't want to talk. It may take weeks to talk, but your frustration must be in check when you do. If you display sarcasm or arrogance, you're history.

Courtesy is essential in overriding bad associations editors have with phones. Phones infuriate many editors. Rude strangers can interrupt them on the phone even when colleagues are shut off by a closed door. What's more, editors, who like to control everything from editorial content to commas, can't conveniently control the phone—and that bugs them. "When the phone rings, editors are put on the defensive, a position they don't want to be in," says Daniel Kelly, former editor of *Minnesota Monthly.*

Be willing to walk away. And take your self-respect with you. Some editors may not like the phone, but they make the time to talk because they appreciate what good writers—who write first—can do for them. Editors who don't take time to talk are most likely doing you a favor by staying out of your life. "If an editor isn't willing to talk on the phone [at some point], you probably shouldn't be dealing with him or her anyway," says Krantz.

Keep your call short. "The longer the call, the less a writer knows about the magazine," says Curtis Pesmen, who has since left *Esquire*. "It's not my job to do a lot of explaining of departments. My job is to help the assignment once it's made."

So do your homework and then can the chitchat. This reduces an editor's annoyance and suspicion of being sold. "Don't be buddy-buddy with an editor," says David Higdon, a senior writer at *Tennis*. "I get this with public relations people mostly. They call and say: 'Hey, how's it going? How's the weather? New York's great.' That's the worst thing you can do. Get to the point."

Know your stuff. Your call should be short, but be prepared to go long and answer questions from the editor. You want questions, because the only alternative to Q&A is "No thanks." If you don't know your stuff and fumble around in answering questions, the editor may just drop you and your idea.

As editors cross-examine, they think. This can easily lead to brainstorming. Your idea per se may not work, but what you say may fit into their plans or trigger a thought. When David Higdon was with *American Health*, he heard a freelancer's idea on fitness in Britain. Higdon wasn't hot on the idea until the headline "Fit Brits" popped into his head. Higdon assigned the story and that was the headline.

Sign off first. Don't be short with an editor, but when you're done, say good-bye before he or she is forced to. Signing off first shows editors you respect their decision and time, and that you are a professional and have your own eye on efficiency. You also save editors the bothersome task of getting rid of one more caller.

Stay in touch. Calling is easier the second time around, especially if you wrote a good story the first time. You and the editor know each other better and trust each other more. Calls are returned quicker. Some editors allow, or often encourage, writers they know to shoot them ideas over the phone before sending a letter on ideas that sound good. That's a timesaver.

Staying in touch doesn't mean you should forget these guidelines and become a pest. In general, write when a letter will accomplish everything a call can. However, I do try to add a personal touch by calling an editor every two to three months, but only if I have story ideas.

Regular phoning can lead to assignments not planned for. When I called Daniel Kelly at *Minnesota Monthly*, he asked what I was working on. I said a book proposal on infertility. Tell me more, he says. Turns out he was planning an issue on family, and a story on infertility had possibilities. I wrote the story, which led to two speaking engagements and a TV talk show appearance.

Calling can't replace talent. No matter how good you are on the phone, you must be better on paper. But if you can back up your phone calls with articles that meet editors' needs and expectations, you may not have to use these guidelines at all. Editors will be calling you.

Responding to Editors' Replies

BY SALLY-JO BOWMAN

My mailbox holds the trigger to my emotions.
Those returning self-addressed, stamped envelopes lying in the box can bring detonations of despair—or explosions of euphoria. Sometimes I'd like to stomp the mailbox to pieces upon receiving a rejection to a query. Sometimes I'd like to dance around the box when I get a go-ahead. Query replies range from nothing to a contract, and there's a smart way of dealing with each.

NO ANSWER

If a magazine hasn't answered a query within the time specified in its writer's guidelines or in *Writer's Market*, send a follow-up letter. Here's a real-life example from my correspondence with *Outside* magazine:

Dear Kathy:
In early October I queried you about a piece on Canyon de Chelly. I enclose a copy of the letter in case it went astray.
I look forward to hearing from you soon. Happy Holidays.

Dear Sally-Jo:
Thanks for sending another copy of your Canyon de Chelly query—the original did go astray somewhere. I apologize for not getting back to you sooner. . . . Unfortunately, we already have a piece in-house on Canyon de Chelly. . . .

This wasn't the answer I had hoped for, but at least it was an answer. Stuff does get lost in the mail; give the editor the benefit of the doubt. I think sending a photocopy of the original query is a better bet than simply repeating the information in the second letter. It saves you work, and it shows the editor that you did query previously.

NO, NO, NEVER

Editors aren't usually *that* rude. But they do send standard, preprinted unsigned rejections that say things like "Thank you for your inquiry. Unfortunately, your story idea is not suited to our current needs."

These can bring on deep despair because they offer no insight into *why* the magazine is passing on your idea. It's easy to read an impersonal preprinted *no* as saying, *You are a rotten writer. You will not succeed.*

But there's another attitude worth adopting. A travel writer I once knew was losing a lot of work time agonizing over her first few No, No, Nevers. Then one day she adopted a new attitude: "This is my opportunity to send this idea elsewhere."

My own policy is to rework such a query for another editor and have it out within twenty-four hours.

THE INFORMATIVE FORM REJECTION

Some magazines use preprinted rejection forms that provide clues as to the reason for rejection.

On the *USAir* form an editor checks an item from this list:

- Subject duplicates material we've recently published or plan to publish.
- Subject is well-covered by other publications.
- We do not publish humor pieces, poetry, fiction or first-person essays.
- We only publish stories that are on *USAir*'s route system.
- The destination is not on this year's calendar.
- The subject comes close, but we can't consider it at this time. Query us again in _____ months.
- The subject is too narrow.
- The subject is covered by one of our regular columnists.
  Other:

At the bottom of the form is a nice paragraph apologizing for the impersonal treatment and inviting the writer to query again. Do it.

THE PERSONAL REJECTION

If an editor takes the time to write a personal note, read it carefully. If it's an overt or implied invitation to try another idea, get on it right away.

In October 1990 I queried *Friendly Exchange* on a travel piece about

Mt. Rainier. The reply: "Great query, bad timing. Try us with another idea."

In November I suggested an article on Steens Mountain, Oregon. This time I got: "Another good query, but we have two Oregon articles already planned in '91. . . . I'll have to wait to return to that locale."

In December I took a new tack. (And by this time I was addressing the editor by her first name.)

Dear Adele:

Thanks for another nice turn down, this time on "Steens Country." I'm starting to feel like I know you just from writing good queries on subjects you can't use. Now I'm writing to let you know of my plans that will take me to areas about which you could consider queries.

I mentioned a Southwest car trip with a dog. I mentioned the solar eclipse in Hawaii. I mentioned Civil War and Revolutionary War/Colonial sites in Virginia. I struck out anyway. But not permanently.

This time the reply told me the magazine plans its editorial content up to eighteen months ahead and that it seldom uses stories outside the continental U.S. west of the Mississippi. By then it was April 1991. I queried on a historical travel article about the Oregon Trail:

Dear Adele:

I haven't given up. Here's a story suitable for early '93. I can't beat it for fitting your geographic boundaries.

In June Adele wrote:

I plan to introduce your topic at our next planning session. If it flies, I'll get back to you.

Months went by. Early in 1992 I checked my log of outstanding queries and pondered what to do. In March Adele called. She was ready for the Oregon Trail story. My persistence finally netted a nine hundred dollar assignment.

Now I always jump on a good rejection right away, and point out in my subsequent query that the editor just gave me a nice turn down. It's important to get that second (or third, or fourth) story idea to her while she still remembers you.

A variation of the personal rejection is something that happened to me with *Writer's Digest*. I queried once on "How to Write a Great Ending, Period." The reply:

Good topic, lousy timing. We've recently assigned a piece on endings. . . . How are you on transitions, though? We've been looking for a good transitions piece for a while. Interested?

You bet I was. "Moving Readers With Ease" ran in December 1991.

THE GOOD, GOOD GO-AHEAD

This is the response we'd like to have *all* the time. When it happens, I am instantly euphoric. But as the news sinks in, I panic.

Often a go-ahead comes in a letter, which allows time to ponder it. But when it comes in a phone call, it's important to have your wits about you.

However that news arrives, prepare for a phone conversation when negotiating the terms of assignment. If the reply was a letter, call the editor within a day or two of receipt. A go-ahead almost always mentions only some of the necessary details. For me it's easiest to talk about the story first and money matters last. Here's what I cover:

• *Deadline*: It's usually negotiable. Build in extra time for problems. Never agree to a deadline you might not be able to meet.

• *Length of story*: How exact does this need to be? Is there room to go over?

• *Approach*: Does my slant in the proposal sound okay? Does the editor want something else?

• *Sidebars*: If the magazine uses them, what should they be?

• *Photos/art*: Should you supply a selection of photos? Does the publication prefer to use a staff photographer? Does the art director need suggestions about where to obtain graphics?

• *Rights to be purchased*: Don't sell more than first North American serial rights if you can help it. (Consult the latest *Writer's Market* for a thorough discussion of rights.)

• *Fee*: What is it? Does it include sidebars, or will those bring extra pay? If you've worked for the publication before or have done a similar story for a similar publication, you may want to ask for more money. If you know the expense policy is liberal, asking for a larger fee may not be so important. Mention at the end of the conversation that you assume payment will be on acceptance. Do all you can to avoid payment on publication—you may wait a long time for your check.

• *Expenses*: Estimate what these will be and tell the editor it would help a lot if she would cover them. If you've agreed to payment on publication, ask for expenses to be paid when you turn in the story.

- *Kill fee*: Ask for the contract to include a kill fee clause. It should specify an amount between 20 percent and 50 percent of the full fee to be paid if the editor rejects the manuscript.

I expect a contract assignment when I write for a magazine. Notice in the list above that I sneaked from *rights to be purchased* through *fee* and *expenses*, never mentioning *contract* except in passing under the *kill fee* section. I end the conversation by saying, "I think we've covered everything I need to know. I can start work as soon as I receive your contract." If the editor says the publication doesn't offer contracts, request a letter of agreement confirming all the points you just covered. If the editor promises the letter but doesn't follow through, write the letter yourself and send it to the editor.

Usually this works. Sometimes an editor will insist that you must work on speculation, which doesn't carry the promise of a kill fee. This is especially true if you've never written for the publication. Even then, though, there might still be room to negotiate.

I recently had this issue come up with *Arizona Highways*. The go-ahead letter for "Hiking Canyon de Chelly" (yes, it's the same article I'd previously queried *Outside* about; like I said, keep them in the mail) read: "We like your Canyon de Chelly idea. We're interested in seeing 1,600 words on the subject. But it would have to be on speculation, a first-timer policy with the magazine."

When I called the editor, I started my conversation by telling him how pleased I was that he was interested in the story. I had already done the research and told him I could have a manuscript to him within two weeks. I asked if the magazine, famous for its photography, would take care of illustrating it. He said yes, but asked me to suggest possible subject matter for the shots. I knew he didn't use sidebars, so didn't mention one. And since he had used that ugly word—*speculation*—I skipped my spiel about kill fee and contract.

Instead I said, "The only problem I see is working on speculation. I generally work only on contract."

"Well, we have a firm policy. . . . We're part of state government. . . ."

"What I really want to guard against is the possibility of submitting the piece and then not having your decision for months. That sometimes happens."

"I can appreciate that," he said. "I would never do that to a writer. Tell you what. If you have the story to me in two weeks, I'll promise to make a decision in the following two weeks."

This seemed like good faith. "Deal," I said.

I turned in the story. In two weeks I got a check and this letter: "Nice work on the Canyon de Chelly piece. Please keep us in mind for other things. I'm sending along a writer's guide to spark your imagination."

Happy ending. And probably a contract assignment in the future.

So the next time you're at your mailbox facing a pile of SASEs, don't be too quick to pull your emotional trigger. Set your sights on success by turning rejection into acceptance.

Your Guide to Copyright

BY JAY STULLER

The phone calls roll into the Library of Congress's Copyright Office by the thousands each week. More than a hundred thousand inquiries arrive by mail each year. The questions are pretty basic: "How do I copyright my work?" "What's the difference between copyright and registration?" Still others concern how and where to get copyright registration forms—many others, because the Copyright Office annually registers more than half a million book manuscripts, poems, articles, computer programs, magazines, motion pictures, newspapers, and, among other creative works "in a fixed and tangible form," musical compositions and lyrics. Since about 40 percent of these works are unpublished—and registering a manuscript costs twenty dollars a pop—it's clear that a large number of folks consider copyrighting serious stuff indeed.

Dozens of books cover the subject. In one, *How to Protect Your Creative Work: All You Need to Know About Copyright* (John Wiley & Sons), author David A. Weinstein spends more than three hundred pages dissecting the Copyright Act of 1976, nuances of infringements, statutory limitations, and what can and cannot be protected. Because the law is downright byzantine, there are attorneys who live off this complex field; not surprisingly, perhaps, Weinstein is a lawyer.

However, for the average freelancer, dealing with rights and copyright should not be complex, time-consuming or expensive. In fact, after more than twenty years in the magazine writing business, after working with roughly one hundred different publications on more articles than I care to remember, I've yet to register a manuscript with the Copyright Office. I can recall only one minor beef regarding copyrights, more on that later.

Copyright law provides basic, automatic protection for writers, whether or not a manuscript is registered with the Copyright Office or even published. Under the Copyright Act of 1976, which went into effect in 1978, an "original work of authorship" has copyright protection from the moment the work is in fixed form. That is, a soon as you have that article, short story or book on paper, on a computer disk or even spoken into a tape if you're Barbara Cartland, it is protected by copyright law.

You created it, you own it. And what you're selling to an editor isn't the article itself, but actually the right to *use* the material. Let's cover the basics of what you should know about copyright.

WHAT YOU CAN COPYRIGHT

Because U.S. government publications aren't copyrighted, some of the following is quoted liberally—and with impunity—from a Library of Congress document called *Copyright Basics*, a circular that attempts to answer some of the questions most often asked of the staff at the Library of Congress. (The free Copyright Information Kit is a handy reference; write the Copyright Office of the Library of Congress, Washington, DC 20559 for a copy. For general information or answers to specific questions, call (202)707-3000; for registration forms and circulars, call the Copyright Office Hotline—(202)707-9100. Business hours are 8:30 A.M. to 5 P.M., Eastern time.)

Copyright protection exists for broad categories of works: literary works; musical works (including any accompanying words); dramatic works (including any accompanying music); pantomimes and choreographic works; pictorial, graphic and sculptural works; motion pictures and other audiovisual works; and sound recordings. Copyright law generally gives the owner of copyright the exclusive right to reproduce the work, to prepare derivative works based on the copyrighted material and to perform and/or display the work publicly.

Note the word *generally*, for copyright law includes a number of limitations and exemptions.

Several categories of material are not eligible for copyright protection, such as titles and short slogans; works consisting entirely of information taken from common sources and public documents, such as standard calendars, lists and tables; and speeches and performances that have not been fixed on paper or recorded. Work in the "public domain" (that is, material whose copyright has lapsed, or that was never covered by copyright), material that lacks sufficient originality, and basic themes and plots can't be protected by copyright. Neither can ideas, which beginning writers often find perplexing. (A minor digression: My personal view is that ideas, especially in nonfiction writing, are cheap currency. Editors rarely steal an idea from an unknown writer and assign it to another. But it's a fact—which I know from speaking with at least two or three magazine editors a day—that no matter how novel a proposal, chances are at least a half-dozen writers have thought of it simultaneously. A journalist is invariably racing against others; you win only when you hit the right magazine with the right proposal at the right time.)

Since the idea isn't copyrighted, what is? The *form* of the idea, how it's expressed, how you've strung together words. Curiously enough, the form of the words in a query letter is copyright protected, even if the idea is not.

In addition, a fictional character who is distinctly and strongly developed is protected. If a film producer were to lift such a character from your short story and build a film around him, this would infringe on your right to create or license "derivative" works. Likewise, an attempt to publish a serious novel about Rambo would buy you a lawsuit, although a parody of an established character is OK, since it falls under "fair use" doctrine. (Fair use, under copyright law, allows people to use copyrighted materials in limited ways: brief quotes in other manuscripts, excerpts in book reviews, small numbers of copies distributed in classrooms, as examples.)

To gain copyright protection, your work must be "original," which means you can't copy from or infringe on another writer's copyrighted work. This does not mean that something you write can't occasionally be similar to what someone else creates, and vice-versa, in terms of the topic, tone and even the substance.

For example, after reading a small story in *Aviation Week & Space Technology* about how high-G turns in modern fighters were knocking out pilots and causing crashes, I figured *Air & Space Smithsonian* magazine might like a detailed look at acceleration forces. The editors agreed: I researched and wrote an article based on the topic, and the piece appeared nearly a year after it was submitted and accepted. Meanwhile, *California* magazine came out with an article called "Living and Dying at Nine Gs."

While the basic idea was the same, both articles were conceived independently. Moreover, I concentrated on Air Force flyers; the *California* writer dealt with Navy flyers.

However, elements from a piece I once wrote on legendary UCLA basketball coach John Wooden's hoop camp for adults—for *PSA*'s inflight magazine—are almost certain to appear in any subsequent article about the coach and his camp, whether taken from my story or not. Simple, factual descriptions of the man's amazing career are frequently going to come out the same way. And since Wooden tells such delightful stories, a writer would be a fool not to weave some into the piece.

Resident experts on any given subject frequently give the same information to journalists—over and over, and often in similar form. But as long as the resulting works are developed independently—no matter the similarity of language—they are copyright protected.

KNOW YOUR SOURCE

You can, of course, use the information and facts found in copyrighted material without infringing on it. Moreover, fair use allows you to use snippets of a piece; this is, after all, what a lot of research is all about. It is best, however, to always put things into your own words, to cite the source, and to be very judicious in the use of other people's material— unless, like a Shakespeare work, it's in the public domain—because not being careful could open you to an infringement action.

Fair use is something of a complex and gray area, which can make an infringement suit a gamble. I tend not to be particularly sensitive if some of my lines are borrowed.

For instance, a descriptive scene from my *PSA* Wooden piece landed in a national magazine article about people at the top of their sport. It was a very small percentage of the borrowing author's total work and helped him make a point. Again, I considered it no big deal. But if someone copies half of your book word for word and makes a bundle off it, by all means unleash an attorney.

My only copyright difficulty came when I wrote a piece on counterfeiting for *Kiwanis* magazine. The Secret Service sent me a packet of material on the topic, including photocopies of typewritten pages containing anecdotes about great counterfeiters of the past. Because the material came from the government and had no copyright symbol on it, I assumed it was open game. (Official government publications belong to the people and—as I've said—can't be copyrighted.)

However, when the piece came out, the author of a decades-old book on counterfeiting claimed that the *Kiwanis* piece infringed on his work. Since I had recast the anecdotes in my own style and they were but a small part of a story on current trends in the bogus bill business, I stuck by my guns. After discussing the matter with the book author, we agreed that if the anecdotes were indeed from his book, he'd have a beef with the Secret Service—not me—for photocopying and distributing the material without the author's permission or appropriate copyright markings.

YOUR COPYRIGHT

For works crafted or first published after 1977, a copyright generally lasts until fifty years after the author's death. However, for anonymous and pseudonymous works, and works made for hire (discussed below), copyright protection expires one hundred years from creation or seventy-five years after publication, whichever is sooner. (The trend internationally is to lengthen these terms, and bills are pending in Congress to do so in the U.S.) These are fixed terms and may not be renewed. (For works published before 1978, different rules apply. For more information, see Section 303 of the Copyright Act.)

Prior to the Copyright Act of 1976, work published without a copyright notice, or an improper notice, could fall into the public domain and the writer would lose all rights to the material. Today, such a problem—even if a work is published without a copyright notice—can be remedied if you make a "reasonable effort" to place a notice on all undistributed copies and to register the work with the Copyright Office within five years of publication.

Most magazines contain a copyright notice: the symbol ©, the word *Copyright* or the abbreviation *Copr.*, followed by the year date and a name. If the magazine you're writing for doesn't carry this notice, you may want to ask the editor to print your copyright notice on your story.

(Should you place your copyright notice at the top of your unpublished manuscripts? Will the copyright symbol provide a useful service? Well, I've run into two theories here. Many commend the habit as it shows an editor that you know your rights and what you're doing.

(But one New York literary agent says this simple little notice screams *amateur*. "Professionals know that the work is copyrighted anyway," she says. "And if that is the first thing an editor sees, he or she is going to think, 'Doesn't this person trust me?' There are enough roadblocks to getting a manuscript a serious read. If I receive one that I feel is worth sending to a publisher and it contains a copyright notice on the first page, I mask it out, photocopy that page and only then send it along." I agree with the agent. Putting a copyright notice on a manuscript is like starting out a query letter by saying "I'm a writer . . ." You wouldn't be sending a proposal to an editor if you weren't.)

To register a work, simply fill out the form provided by the Copyright Office—include the twenty dollar fee and one copy of the work if it's unpublished, two if published—and send the packet to the Register of Copyrights, Library of Congress, Washington, DC 20559. Moreover, you can register a large number of articles or stories simultaneously for the same twenty dollars; check with the Copyright Office for information on "group registration."

Why bother to spend the twenty dollars to register unpublished material if it's automatically copyrighted from the moment it's in a fixed form?

"I don't think I've ever mailed in a copyright form," says Bill Hogan. Glen Martin hasn't. I haven't, and neither had the four other professional freelancers I asked.

On the other hand, the Copyright Office recommends registration of unpublished works mainly for legal reasons. If your work is infringed upon, registration establishes a public record for your claim and prima facie evidence that a court will accept.

Before you can bring an infringement suit to court, your work must be registered with the Copyright Office. If you've registered *before* an infringement takes place, you can sue for actual damages—the income you lost or the benefits gained by the party who improperly used your material—plus statutory damages and attorney's fees.

You can also register *after* an infringement and then take the case to court, but the case is weaker than if you had registered before, and you can sue only for actual damages. Remember, if the material was stolen from a copyright-registered magazine or book, registration has already been taken care of. (If you're going after damages, you must coolly consider the stakes. Should the offending party have made fifty dollars by swiping a portion of your work, you might win a judgment, but the time and trouble is an expensive way to uphold a principle.)

I'd rather spend the twenty dollar registration fee on phone calls and postage hawking new ideas for articles. If I couldn't sell a particular manuscript, anyone who tries to steal and market it has a car with a dead battery on his hands. But registering work with the Copyright Office is a personal choice; if you feel more secure, go ahead.

The fact of the matter, though, is that copyright problems are relatively rare. I checked with a New York law firm that handles a considerable volume of copyright business. "I don't believe we have that many infringement cases," says a legal aide there. "Most of our work involves the licensing of copyrighted material and reviewing questions of whether material is in the public domain."

"There's a lot of paranoia out there among people who worry too much about copyrights and register unpublished work," says one New York literary agent. "The fact is, it's hard enough to get someone to buy a book manuscript, much less steal it."

Says writer Glen Martin, "If you worry about whether your article on current chain saw models for a regional magazine isn't sufficiently protected, or that somebody would actually want to heist it, you're in the wrong business. It's a concern that can stand in the way of productive writing."

Worrying that someone will infringe on your unpublished work is akin to posing for a book jacket cover or planning the dedication before writing the first chapter. If you take a balanced view of your work, and hold onto as many rights as possible to writing that may have resale value (while not jeopardizing the sale of material with limited worth), your business will run smoothly. And with hard work, profitably, too.

Work for Hire:
A Red Flag for Writers

BY ELLEN KOZAK

Though most editors and writers understand that copyright for a piece of original writing belongs to its author from the moment it is set down in any form, confusion often reigns regarding the one glaring exception to this general rule—works made for hire.

A true work made for hire turns the copyright law around, giving the copyright in a work to whoever commissioned it. The person who does the actual writing has no rights at all—if you wrote it, you may not resell it, read it aloud in public or even run off copies of it and send them out. You have no control over adaptations or resales. Indeed, if you are foolish enough to write fiction under such a contract, you can't write any other stories about the characters you invented, because those stories will be considered *derivative works*, and the right to prepare derivative works belongs exclusively to the copyright owner unless he or she signs it away. And a special variation on Murphy's Law designed just for writers guarantees that the piece to which you give up all rights is the one that will turn out to have the most lasting value.

Writing something as a work for hire can be appropriate when you are employed to write copy—for example, by a newspaper or an advertising agency. But it makes little sense—with rare exception—for a general freelancer to do so. Nor does it make sense to make an agreement that is closely related to writing something as a work for hire: selling all rights to a piece of writing (I'll discuss the differences and similarities between the two in a moment).

Authors sign away *some* rights to their work every day in the normal course of business. Whether you're assigning first North American serial rights or English language book rights or giving permission for someone to prepare a T-shirt based on the description of the hero of your novel, selling rights to your works is what you're in business to do.

But each right you sell—whether it's first serial rights, or book rights or filmstrip rights or the right to write a short story using one of your characters—can be worth additional money to you. The more rights you keep, the more you can sell later.

When you sell "all rights," you give away the whole ball of wax. Assigning all rights and assigning the copyright are identical, since "copyright" is merely the name given to the collection of *all the rights* you have in your work.

When a work is termed "made for hire," however, you have no rights to assign. Whoever commissioned the work is considered, under the law, to be the author of the work.

Whether you give away all your rights or never have any to give away may not seem to make much of a difference, and, in truth, for the first thrity-five years after an assignment is made, perhaps it doesn't. But the difference between *ever* owning and *never* owning is found in a special escape clause provided by the law. To keep some future Edgar Allen Poe or Charles Dickens from coughing out his lungs in debtors' prison while his publisher grows fat on the fruits of his genius, Congress stuck a special termination provision into the copyright law. When you have made an all-rights assignment, assigned the copyright—or even just assigned more rights than you should have—you or your heirs can, after thirty-five years, take back the rights you've given away.

This procedure is *not* automatic. It requires specific action on your part, following the somewhat rigorous rules for notice and reclamation laid out in the copyright law. And if your work is of ephemeral value, this may not be worth doing. But if you've given away all rights—or even just serial rights or movie rights—to the Great American Novel, it's nice to know that you—or whoever inherits your estate—can get them back before the copyright runs out.

Unfortunately, you and your heirs cannot exercise this termination in works that fall *legitimately* (remember that word) into the category of works made for hire. You can't take the rights back because you never owned them. They belong to the "author"—who isn't you!

In addition to this ownership problem, there is a second way in which works made for hire differ from works in which you assign rights. This is the duration of copyright protection. Under law, copyright lasts for the life of the author plus fifty years. But in works made for hire, the work enters the public domain seventy-five years from the year of its first publication or one hundred years from its creation, whichever is sooner. Depending on how long you live, this can either lengthen or reduce the term of copyright protection.

But remember, I said this applied only to works that are *legitimately* works made for hire. Different federal appeals courts have come to different conclusions about how the work-for-hire law should be read. The U.S. Supreme Court attempted to resolve those differences with its ruling early this summer in *Community for Creative Non-violence v. Reid*. The Court concluded that Congress meant what it said when it provided two distinct means for classifying a work as "made for hire."

The first gives the rights to works created by employees *within the scope of their employment* to the employer. This clarifies copyright ownership in works produced by newspaper reporters, advertising copywriters and company publicists, when those works are created within the scope of their normal duties as employees.

But watch out for the term *employee*, the definition of which was the subject of the recent Supreme Court ruling. To establish an employment relationship, the Court relied on a multi-faceted test that includes such elements as where the work was done, who provided the materials and who set the working hours. However, the Court rejected a standard of formal salaried employment.

Thus, it is still possible for some freelancers to fall into the employee category. For example, you don't have to be paid to be an employee; volunteers may fall into this category, if their regular duties include preparing works under the supervision of the organization for which they work.

Of course, the copyright in works that employee-writers create outside the scope of their employment belongs to them. Thus, if you are a newspaper reporter and write a novel in your spare time, the novel's copyright is *not* the property of the newspaper—nor, unless you have a specific contract that says so, is the book you write based on information you have gathered in the course of your job.

This is because, since there is no copyright in facts, *copyright* law will not prevent you from using facts gathered in the course of regular employment to create a book based on those facts. (However, other areas of law, such as unfair competition or employment contracts, may prevent you from doing so.)

Unless freelancers fall within the definition of employees, their works are generally covered by another section of the law. This section has specific requirements—so just because a publication says that it buys "works made for hire" doesn't mean that it does. Three carefully defined conditions must be fulfilled before a freelancer's work can be termed a work made for hire.

1. **The work must be "specially ordered or commissioned."** This means that work that comes in over the transom can never be considered a work made for hire. A work that is complete before it is ever seen by the buyer obviously couldn't have been "specially ordered or commissioned."

Of course, articles written on assignment *are* specially ordered and commissioned. Does this mean that such works are made for hire? The law says no—not unless all three conditions are fulfilled, and specially ordering and commissioning a work is only one of them.

2. **The parties "expressly agree in a written instrument signed by both of them that the work shall be considered a work made for hire."** The law is quite clear on the requirement of an *express* agreement signed by *both* parties. It must contain the words *made for hire*. It requires at the very least an assignment letter, countersigned by the writer and mailed back, containing those words. A contract with your signature and that of someone representing the publisher is the more formal way to handle this.

The copyright law is also quite clear that where there is no contract, copyright in contributions to collective works (such as magazines) remains with the author. Issuing guidelines that say all contributions will be considered works made for hire does not put them into that category without a written document, signed by both parties, agreeing that they are.

And note that word *shall* in the part of the law I quoted. Many lawyers read it as requiring that such a contract be signed *in advance* of creating the work. Otherwise, Congress could have said *is.*

3. **The work must be "for use as a contribution to a collective work, as part of a motion picture or other audiovisual work, as a translation, as a supplementary work, as a compilation, as an instructional text, as a test, as answer material for a test, or as an atlas."** While articles written for magazines and encyclopedias are collective works—you'll note that nowhere in the list do the words *booklet, book* or *novel* appear. A freelancer who writes a promotional booklet owns the copyright in it unless he assigns it. And a freelancer's novel can never be a work made for hire.

This, of course, hasn't deterred some publishers from trying to get around the law. I know of several writers who have been asked to sign contracts that state that the writers are employees for the purpose of writing a book, but that they are waiving all the rights they would have as employees under the law.

The law looks askance at such contracts. It is normally considered against public policy for an employee to waive protections the law provides for all workers. As a result, such waivers are likely to be void, and may even backfire if, for example, a writer were to be injured in pursuing such an assignment and chose to file for worker's compensation.

Although allowing a piece to be termed a work made for hire is generally the most complete way of divesting yourself of your rights, if all three requirements discussed above are not met, the work may actually fall within the category of *all-rights* assignments instead.

To protect yourself and your rights:

Employ a little communication. The rule of thumb is: It Never Hurts to Ask.

For example, inquiring why the publisher wants all rights may turn up the fact that he or she actually seeks some sort of exclusivity, say, a guarantee that you won't sell the piece for a year after its original publication. Because a contract can contain anything the traffic will bear (as long as it is not illegal or "against public policy"), you can draft an agreement giving the publisher just those rights—exclusive publication rights for one year—while retaining the rest of the rights for yourself.

If the publisher still insists on an all-rights assignment, you can often negotiate a reversion clause, which *returns* the rights to you either after the work goes out of print or after a certain period of time has elapsed. In your contract, ask for a built-in reversion clause, something on the order of: "After publication, the rights automatically return to the writer." I prefer this to a reassignment of rights, in which the buyer writes a letter reassigning the rights to the writer. The reversion clause doesn't require any action on the part of the publisher—who may go out of business before he reassigns your rights to you.

The equivalent clause in a work-for-hire contract would be one that automatically *assigns* the rights to you after a certain amount of time has passed. Because you didn't own them in the first place, they can't revert.

All manner of variations can be negotiated into any work-for-hire contract. I once dealt with an encyclopedia publisher that insisted on buying articles only on a work-for-hire basis. I obtained permission for the author I represented to reprint her individual article for distribution to her clients, and that permission was incorporated into the work-for-hire contract. This was necessary because the rights you normally assume are yours as the author of a work must be specifically granted to you by the legal "author" if the work is classified as made for hire.

Another reason It Never Hurts to Ask is that I've found that many editors who claim to make work-for-hire assignments don't fully understand what the phrase means. Some assume that making work-for-hire assignments means the same as making assignments in general.

Charge more for selling all rights. One writer who has written a number of works for hire says, "I find it an ideal way to boost my income into what must be the top bracket for full-time writers, or at least the top 10 percent."

Sometimes the money *is* good—but more often than not, it is the publication that pays a penny a word that insists on the work being made for hire. This is usually because such publications can't afford to pay for legal advice, and assume that they *need* all possible rights in any work they publish. When dealing with this kind of publication, your best move is to negotiate rights you are willing to sell—or to forgo publication.

How much money is enough for you to accept a work-for-hire assignment? Only you can decide that. Much depends on the ephemeral nature of the work. If you don't think you can resell it elsewhere (such as work for an ad agency or PR firm), or if it will be outdated anyway by the time the exclusive rights you would normally grant would expire, perhaps it doesn't matter if it's a work made for hire. And if your mortgage payment is due and the payment for the article will cover it, perhaps you have no choice.

Tap what you haven't sold—your research. Even when you sign a contract designating a work as made for hire, there is no copyright on facts—which means you *can* write a totally different article based on the same research.

A caution, however. The test for infringement is access plus substantial similarity. If you wrote the original piece, there can be no doubt of your access to it. So if your second piece is substantially similar, you would be guilty of infringing on the copyright of the publication for which you wrote the work-for-hire piece.

Of course, it's easier to resell the same work than to rewrite, and it's much better not to have to compete with your own work, which someone else now has the right to sell.

Therefore, the safest thing you can do is never sign anything that calls your work a "work made for hire" if you can avoid it, and to negotiate modifications, if at all possible, when you can't.

Your Best Defense

BY HOWARD G. ZAHAROFF

F ew people become writers believing they'll make a mint. Even fewer expect to lose their shirts. But it can happen in our hyperlitigious society. To avoid that unhappy event, writers must learn to practice what I call "defensive authoring."

Defensive authoring has two elements: a *commonsense* self-testing of your manuscript for problems, and an understanding of certain basic principles of publishing law.

Step 1: Self-testing. Begin by asking if anything in your manuscript (be it an article, book, short story, novel or script) might do the following:

- make someone feel you have used his or her work unfairly;
- harm anyone's reputation or invade anyone's privacy;
- misstate a fact that, if relied on, could cause injury.

If the answer to any of these questions is *yes*, you *may* have a problem. Since the best way to solve a problem is to avoid it, you should consider whether you can revise the piece to make the answers to all these questions *no*.

Step 2: Know the Law. A *no* answer, however, is not always required. To determine when it isn't, you need to understand certain basic points of publishing law. What follows are brief summaries of the key issues in copyright, libel, privacy and negligence law. Reading these is no substitute for consulting with a knowledgeable lawyer (not does it cover all legal issues of concern to writers), but these guides should help you decide when *yes* answers to your self-tests are OK . . . and generally help you stay out of trouble.

COPYRIGHT
What is the Fair Use of Another's Work?

The Copyright Act gives authors five exclusive rights: reproduction, adaptation, first sale, public performance and public display. The most important of these is the first: In general, you may not copy another author's works without permission.

There are exceptions, however, and the most important is the one that allows *fair use* of another writer's work. Although the Copyright Act never defines what use is "fair," it does list four factors to consider. So, to determine if your use of another's work is fair, ask yourself these questions:

What is the purpose and character of the use? Certain uses receive more latitude for copying, such as nonprofit educational uses, noncommercial research and scholarship, news reporting, criticism and comment, and satire and parody. (Also, it counts against you if you obtained the work through theft, fraud or bad faith.)

What is the nature of the copied work? Works of fiction and imagination receive more protection from copying than do works of fact and information. Similarly, unpublished works receive far greater protection than do published works (we'll discuss this in a moment).

How substantial—quantitatively *and* qualitatively—are the portions I'm using? Taking less is safer that taking more, but there are no absolutes. Courts have permitted certain copying of *entire works* (government copying of journal articles, copying broadcasted movies for later home viewing), while prohibiting *any copying* in other contexts (J.D. Salinger's unpublished letters). The more important the portion taken is to the original work (such as the story of Richard Nixon's pardon within Gerald Ford's memoirs), the more "substantial" the taking is considered to be—and, thus, the less likely that the taking will be considered fair.

What is the effect of my use on the market for the work? The Supreme Court has called this the "single most important element of fair use." In general, if the second work substitutes for the original, or harms the market for the original (other than through negative comment), the use is not likely to be considered fair.

One critical issue, especially to biographers and historians, concerns when you may quote from *unpublished* sources. Cases in the 1980s suggested that copying from unpublished works without the author's permission is almost inevitably an infringement. As one court wrote in a 1989 case concerning an unauthorized biography of Scientologist/SF writer L. Ron Hubbard: "Unpublished works normally enjoy complete protection" from unauthorized copying.

But then, in a 1991 case concerning Margaret Walker's biography of author Richard Wright, the same court allowed the biographer's "modest" use of Wright's unpublished writings. Concluding that this use served "to illustrate factual points or to establish Dr. Walker's relationship with the author," the court found the use fair.

The final development in the saga occurred late in 1992, when Congress amended the Copyright Act to state that the unpublished nature of a work does not bar a finding of fair use. This should produce more *Wright-like* decisions, but it will always be hard to guess how modest the copying must be to be accepted by the judge who hears *your* case. Therefore, it remains safest to seek permission; lacking it, you should limit yourself to brief quotations that convey information that could not easily be communicated in another way (and that do not simply enliven the text by displaying the writer's style).

LIBEL
Can You Defame Someone by an Opinion or Misquote?

In general, you are guilty of libel (or defamation) if you are at fault in publishing false statements of fact that hold a person up to contempt, ridicule, hatred or scorn. Although you should always double-check to be sure your statements—particularly critical comments—are accurate, court cases suggest guidelines that may help you allocate your research time:

• *Does the subject still exist?* In general, there is no liability for libeling deceased individuals or defunct organizations.

• *Is the subject recognizable?* If the identity of your subject cannot be inferred from your words or the context, he or she has no claim against you.

• *What is your subject's status?* When referring to matters of public concern, you generally cannot be liable for defaming a public official or public figure, unless you knew your statements were incorrect or you "recklessly disregarded" their truth or falsity (in general, if you seriously doubted their truth).

Two libel issues that have received recent attention concern opinions and misquotes. Regarding opinions, many courts has assumed that, since defamation requires the publication of false statements of fact, opinions could never be libelous because opinions are not statements of fact and can't be proven true or false.

That view was rejected by the U.S. Supreme Court in the 1991 case *Milkovich v. Lorain Journal Co.* The court held that a writer can be liable for opinions if they imply the existence of underlying facts that are false and defamatory. Thus, although you couldn't be found guilty of libel if you referred to someone as "scum" or "pig," you could be guilty if you called someone a "liar" in an article discussing his testimony at a public hearing (as in *Milkovich*).

So when you proofread your article for defensive-authoring problems, don't assume that only the statements you assert as facts must be true to avoid defamation. If your opinions or beliefs imply underlying facts, those had better be correct, too.

Attention also has been paid recently to accuracy in quoting. In a 1991 case in which psychoanalyst Jeffrey Masson sued *The New Yorker* over various quotes falsely attributed to him by author Janet Malcolm, the U.S. Supreme Court concluded that even deliberate alterations of the words of a public figure or public official aren't libelous, unless the alteration results in a "material change in the meaning conveyed by the statement." If the altered quotes of a public figure preserve substantial truth (in essence, the court's finding in the 1992 dispute between Gordon Lice and *Harper's Magazine*), the altered quotes should not subject the author to liability. Thus, you can change quotes for grammar, syntax or other legitimate reasons. But if doing so changes the meaning, and the result creates a comparatively unfavorable portrait of the speaker, you could be in trouble.

PRIVACY
Can I Tell That Great Story I Heard Last Night?

This is an area of growing importance to nonfiction writers. Traditionally, privacy was divided into four categories: public disclosure of embarrassing private facts; publication of information that creates a false and offensive impression (*false light*); improper entry or observation of private areas; and commercial misappropriation of someone's name or likeness.

To avoid an invasion of privacy claim, ask yourself the following:

• *Is the information true?* Truth will prevent a finding of defamation. However, it will not preclude a finding of invasion of privacy.

• *Is the information private?* If the information is available in public documents, such as court papers, there is no liability for further publicizing it. If it came from private, unpublished sources, you're at risk.

• *Is the information offensive?* If the information is private but benign (that is, the person was treated for the flu), it shouldn't create liability.

• *Is the subject a public official or public figure?* As in the law of libel, more latitude is usually given to reports about people in the public eye. Although not all information about public figures is publishable, the more it relates to their public status, the more defensible its publication.

• *Is the information newsworthy?* Even if the subject is not a public figure, courts normally allow more latitude for reporting private information that is relevant to the public (for example, that someone had a long-term affair with a presidential candidate or European monarch).

• *How was the information obtained?* You have a stronger defense against liability if you witnessed your subject's private behavior by observing their antics through an open window from the street outside their home, rather than from their enclosed backyard.

NEGLIGENCE
Can You Be Liable if Someone Suffers Physical Injury as a Result of Your Words?

Courts have considered a number of theories for holding authors and publishers liable for physical injuries that "result" from their words.

One theory is *incitement*—that is, actively prompting someone to commit dangerous or unlawful acts. However, there are no reported cases in which liability for incitement has been imposed on the written word alone.

A related theory, which shocked publishers in late 1992 by producing a $4 million-plus verdict against *Soldier of Fortune* magazine, is liability for publishing advertisements that, on their face, "present a clear and present danger of causing serious harm to the public from violent criminal activity." Liability under either theory should be relatively easy for an author to avoid: Make sure your works don't actively solicit or encourage unlawful or unreasonably dangerous behavior.

Liability for physical injury resulting from the written word has also been imposed in a very different context: the reckless or negligent publication of erroneous information that is expected to be relied on, such as information in how-to books. Most cases concern the liability of publishers rather than authors, because publishers are often the more inviting target. One example was a 1980 case that found Rand McNally liable when students were injured performing an experiment described in a textbook that did not include adequate warnings.

More often, publishers win. A good example is *Winter v. G.P. Putnam Sons*. This 1991 case concerned two people who, relying on Putnam's *The Encyclopedia of Mushrooms*, became critically ill from eating poison mushrooms. They sued on the grounds that a book is a product, so publishers should be subject to "strict product liability" (that is, liable if their product is defective even if they weren't negligent), and that Putnam *was* negligent in publishing a book with erroneous information.

The court rejected both arguments, ruling that a book is not a "product" (the threat of strict liability would pose too great a risk for the unfettered exchange of ideas), and that a publisher "has no duty to investigate the accuracy of the contents of the books it publishes."

Writers should not expect the same latitude, however. For example, one court wrote that, although publishers ordinarily aren't responsible for the contents of their books, "author liability for errors in the contents of books . . . is not firmly defined and will depend on the nature of the publication, on the intended audience, on causation in fact and on the foreseeability of damage." In short, authors should expect their liability to be determined under more conventional negligence principles: If they fail to exercise appropriate care in the context, and someone is injured, they are responsible.

So what should you, as a writer, do to guard yourself against such liability? Be guided by your answers to the following questions:

- *May your words be relied on for action?* The more likely that people will do what you say or describe, the more careful you must be. Thus, if you're writing fiction, you probably needn't worry that your readers will act like your characters (imitate James Bond's stunts, for example). However, if you're writing fiction for children, at least *consider* the issue before making some dangerous activity look too safe and inviting. Where you must take great care, on the other hand, is in writing how-to and similar texts, where you clearly intend your audience to rely on your words. This leads to the second question:

- *How dangerous are the activities I describe or recommend?* If your work explains how to identify certain birds or butterflies, there is less likelihood of harm (and therefore less cause for concern) than if your work identifies edible mushrooms, provides instructions for chemistry experiments or describes safe places for swimming. Which leads to the final question:

• *How much care must I exercise?* Don't assume your readers will appreciate the dangers (even obvious ones) involved in the activities you describe. Therefore, give the most precise instructions, describe the safest (reasonable) procedures to follow and offer the clearest possible warnings. If you're describing places to visit or activities to do, visit or perform them yourself, be alert to both obvious and subtle risks, and include appropriate warnings in your write-up. If you're describing experiments where there's a risk of injury, perform them yourself (better yet, do them two or three times), at each step considering the dangers involved and how to prevent them. You should also examine how similar texts have handled similar activities, ask experts in the field to review your work before publication, observe nonexperts (such as teachers and students) conducting the experiment following your directions, and obtain safety feedback from users of your writing.

In general, assume you'll be held responsible for the accuracy of what you write. Therefore, the greater the potential for harm, the greater the care you must exercise.

Dodging lawsuits should never be your highest goal as a writer. Still, take it from someone who has seen our legal system from both the outside *and* inside: You'll be much happier if you're never sued, subpoenaed, deposed or otherwise dragged into our judicial system as a result of your writing. Although following these defensive authoring strategies will not immunize you from lawsuits, it will reduce your risk.

How to Set Your Rates

BY TOM YATES

I f you're a writer who loves to write, money can be an unpleasant subject. I know I'm uncomfortable talking about it, especially when a prospective client asks, "So how much do you charge?" If you write for the sheer pleasure of it, forget about making money; keep the day job and write for personal satisfaction. But if you look at writing as an income-generating *business*, you must make some serious business decisions. After all it's your job. It only makes sense to set rates.

CALCULATING YOUR RATES

After about twenty years of part-time, then full-time writing, I've formulated three rules about writing for pay. The first: *You must set rates in advance.* While you normally don't quote rates to magazine editors, you may find yourself taking on other clients such as advertising or marketing and communications agencies. When you do, the first question they'll ask after you've shown your samples is, "What are your rates?" They may want those rates quoted per page, per hour, per day, per week or some other unit, depending on the size of the project. When these prospective clients ask, you must have something ready. "Let me get back to you" is not the answer they want to hear.

The first few times I quoted rates to potential clients, they seemed *too* willing to accept them. That was my first clue I was charging too little. That gave birth to my second rule: *If the client quickly accepts your initial rate or price, it's too low.* (It's too late to raise them after you quote them, but you'll know for next time.) I now charge about the same as a good electrician or other skilled tradesman, which is about $65 per hour or $470 per day. In the Detroit area, and in most big cities, that's a reasonable rate. But what about a small town? Sixty-five dollars per hour may seem a trifle stiff there. How do you decide what to charge? Like writing a story, you do some research.

Determine what your basic costs are. This is where most of us fall down. We tend to think in simple terms: "Gee, $40 per hour sounds pretty good to me." We may even sit down and make up what we feel is a pretty comprehensive list of our basic expenses: food, rent/mortgage, electricity, heat, water, car payment, insurance (car, life, health and homeowner's) and something for clothes and entertainment. But we always seem to forget incidental items like state and federal (and maybe city) income taxes, Social Security (FICA) and savings for retirement. Obviously taxes vary with your income, but the other expenses listed are fairly constant and must be figured in when setting your pay rate.

My second and biggest clue that my rates were too low came at income tax time. I wasn't too concerned. After all, I hadn't made a lot of money and had a couple of hundred dollars in the bank—more than enough to cover my taxes. Or so I thought. After an hour of nervous answers to my accountant, it was clear I *hadn't* set aside enough. His first question was if I'd been filing quarterly income estimates with the IRS, and paying the taxes on those receipts. *Gulp!* Then there was FICA and state income tax. *Whoops!* I had remembered to put aside 10 percent in my IRA, so at least I had a deduction to reduce my taxable income and partly compensate for my mistake. But I still had to make up the difference.

To avoid such future shocks, I sat down to figure out my taxes in advance—*and* what I'd need to charge clients to cover this expense. Determining my personal tax bite was the first step to setting my writing rates. The top federal income tax rate is 39 percent, so to be safe I now put aside 24 percent of every check. Twenty-four percent may be on the high side, but in the long run it's better. I'll have money left over after I pay my taxes. (Not only that, but I collect interest while saving for taxes. After I've paid my taxes I can take the extra and blow it on a good dinner, more software or something frivolous like a house payment or tires for the car.) To the fed's 24 percent, I added Social Security: FICA tax is 7.65 percent, but, since I'm my own employer, I must also kick in the employer's 7.65 percent, for a total of 15.3 percent. then there's state and local government cuts. I live in Michigan where the state income tax is 4.69 percent. Luckily, my city doesn't have an income tax; if yours does, add that percentage to the others. The chunk out of my check is 43.9 percent.

Beyond the income set aside for taxes, I need to put something aside for retirement. Five percent is okay for retirement but 10 percent is better. (Once I got used to taking "ten off the top," it was fairly painless.) by the time I finished my calculations, 53.9 percent of my income was gone before I did anything with a check.

Now it was time to calculate how much the other 46.1 percent of my income needed to cover. Look at all your receipts and be extremely detailed. Start with the basic expenses I listed a few paragraphs back. Don't forget your business expenses: paper, printer ribbons, floppy disks, computer upkeep, a fund for new equipment, a travel fund for out-of-town stories, a savings account to smooth out the low spots in your income, etc. *Any time you spend money, it's an expense.* And always plan for the worst when calculating. Use your highest heat, electricity or water bill, the most Dove bars you ate in one month, etc. Multiply the total by twelve; this is your basic yearly expenses.

Now you have your total basic expenses and what you should put aside for taxes. The other number you need to calculate your final hourly rate is a *work year*. Assuming you work eight hours per day, five days per week, fifty weeks per year (you owe yourself a vacation), your work year is two thousand hours. Take your basic expenses and divide by two thousand. That figure is the basic hourly rate you need to make your nut (basic living expenses). But wait, you still need to adjust this number to cover taxes.

Because 53.9 percent of your earnings goes to taxes or is otherwise untouchable, the basic rate you calculated in the last paragraph represents just 46.1 percent of your final rate. To determine that final rate, divide the basic rate by .461. As an example, assume you've calculated you must earn $30 per hour to cover your basic living expenses. To determine the hourly rate you need to pay that *and* your taxes *and* retirement, divide $30 by .461. The result is $65.08 per hour; round it off to $65 to make things neater.

Don't put away your calculator yet. You should be able to quote hourly, daily, weekly or even monthly rates. For a daily rate, I take my hourly rate, multiply by eight and deduct 10 percent. For weekly or other rates I multiply the daily rate by five, ten, twenty or however many days the time span includes. I give a 10 percent or even 20 percent discount for long-term projects because it's assured income for that period of time. Often that discount can help you land a job.

Once you've set your rates it's easy to budget your money. When you receive a check, immediately set aside money to cover your taxes and retirement. When you do that you find the $65 per hour rate I quoted earlier is about $30. That may still sound like a lot, but that's what you have to pay for everything else—business and personal. Checks for $500 or $1,000 cover just $230.50 and $461 worth of expenses.

That brings us to my third rule: *Set aside and never—never—touch money for taxes and retirement unless it's April 15 or you're retiring.* No matter the temptation, don't touch the tax fund.

STICKING TO YOUR RATES

The most important thing to remember after setting your pay rates is that it's only the beginning of the writing business. Now you need to stick to them. Whether you're tackling a magazine, ad agency or ghostwriting job, do your best to make sure your income for a given project stays at or near your hourly rate. That rate is a target that keeps your time under control, your yardstick to measure the time investment in whatever you write.

One magazine I write for pays me $250 per page, including photographs. Measuring that payment against my $65 per hour rate, I know I can only allow 3.85 hours per page. That time constraint means any photos I use will probably be from a company's PR department, unless I'm pretty sure I can shoot enough usable photos to fill a page or to recycle for another feature. Otherwise, I have to spend time writing copy, though most features seldom run more than 2,000 words. Another magazine pays me 20 cents per word and $25 per photo. In this case, one picture is worth, contrary to the cliché, 125 words or half a manuscript page. But to set up, shoot and arrange for the processing of that photo can take two or three hours, much longer than it takes to write half a page.

Overall, I try to limit my time investment in a story that's only going to pay $300 to $400. Eight hours is the maximum for a 2,000-word feature and 20 cents per word, and that time includes photography, because I can't be sure I'll sell any photos. That rate is still lower than I usually want to go, but this particular magazine uses my work on a regular basis and the steady income smooths out the lows from other freelance work.

Don't fall into the trap of taking extra time on a current project just because you don't have another assignment waiting. The time you're investing at the lower rate can be put to better use outlining new stories, pitching story ideas to editors, researching basic information

YOU FIGURE IT OUT

Use this worksheet to determine your own hourly rate. Your costs will be divided into two percentages: a percentage to be set aside for taxes, and a percentage to cover your basic expenses.

Taxes		
Federal Income Tax		%
FICA	(for yourself)	7.65%
	(as your own employer)	7.65%
State Income Tax		%
City Tax (if any)		%
Retirement Savings		10%
Total		%
Subtract **Total** from 100; this is the percentage of your income available to cover basic expenses.		%

Basic Expenses	
Figure these expenses based on one month. Be as detailed as possible, and use the highest possible monthly values.	
Personal	
Rent/Mortgage	
Food	
Electricity/Gas	
Water	
Phone	
Car Payment	
Medical/Other	
Insurance (car, life, health, homeowner's)	
Business	
Paper	
Printer Ribbons/Disks	
Computer Upkeep	
Postage	
New Equipment & Travel Funds	
Savings/Other	
Total Monthly Basic Expenses	
Total Yearly Basic Expenses	× 12

Now, figure your work year. Hours per day × days per week × weeks per year.

Work Year Hours	

Divide Total Yearly Basic Expenses by Work Year, and that's your Basic Hourly Rate. Divide the Basic Hourly Rate by the percentage of your income used to cover basic expenses, and you have your hourly rate.

	÷	=	÷	=
Total Yearly Basic Expenses	Work Year Hours	Basic Hourly Rate	Income % available for Basic Expenses	Hourly Rate

you'll need in the future, or even just catching up on your reading (which really is legitimate research).

Sticking to your hourly rate also makes it easier to control the normal outside interruptions a writer's life seems to have. If you're trying to decide whether you should run an errand or do a chore during your normal writing time, ask yourself, "Would I pay someone my hourly rate to do this job?" If the answer is no, put the job off until you have free time or until after your regular writing hours. You can combine personal errands with story-related travel or running around, reducing its cost. Obviously there are things you'll have to do during your writing time, but remember your hourly rate and keep your costs to you low.

I usually manage to stick to my hourly rate. The reality of the writing business, though, is that while I make $65 per hour for the work I sell, I don't always sell enough to maintain a gross income level of $65 per hour. Based on a two thousand hour work year, one year I earned $5 per hour; just above minimum wage. Luckily, another reality of writing is, as you gain experience, you become a faster, more efficient writer.

Another advantage that experience gives writers is the ability to recycle stories. By reslanting or changing emphasis you can sell stories in several different markets. Sometimes a resale involves nothing more than eliminating specific regional information. Other times it's taking a different view and rewriting. The result is almost "found" money. You already have the basic research time paid for by the original payment. Any additional payment is for the time you spend on reworking the story. Thus, a four-hour rewrite that nets you $30 is worth $75 per hour. By recycling stories I've made as much as $20 per hour. Currently I have two evergreens at work for me. One has earned me more than $1,200 in three sales; I spent about ten hours on interviewing, photography and writing. It still has more lives to go, too. The second story has been resold five times, more than doubling my original fee. Each time those stories are resold my hourly rate goes up.

It always bothers me to talk about writing in such a cold, business-like way. Freelancing is the best job I've ever had; and I've had maybe thirty-five or forty. But I keep reminding myself that, like the guy who owns the local gas station or the flower shop, I'm a businessperson. I have to set rules and follow them or I won't be in the business long. I'll lose the best job I've ever had.

The Art of Negotiation

BY GREGG LEVOY

Many years ago, one of the magazine editors I regularly sold to left his spot on the masthead to become a fellow freelance writer—an irony only a writer can fully appreciate.

He was now considerably easier to reach, and during a phone conversation he told me something he never would have revealed while an editor: "You should have been asking for more money, more often, especially once you began writing for us consistently. You always took whatever we offered."

When breaking into a magazine, he said, writers *should* take whatever terms are offered. Continuing this practice after breaking in, however, is like turning down raises.

I was guilty as charged. My views on asking editors for more money, or more anything, could best be described as approach-avoidance: If I didn't approach the subject of negotiation, I could avoid rejection (which I'd already had plenty of, thank you).

I'd also thought of negotiation as something only for J.R. Ewing types. I didn't realize that the very qualities that make me a writer and made me think I'd be eaten alive at the bargaining table—sensitivity, thoughtfulness, creativity—are also typical (when combined with a bit of assertiveness) of the best negotiators.

But the former editor's remarks fired me with both insight and indignation. I began experimenting. When a trade magazine editor asked to reprint one of my stories for $75, I screwed up my courage and said, "How about $125?" He said, "How about $100?" I said, "OK."

I made $25 for less than ten seconds of talking! That would make a dandy hourly wage.

Not all negotiations have been this easy, but each time I managed some success I was emboldened. Within a year I was negotiating with some of the buck-a-word magazines for money and rights that would eventually double my income. I learned three lessons in short order:

- *It is astonishing what you can get if you ask.* One editor I know told me that nine out of ten writers never ask for anything, and she almost always says yes to the one who does.
- *The worst thing an editor will do is say no.* Not one editor in twenty years has hung up on me because I asked for more money.
- *Everything is negotiable,* from money and rights to deadline, expenses, payment schedule, kill fee, length, tone and editing.

COLLABORATIVE BARGAINING

There are more than a few writers who feel they couldn't warm to editors if they were burned at the stake together. They approach negotiating in an atmosphere of trust not unlike that surrounding two nations exchanging captured spies at the border.

Editors, however, aren't our enemies. They are hardworking people trying to be recognized for their efforts. They're also not people you're selling used cars to. You want to develop long-term relationships with them, because the more steady customers you have, the more steady income you have. Your negotiations must be collaborative, with both sides feeling good about what they get.

So how do you manage a win-win outcome when editors have all the power?

First, understand that editors *don't* have all the power. It's a buyer's market for some writers, and a seller's market for others, as determined by the law of supply and demand. If most writers offer roughly the same thing—passably good writing, fairly good ideas, occasional reliability, a modest stamina for rewrites and a deep-seated fear of asking for anything more than editors offer—it's a buyer's market, and editors will buy the cheapest work available.

But when you begin giving editors what they want most—bang-up writing, imaginative ideas, a firm grasp of the audience, punctuality and a product that sells magazines—and when you then ask for payment commensurate with that quality of performance, it turns into a seller's market, with editors favorably disposed to negotiating to keep you.

USING YOUR BARGAINING POWER

Negotiation is not an event, but a process. It's more than just a quick pitch; it's the whole sales campaign.

It begins not when you pick up the phone, but when you pick up the professional relationship; bargaining power is the cumulative effect of everything you do in that relationship. Most writers don't recognize this and badly underestimate their bargaining power.

These five "power tools" will help you build a strong negotiation position.

1. **Performance.** Several years ago, I told one of my regular buyers of short pieces, Allied Publications, that I wanted to renegotiate the fee, which had held steady at $25 per piece for two years. He told me to put it in writing and let him think about it. I wrote the following letter:

Dear Richard:
It was nice chatting with you on the phone yesterday. I look forward to putting together more pieces for Allied. As for the business: After having written eight or ten pieces for Allied over the course of two years, at $25 each, I am hoping we can consider a higher fee, $50 each. I hope that given the consistent quality, fast turnaround and minimal editing my articles require, this will seem like a fair price. Give me a ring and we can discuss it.

His reply: He raised my rate to $35 and suggested we could discuss another adjustment in six months. Meanwhile, 45 percent raise.

When you deliver the goods and give editors more than they bargained for, don't let the fact go unnoticed at negotiating time.

2. **Presentation.** From the first impression on, your presence should communicate enthusiasm, self-motivation, attention to detail, resourcefulness, humor, patience and, above all, confidence (fake it if you must; it has a way of becoming a self-fulfilling prophecy anyway). How you present yourself is conveyed, whether you know it or not, through your phone manner, correspondence, query letters, stationery and writing.

3. **Professionalism.** During the negotiation that led to my first piece for *Pursuits Magazine*, the editor wanted me to pay expenses up front for a trip to Seattle to do the article, for which she would reimburse me.

I explained, though, that I was currently on assignment for two other national magazines, both of which wanted me to pay out-of-pocket expenses for trips (one to South America) and doing so was fast depleting my savings account. I asked her to reconsider her request and send me a check before the trip to cover my expenses. I also offered to send her an itemized list of exactly what I anticipated spending.

She sent a check for $600 that week.

I had, in this case by implication, demonstrated that I was a professional with credibility and competence, that I was *worth* sending not just to Seattle but to South America, but that I nonetheless had a limited bank account. Bringing self-esteem into your business and writing affairs can have a commanding effect.

"Professional" writers, for instance, are those most likely to succeed at changing "pays-on-publication" clauses to "pays-on-acceptance," simply because they know that in no other business do people, professional or not, stand for not being paid their wages on time. At the least, these writers appeal to an editor's sense of logic, fairness and business principles by pointing out the time-honored tradition, common to all deferred-payment plans (such as credit-card payments), that a buyer pays a higher price for delayed payment, and a seller gets a higher price for waiting.

4. **Polish.** Go the extra mile for editors: burn the midnight oil to give a story that extra shine; help them track down photos; do your own editing; double-check your facts; oblige all reasonable requests for rewrites; get work in *before* deadline. Then remind your editors of these facts at negotiating time.

5. **Personal contact.** People enjoy doing business with those they identify with. So give editors lots of opportunities to identify with you. Drop them notes, call with updates on stories, go visit them and break bread. And once you've broken into the stable of writers, cultivate your editorial relationships as if your livelihood depended on it. Remember: The stable is usually not far from the pasture.

THINK BIG

Several years ago, a *Vogue* editor called to buy a story idea from me. Not the story, just the idea. "How much do you want for it?" she asked.

Now what is a story idea worth? They're a dime a dozen—$100? I did save them time, though, by already doing the outline—$200? And now they wouldn't have to pay me to write—$300? "How about $400?" I finally said, thinking big. "Sold!" she said. There was a moment's silence, during which I thought to myself, *Damn.*

Anytime a buyer accepts your first offer, you've blown it. You've undersold yourself. Your writing is worth whatever someone will pay for it, and that is determined by how much they need it, how valuable they perceive it to be, the going rate, the budget and your bargaining power. But set high aspirations. Come in with a price before the editor does, one that is perhaps a third to a half higher than you expect to receive, or expect them to offer. Often your expectations of both are too low.

Remember, aspirations can always be lowered. Once stated, they can't be raised.

APPROACHING YOUR NEGOTIATIONS

You just asked an editor to pay you on acceptance instead of on publication. She flatly said no, sorry, company policy. Quick, what's your response?

You don't want to be reduced to responses like "Well, it doesn't hurt to ask, huh?" You need instead studied comebacks that grow out of planning your negotiations. Do not go into them thinking you'll just see what happens. Rely on homework, practicing what you'll preach, knowing what you'll say if an editor invokes "company policy." Script it out if need be. Above all, know what you want out of the negotiation, and what you're willing to settle for.

Another form of planning I undertake is keeping notes on all my conversations with editors. Several years ago, an editor at *Health* mentioned to me that rates were probably going down for shorter pieces and up to a dollar a word for longer features. I jotted it down. Four months later she called with a go-ahead on a query and offered me $1,500 for a 2,000-word piece.

I pulled out my file and there was the note about a probable rate change. I asked her about it. After much squirming, she finally offered me $1,800 for 1,800 words. Less work, more money.

You can also brainstorm advance solutions to potential negotiation deadlocks. For example, both sides usually want more money, and conventional wisdom suggests that more for you means less for them, and vice versa. Not necessarily. The pie can be expanded.

When I travel on assignment to a city where I have friends, I offer to stay with them instead of at a hotel, if the editor will kick back half the savings into my fee.

If the deadlock is over editors taking all rights, denying you the chance to make extra income from your writing, try this: Offer to retain "syndication rights." You can sell your pieces again, but only to newspaper syndicates that agree to put at the top of the story "Originally appeared in *XYZ Magazine*." The magazine gets its exclusivity; you get your extra income.

But you must think of these *before* you begin to negotiate.

EIGHT MORE NEGOTIATION TACTICS

All of these strategies are based on collaborative principles (or at least aren't contrary to them):

1. **Listen.** Sometimes the cheapest concession you can make in a negotiation is simply letting an editor know he's been heard. And remember, listening is not necessarily agreeing.

2. **Be quiet.** Nature abhors a vacuum. People will naturally rush in to fill silences, but if that silence is going to be broken with a compromise, let it be theirs, not yours.

During the negotiation with an inflight magazine editor about his pays-on-publication policy, I mentioned that as a business practice it didn't seem fair, and then I shut up for a moment. In the awkward silence that ensued, the urge to blurt out something—anything—to ease the tension, was excruciating. He broke first, and he did so with a compromise, effectively talking himself right out of his position.

3. **Attack problems, not people.** In the inflight negotiation, I made sure to focus my attention and displeasure on the issue, not the editor. It was the policy that was unfair, not the person trying to uphold it even against his own principles.

4. **Ask open-minded questions.** The more information you have about an editor's needs, interests and dilemmas, the better your bargaining position. So get them talking (before and during the negotiation) by asking questions that do not elicit *yes* or *no* answers: Why do you have a pays-on-publication policy?" or "Are there improvements I could make in my writing that would make it work better for you?"

5. **Have a concession strategy.** Acrobats are the only people who make any sort of a living bending over backwards. Don't give in just to avoid conflict (but don't dig your heels in either, biting when a simple growl would do). If you come in with a price of $900 and your editor counters with $500, don't immediately whittle away at your initial offer by suggesting $700. Tell him why you believe you're worth $900.

When conceding, make small concessions. Don't jump from offering $1,000 to backing off to $500 in one giant step. It will appear you can be bought for even cheaper than *that*.

6. **Discuss fees last.** Fee is the area you're most likely to disagree about, so start, if you can, discussing more easily agreeable areas. If an editor suggests a three-month deadline, say you can get it done in two and a half. If she says $50 is all she can give you for phone expenses, say you'll make your calls in the evenings and weekends and save her $20. Then, once you've built up common ground, and warmed the editor's heart with your conciliatory nature, talk price.

7. **When you stop negotiating, stop.** Make sure you discuss all negotiables in one session, not piecemeal. And once you've made your final agreements, don't try to better them.

8. **Get it in writing.** When you finish negotiating, make sure you commit your agreements to paper, be it a written contract or a simple letter of agreement. If an editor suggests you forego a written contract and just leave it at a friendly handshake, politely tell him that you'd like to *keep* the relationship friendly, so you would much prefer to work with a written contract—you can even tell him that's *your* company policy.

Bill 'Em!

BY DAVID FRANCIS CURRAN

A while back I roamed the Eastern U.S. confidently looking for a magazine job. The job never came. But a career did, partly because in Washington, DC, an editor who obviously didn't want me for the job she had open, gave me the most valuable writing advice I have ever received.

"We do depend a good deal on freelancers," the editor told me. "Obviously, we can't produce all of our material ourselves. We have a number of professionals, and by professionals I mean people who make more than $20,000 a year with their writing and who submit to us regularly."

"How much do you pay for articles?" I asked.

"Well," she said, "it depends. Normally around $500 to $600. More for a big-name writer, of course. Our writers are usually paid after publication. Unless they send an invoice when they submit the article."

"An invoice?"

"Yes. If they send an invoice with the work, if it was commissioned, or accepted, the accountants pay for it right away. Otherwise, the writer has to wait until after publication for payment."

"Wow," I said, "do a lot of writers do that?"

"Oh, quite a few professionals do," she said. *"An editor may not understand a writer's need to be paid, or may not be able to do anything about it, but an accountant understands an invoice."*

I've italicized her words because they are ones that every writer struggling to make a dollar should carve in granite and post next to his checkbook.

My first question, of course, was, "Will it work for me?"

When I got back from my unsuccessful job hunt, I sent out my first bill. Not to the editor who, despite promises, had delayed using and paying for some material I had written for him, but to the business manager of the publication. My bill was for $132. Within days I received a $100 settlement. (I did demand the extra $32, but more on that later.)

Over the years, invoices have proven useful to me. There always seems to be an accountant out there who is ready to help—and ready to pay. Invoices also serve as useful reminders for slow or forgetful editors.

For example, I was assigned a story by an editor at the *National Enquirer*. However, the story, which involved a substantial investment of time and energy, never appeared and I never heard from the editor about it. Months later, I sent the *Enquirer* an invoice asking for a $250 kill fee. Again, within days I had my check.

Just the name—*invoice*—sounds formal and businesslike, yet it is nothing more than an itemization of goods delivered—a manuscript in this case—and the amount due.

The format of the invoice isn't important. It could be typed on a plain sheet of typing paper. Simply remember to make carbon copies or photocopies for your files. You can also buy preprinted invoice forms, or you can go to a quick-printer, who can supply you with forms that have your name and address printed on them. You can order printed forms in what are called "carbonless sets." This means that the forms are attached in sets of two or three, and when you fill out the top form, copies are automatically made. I use triplicate forms. I use the second copy as a reminder if the bill isn't paid within thirty days and the third copy is a permanent copy for my files.

Provide as much information as possible on your invoice. Start with your name and address, and then the name of the company you are billing. Address your invoice to the business manager, whose name will often be listed in the masthead. But if no business manager's name is listed, direct your invoice to Accounts Payable.

Next list the article or articles sold by name, and the agreed-on price for each. Then list any charges for expenses, the name of the editor who ordered the work, the date of the order, the deadline date, and the date the article was submitted. If you received a story assignment number, include it. You might also include the agreed-on kill fee; it might save time in getting the money to you if your article is killed.

Two points. I use invoices only when a problem arises, and I try to be as tactful as possible when I do use them. Try to settle accounts with the editor before you go over his head by submitting a bill to the magazine's accounting department. After all, you don't want to sour a potential market. On the other hand, you should be paid what you deserve. As I mentioned before, I demanded the $32 difference between what I had billed and what I was paid by the magazine I first tested the invoice system with. Because of my demands and because of some mutual feelings of hostility that resulted, I will probably never sell to that publication again. Then again, is it worth submitting to a publication that quibbles over $32?

Now when I send an invoice, I also send a note to the editor explaining that using the invoice is simply the way I do business.

There's another drawback to using invoices. In my state, businesses must use the "accrual" method of accounting. Your state may have similar rules. This means that money you are owed is considered to be earned as soon as the bill is sent out and it must be declared as income on your taxes whether you get it soon or much, much later. (On the other hand, expenses are deductible when you are billed whether you pay the bill or not.) Check the rules in your state. Although this may seem a complicated bit of red tape, the quicker payment you will receive when you start to use invoices will have you happily untangling that red tape on the way to the bank.

What to Do When the Publisher Won't Pay

BY DEAN R. LAMBE

T he checks and contracts will go overnight mail this afternoon," the soft-spoken editor said. I stared at the telephone. Should I believe her this time? She did claim to be calling from the New York office of the giant publishing corporation, an office that she rarely occupied. Perhaps the lawyer's letter had finally opened the piggy bank. Yet, I had heard many similar promises from this woman before, during the eight months that I worked to solve this particular grievance for two of my colleagues. Payment was long past due.

As it turned out, the editor's "this afternoon" translated into another five days. Delivery was hardly via express, but my fellow writers did receive their money—plus interest, as was fair under the circumstances. Sometimes it's easier for freelancers to push a snake uphill than to collect for their efforts at the keyboard.

How—and why—did I become involved in other writers' problems? The "how" is easy: I volunteered to be co-chairman of the grievance committee of the Science Fiction Writers of America. As for "why," unfortunately the above example is not uncommon. Whether you write romances, locked-room mysteries or software reviews, at some point you will probably have a grievance with an editor or a publisher. In the freelance writing world, the buyers of our work often seem to hold all the cards. Yet, we do have rights. Workable methods exist for resolving grievances. And you can take steps from the start that will minimize grief.

GET EVERYTHING IN WRITING

Years ago, the science fiction anthology market was dominated by one person (who, like all the grief-givers and victims in this article, shall remain nameless). That former editor was notorious for making deals over the telephone. Contracts and editorial changes were often strictly verbal, as well. Chaos reigned; promises broken; writers suffered.

Verbal contracts do have force in law, but justice is blind and lawyers and judges prefer the feel of paper. Always bear in mind that you are in business. Whether your product is greeting cards or slick-magazine copy, your work belongs to you from the moment of its creation. You, therefore, must agree to sell rights to your creation to another party. Make all such agreements on paper with appropriate signatures.

UNDERSTAND THE RIGHTS YOU ARE SELLING

I once received a call from a West Coast writer who had just seen his first novel appear in translation. In the flyleaf, however, he found reference to European publication of several of his short stories—publication without his knowledge or permission. The fellow was upset, sure that he faced a messy international copyright lawsuit. Fortunately, I read French, and knew that the European magazine in question was a sister to the American magazine where the stories had appeared originally. Foreign serial rights had been included in the first sale. When I explained this, the writer was much relieved. He could have avoided all that anxiety had he truly read what he signed.

SAVE EVERY BIT OF PAPER

If you wish to save your notes, sketches, second drafts and used ribbons for your memorial library, that's between you and the space in your basement. However, wise writers do retain all relevant documents at least until the checks are in their accounts. Save all correspondence with editors and publishers. If agreements are made over the telephone (or electronic or e-mail), make a dated memo or printed copy and have it initialed by the originator.

If the sample that crosses my desk is representative, most writers' grievances concern money—how much and when. The above points represent common business practice. They should help you avoid problems with contractual terms—the "how much." Should grief occur with the "when" of payment, however, proceed as follows:

PUT YOUR AGENT TO WORK

Any agents worth their 15 percent try to collect promptly, and in full, for their clients. When payment is late, talk to your agent first. Unfortunately, much freelance work is not agented. Even when book-length projects are represented, writers are often on their own for shorter material. If you have a good agent-client relationship, however, it doesn't hurt to ask for advice.

WRITE A POLITE INQUIRY LETTER

Do not, as one writer I know did recently, "let fly" with letters to everyone from the corporation's CEO to the mailroom clerk. Write first the person with whom you make the deal: editor, vice-president, etc. While the phone or e-mail may seem faster, you want your grievance in writing. Be polite, because honest errors do happen. Even the Postal Service has been known to lose checks. Legitimate business practices sometimes justify weeks of travel time for an editor's payment authorization to go "just down the hall" to the comptroller. Perhaps the little person with the green eyeshade really does come in only once a month. State your grievance specifically, in terms of the contractual agreement, and the date of expected payment. Request resolution of your complaint within thirty days.

WRITE THE PUBLISHER

Your letter to the editor may produce no champagne and T-bone steaks. If (as is often truly the case) the editor tells you that payment disbursement is out of her hands, write the publisher and/or chief executive officer of the company. Again, be polite and state you complaint in detail. Vituperative, threatening letters from a stranger are likely to be deposited in the same round file that you use for similar mail. Enclose a copy of your contract. Request that your contractual provisions be honored immediately.

If you are a member of a writer's organization, say so in your letter, and note that your organization shares your concern for publishers who fail to pay on time. Send copies to the grievance committee of your writer's group. Allow another fourteen business days for your check to arrive (sorry, but that's the pace of North American business).

SEE A LAWYER

Had the complexities of trademark or patent registration been involved, you should have seen a specialized attorney before you signed anything. For most aspects of copyright assignment, however, writers know (or should know) more about their rights than the average lawyer. Most anyone behind a legal shingle understands when a contract has been violated, however, and can write a letter to that effect. Note that an actual lawsuit, especially when an out-of-state publisher is involved, would be expensive, and unjustified unless thousands of dollars were involved. All you want a lawyer to do is write, under the lawyer's letterhead, a letter to the publisher demanding payment. A formal threat of legal action is difficult for any company to ignore, as can be seen from my opening example. If you can't find a lawyer to write such a letter for less than $75, keep looking (and complain to your local bar association). In most cases, that letter will suffice, and your check will appear.

TAKE LEGAL ACTION

Should repeated requests for payment be ignored, and your frustration continue for several months, consider action in small claims court. A call to your nearest clerk of courts will provide the necessary information about filing a small claims suit. While the upper monetary limit varies from state to state, in most cases the amount promised for an article or a short story, or royalty payment, will fall under that limit. You usually do not need a lawyer to file a small claims suit, although a small fee is generally charged by the court. You may also claim interest on amounts past due.

Since these are state courts, both you and the publisher in question must be doing business in the same state. In practice, such suits would be most convenient for writers who share the same city with the publisher. Whether the sale of a New York publisher's magazines on newsstands in Iowa constitutes "doing business" in Iowa for purposes of small claims actions is an interesting legal question (at least it was to the trial attorney I was married to). Recent precedents clearly favor a "long arm" interpretation. The Supreme Court has concurred, in cases of libel at least, that a publisher may be brought to trial in a state he has never previously visited, so long as that state is where the wronged party lives. Freelancers should check on such "cross-state" legal precedents in small claims actions as well.

A second, inexpensive legal avenue—given that interstate commerce is often involved between writer and publisher—is the Postal Service. If the manuscript was mailed to the publisher, business was conducted through the mails, and some aspect of mail fraud regulations may apply if the publisher refuses to honor the agreements. A copy of your letter to the publisher also should be sent to the Mail Fraud Division of the Postal Service in the city where the publisher is located. You may also contact your local postmaster for appropriate forms. As with formal notice of a small claims action, a letter from a regional postal inspector may well be enough to shake loose that tardy check.

FILE A CLAIM IN BANKRUPTCY ACTIONS

In the sad (but not unusual) event that the publisher stiffs you by declaring bankruptcy, always file a claim. With bankruptcy, you deal with uniform federal law. In many cases, some money is eventually pried loose for the creditors. But you don't become a creditor of record unless you file a claim. A local attorney can tell you which district bankruptcy court is appropriate (usually the one in a major city nearest the publisher's business address). Call or write the clerk of that court for the proper claim number of the case file, and ask for a copy of the appropriate claim form. In my experience the only cost for filing is your postage.

If you don't know a helpful attorney, the reference librarian in a major library may help you track down the address of the appropriate bankruptcy court. City and county courthouse law libraries are also available to the public for questions of this sort.

SHARE YOUR GRIEF

If all else fails (and especially if a bankruptcy filing is pending), let your fellow writers know about your problems. Unless you are a member of the few legally chartered writer's guilds or unions, a call for a strike or boycott is illegal. But you are quite within your rights to state the facts of a bad situation. Spread the word within the group to which you belong, in newsletters and in writer-oriented publications.

Freelancers generally work in isolation, feeling that they have little individual "clout," and often fearing that "making waves" will hurt their careers. The formal grievance procedures of writer's organizations do provide more protection for writers who encounter problems. As long as a writer remains polite and businesslike in pursuing legitimate grievances, however, reputable editors and publishers are likely to keep the doors open. As for those few incorrigible publishers, what have you really lost if you never hear from them again—after the checks *are* finally in the mail?

Five Strategies for Beating the Tax Man

BY PETER H. DESMOND

B y the time April 15 creeps onto our calendars, most writers feel like forgetting forever about taxes, and taking a chance the IRS "might not notice."

Of course, as self-employed people, you had the opportunity to file quarterly. However, a typical writer's twelve months of stony Yeatsian sleep are not vexed to nightmare by the flipping calendar and the passing estimated tax payment deadlines (June 15, September 15, January 15).

But April's hour comes round at last, and a hard time is had of it. Adding figures all night, sleeping in snatches, we hear the voices singing, "This is all folly."

Sound familiar? Why be so reckless with your taxes when you're so professional in other aspects of your business? If you simply feel ignorant of tax law as it applies to freelancers, read on: Revelation is at hand.

Although each year brings taxing new plot twists from Congress, the courts and the IRS, let's look at some of the more important ones from recent times.

SECTION 179 DEDUCTIONS

You can currently deduct as much as $17,500 in business equipment in the year you buy it. This is much more immediately gratifying than depreciating it over a period of years, and it reduces your taxes quite nicely. (Sorry, this offer is not valid for automobiles, where certain limits apply.)

Let's pause to look at Form 4562. Part I is where you claim the immediate write-off for items you bought in the past tax year; Part II is where you take things off a bit at a time. If the past year is the first year for which you're filing as a freelance writer, Part II is where you'll get tax benefits from the stuff you bought in previous years. Thumb through your checkbook register, your credit card statements and any receipts you've tucked away. Can you prove how much you spent on that desk, that computer, that impressive collection of how-to books? Good. Now reduce the amount to reflect wear, tear and obsolescence, and you're in business.

Incidentally, you use Form 4562 only for expensive and durable items. Write off the little stuff directly on Schedule C, Profit or Loss From Business; use line 22, Supplies. Does IRS prose leave you feeling worn and torn? Sorry, that's not depreciable. You can always hire a tax pro to prepare your business forms. Next year deduct his or her fee on line 17, Legal and Professional Services.

MEALS AND ENTERTAINMENT EXPENSE DEDUCTIONS

In this chapter our protagonists run into an obstacle. As of January 1, 1994, freelancers can deduct only 50 percent of the cost of meals they eat on business trips and the cost of business entertainment. (Check out line 24 of Schedule C.) This measure was aimed at the three-martini-swilling, corporate-skybox crowd, but it will also pinch struggling writers. Four possible remedies spring to mind:

• Try to persuade your parsimonious editors to reimburse you directly for your meal expenses while on assignment. Then they'll be stuck with the 50 percent limitation, and you won't be penalized for treating your sources to lunch or a round of beers.

• Take advantage of the IRS's standard meal allowance. Instead of keeping the actual receipts for the meals you bought on business trips, you can claim you spent from $26 to $38 a day, depending on where you traveled. Publication 463 lists the more expensive U.S. cities and counties, with the per diem amount allowed in each. It is perfectly legal to claim expenses of $38 a day for food in New York City, even if you ate only two Nathan's hot dogs. Note, however, that you will be able to deduct only $19 a day—the 50 percent limitation applies.

• Freelancers must prove how much they spent on lodging during their business trips. Fortunately, lodging costs are 100 percent deductible. But what if friends put you up for a couple of days while you do your research? Your normal impulse might be to take them out to dinner in gratitude for their hospitality. Change your ways: An auditor may claim that the restaurant tab was only 50 percent deductible. A better strategy would be to buy your friend a gift (fully deductible up to $25). Less gallant: Pay them for their trouble and ask for a receipt. They may not be as offended as you expected.

• Buy $17,500 worth of edible office equipment.

HOME-OFFICE DEDUCTIONS

Two rules govern whether the home office is your principal place of business, and therefore deductible. The first is whether you conduct your most important money-making function there. Assuming the role of literary critic, the IRS concluded that an author's crucial activity is tapping the keyboard or pushing the pen, not lunching with editors or appearing on *Oprah.*

The second rule has to do with how much time you spend in the home office, as opposed to other locations. If you write only at home, you can be serene. If, in addition, you conduct a lot of your interviews and research using the home-office phone and bookshelves, you can relax profoundly. Your home office is your principal place of business, and you can deduct part of your housing costs as a business expense. (But do try to get outside every once in a while, if only for your health.)

Things may be trickier for people who do their writing in two or more locations. It would be good if you spent 51 percent of your total work time (writing, rewriting, researching, fabricating quotes, querying, billing) in the home office. Better still would be to do 51 percent of your actual writing there, or to earn 51 percent of your writing income from stuff you wrote at home.

Aside from being a principality, the area must be used regularly and exclusively for your business. Sorry: No investment tracking or charitable paperwork at that desk; no recipe files or games for the kids on the computer; no hanky-panky on the office couch. The law is rigorous but clear on this point. Banish such activities to the den, the kitchen, the nursery or the polar-bear rug in front of the living room fireplace.

Get Publication 587 to read about business use of your home. Freelancers claim home-office expense on Form 8829; the deductible amount then transfers to Schedule C, line 30.

AUTOMOBILE EXPENSE DEDUCTIONS

Before we cut to the chase, I want you to promise to keep better records of your automobile use. What is so difficult about noting the odometer reading on January 1 and whenever you're warming up the car to drive to the writer's colony? At least keep track for a couple of representative months during the year; the IRS will accept a random sample of your auto usage as sufficient proof of your yearly expenses. Keep your log in the glove compartment, and note the business purpose of each trip. If you don't have such records, a gimlet-eyed sadist will disallow the expense at your audit, and in the afterlife you will be forced to attend a nonstop literary reading by Norman Mailer.

Why all this brouhaha? You want to arrive at two figures: your business mileage and your total mileage for the year. These establish the percentage of your actual car expenses that you can deduct; in addition to these expenses, you can factor in depreciation. (Fill out Part V of Form 4562.) Or you might prefer simply to use the IRS's mileage allowance. Either way, be sure to deduct tolls and parking, in addition to the business portion of your car loan interest and car excise tax (lines 10, 16b and 23 of Schedule C). Read all about it in Publication 917.

To determine what you include as "business mileage," we must look at the legal landscape, which is littered with the wreckage of IRS cruisers. The IRS does not let employees deduct commuting expenses. It has repeatedly tried to widen this dragnet by flagging down freelancers on their way from their home offices to other work sites. The result is usually a Keystone Kops routine.

A typical case is that of Leroy K. Kahaku. In 1990 the Tax Court pointed out that the law allows everyone to deduct travel between two different work sites, and that a home office is a work site; ergo, Kahaku's driving was not commuting. He commuted when he walked into his home office with his morning cup of coffee and planned the day's business activities. Had he tried to depreciate his slippers, the Tax Court would have found against Kahaku. Instead, it ripped up the IRS's ticket.

What's more, anyone can deduct travel to and from temporary work sites. After their 1993 high-speed chase of Charles W. Walker, who didn't even have a home office, the IRS lost this point (and their tempers). In 1994 they turned on the sirens again and took off after David W. Burelson, who didn't have a home office; the Tax Court sternly reaffirmed its stance, and the IRS-mobile was totaled.

Journalists who use their cars to cover a quick succession of stories in various locations should be able to deduct their driving (and parking) expenses under this doctrine, which purrs smoothly past the barriers involving commuting.

Here's an idea for the home-officeless: Drive to the nearby public library every day to do necessary research; afterwards, gad about conducting interviews. As the sun sets, return to the library to organize your notes and verify facts; then go home. None of the trips between your home and the library are deductible—you're commuting to and from a regular work site—but the rest of the day's driving counts as a write-off.

INTEREST EXPENSE DEDUCTIONS

Everyone, including IRS employees, thinks that you can't deduct credit card interest on your taxes any more. Everyone is wrong. The guiding rule since 1986 has been, for what purpose do you use the borrowed funds? If writers use a credit card to buy a new computer or pay for a research trip, they should list the credit card interest on line 16b of Schedule C. And there's no 50 percent limitation for the interest on charged restaurant business meals.

The IRS's record-keeping requirements can be rigorous, so it's best to use a separate credit card for your writing business. If you're short of cash at the end of the month, pay off your personal (nondeductible) card and let the deductible business interest accumulate. Business interest is deductible even if you only have one card, but prepare to spend hours and hours trying to determine how much you can reasonably write off—deducting personal interest expense is a strict no-no.

Taxes are never easy, no matter what profession employs you. Proficiency is really a matter of efficiency: Keep complete and accurate records this year, and next year might not seem like so much folly.

Twelve Tips for the Taxpaying Writer

BY PETER H. DESMOND

UNCLE SAM'S WRITING TIPS

• **Write more.** The more time you spend writing, the more serious you appear to the IRS, regardless of genre or content. Jack Nicholson's character in *The Shining*, even though he only typed and retyped the same sentence day after day, would not have flunked this part of the audit.

• **Don't give up your day job.** You can write evenings and weekends as a sideline; this is perfectly okay with the IRS, as long as you intend to make a profit from your writing. But how do you prove you're in it for the money?

• **Submit to paying markets.** If you send poetry to magazines that only pay in copies, you're acting like a hobbyist. Don't bother filing Schedule C, "Profit or Loss From Business." Do you pay reading fees and enter contests that offer cash prizes? That's more like it! You're spending money to make money. Once you've got a fistful of clips, woo editors who actually write checks to their contributors.

If you're a journalist, raise your sights from stingy local weeklies to trades and slicks. Though not written into the Code, Dr. Samuel Johnson's dictum prevails in spirit: "No man but a blockhead ever wrote, except for money."

• **Avoid the passive.** To make it as a writer, you have to hustle. Don't let rejection get you down! Send that short story right out again. IRS auditors don't care if you submit simultaneously; they just want to see that you're active. The fact that you wrote an article three years ago will not impress them as much as it did your mom. (In fact, she's probably getting impatient with you herself.)

• **Track your submissions.** A chart will help you keep all your pieces out there all the time. It also makes for dandy evidence at an audit. Bring along copies of your cover letters and every rejection slip you've ever received, and the auditor will begin to see the light: This person is serious about writing. The payoff? Write-offs.

• **Consult experts.** The IRS frowns on entrepreneurs who launch a new venture without getting expert advice. So stock up on writing books, take those classes, attend those workshops, subscribe to *Writer's Digest.* Boldly claim the cost on Schedule C, with the government's blessing.

• **Computer, typewriter or pen?** Whatever tool of the trade you favor, you can deduct the cost as a legitimate business expense. For pricey purchases that have a useful life longer than one year, add Form 4562, "Depreciation and Amortization," to your tax return. Either write off the cost over a five-year period or, if you had enough earned income, deduct up to $17,500 worth of equipment in the year you buy it. (Ribbons and refills go right on Schedule C as "supplies," whether you earned any income or not.)

• **Keep a journal.** Just as you take note of fleeting inspirations for later use, jot down those evanescent expenses you run up. The information will be handy come April, when you're working on the final draft of your tax return. Remember to pick up receipts at the post office and the stationer's. Routinely log your auto mileage in a glove compartment notebook (you can claim 30 cents a mile for work-related car trips in 1995). If you already rely on an appointment calendar, the record-keeping battle is half won.

Mind you, the IRS's requirement for receipts isn't absolute. It used to be that you didn't have to keep a receipt if you were claiming an expenditure for business travel or entertainment of less than $25, as long as you jotted down the time, place and date of the expense, and the business purpose, and your business relationship with the people you fed or entertained. Starting October 1, 1995, this limit rose to $75.

But think for a minute before opening up the window and tossing your receipts like confetti. The handy thing about receipts is that they already have the amount, date, time and place on them, as well as the name of the restaurant. Isn't it easier just to keep the receipt and scribble on it, "Lunch with Deep Throat—RMN knew"? Also be aware that you must keep receipts for lodging on business trips.

You still can't deal with collecting and filing little pieces of paper? The IRS will allow you to use a per diem allowance for meals while you're on a business trip. Depending on your destination, you can legally claim you spent from $26 to $38 a day for food when you traveled away from home overnight. (You can then deduct only 50 percent of this amount; the tax laws are convoluted and badly in need of editing.)

• **Set aside a place for writing.** Your writing coach may have talked up the advantages of having a cubby where nothing can distract you from the page or screen. The IRS feels the same way and will reward you for such devotion to your craft. This boon applies only when the home is your principal place of business.

If you have a net profit from writing and use one-fifth of your home regularly and exclusively for writing, you can deduct one-fifth of the utilities, insurance, repairs, cleaning and rent (or real estate tax and mortgage interest) on Form 8829. Incidentally, when novelist Georges Simenon lived in Connecticut, he successfully wrote off half the expenses of his farmhouse. The percentage you can take will depend on how big your cubby is and how many bookcases are scattered around the rest of the house.

Note that you must have a net profit in order to take the office-in-home deduction in the current year. What's more, you can't create a loss by taking the entire home-office deduction, though you can reduce your net profit to zero. However, Part IV of Form 8829 allows you to carry forward any unused loss to the next tax year, and the next and the next, until you finally hit the bestseller charts and auction off the movie rights. (Hint: Keep those part-year rent checks in your tax file, so that you can haul them out at your audit in the year 2001.)

• **Take care of your health.** Try to get out of the home office every once in a while, even if it's only for a spin in the car. Unlike company employees, who cannot deduct their morning and evening commute, people with home offices can deduct every business trip of the day. As long as it doesn't take you out of your way, no auditor is going to complain if you stop halfway between the library and the copy shop for a jog around the pond.

There's a small break on the health insurance front, too. If you pay for your own health insurance and you showed a net profit from writing in 1995, you can now deduct 30 percent of the premiums you paid on line 26 of Form 1040. This figure is up from 25 percent last year. However, the dollar amount you take off cannot exceed your net profit.

• **Some day you'll make it.** If you're serious, you'll keep plugging away. While you're at it, keep writing off your expenses. True, the IRS has a presumption that you must show a profit in three years out of five in order to take deductions on Schedule C. Note, however, that

STILL ANOTHER TAX TIP

BY CINDY ROBERTSON

Here's a tax fact to consider before you move your writing business from your home to an office: The IRS allows transportation deductions only for expenses involved in getting from one workplace to another.

This means that if your office is in your home, your mileage count or other deductions begin when you leave your house for writing-related work. But if your office is in town, and you leave from your house to do an article interview or other writing business, and then return home, you cannot claim any transportation expenses for the trip. The IRS says that transportation from home to work is commuting (even if you conduct business on the way, on a car phone, for instance), and is not deductible.

However, if you do have a separate office, you can still deduct local travel expenses if you do some work at your office first, and then begin your business-related driving.

this is a rebuttable presumption.

If you can show at an audit that you've followed the IRS's own tips for writers—devoting time to your craft, trying to sell your work, honing your skills and keeping good records—the auditor may throw in the towel. Consider hiring a knowledgeable advocate (a CPA or EA).

• **To be a great artist you need not suffer.** IRS auditors are somewhat suspicious of people who may actually enjoy their work. Don't let that faze you. As a Tax Court judge once remarked, "Suffering has never been made a prerequisite to deductibility." What's more, your intention to make a profit need not even be reasonable, but merely genuine. Viewed in this light, Jack Nicholson's demented author might have breezed through an audit.

Do You Write for Business—or Pleasure?

BY JAMES MCKECHNIE

From the Internal Revenue Service's viewpoint, the difference between a "not-for-profit activity" (the taxman's term for hobby) and a real business or profession is the motive for pursuing it. A hobby, whether stamp collecting, photography or writing, can produce an income and still be a hobby. A business can produce a loss and still be a business. However, a hobby is not primarily pursued for profit while a business is.

If you consider your writing a business, report all writing income, then reduce that income with the expenses incurred to produce it. If you have more deductions than income, you have a business loss. This loss reduces other types of income reported on your tax return. Hobby losses do not reduce other income.

Federal Regulation 1.183-2(b) lists nine elements to consider in deciding whether you are writing for profit.

• **The manner in which the taxpayer conducts the activity.** Writers must conduct their careers in a business-like manner. Maintain complete and accurate books and records to show the activity is for profit.

• **Expertise of the taxpayer or advisors.** Prepare for a writing career by studying accepted principles and economic practices . . . perhaps by consulting with those who are expert. You can provide evidence of your profit motive by carrying on the activity according to such practices.

In cases where a writer has that preparation or gets expert advice, but ignores the prescribed practices, an auditor may conclude you lack intent to make a profit. For example, writers know most query letters will not be answered unless a self-addressed, stamped envelope (SASE) is enclosed. If you violate that procedure and mail query letters sans SASE, you may be showing lack of intent.

• **Time and effort the taxpayer spends on the activity.** The amount of personal time and effort a writer devotes to carrying on a writing business may indicate an intent to make a profit.

That a writer devotes a limited amount of time to writing does not, by itself, indicate a lack of motive. Time and effort are considered in relation to other activities, such as a full-time job. Maintaining regular and steady hours for writing-related tasks will help show you're spending as much time as you have reasonably available. For example, a writer who devotes limited time to writing, but who hires a qualified agent to do the selling, could still be considered in business. A few isolated sales, however, will not qualify your writing activity as a business.

• **Expectation that assets used in the activity may appreciate.** The term for profit also encompasses assets that increase in value. Suppose a magazine writer realizes there may not be a profit from current writing activities. However, if the writer expects to gain an overall profit from the sale of a book or copyright (an asset), then the writer could be considered profit motivated.

• **Taxpayer's success in similar activities.** If the writer had success and profits in prior years for similar activities, that's evidence that the current activity is for profit. For example, if a successful magazine or short story writer decides to write a book, there is a reasonable expectation the writer will succeed based on past performance.

• **Taxpayer's history of income or losses in the activity.** A series of business losses during the initial or start-up years of writing may not prove lack of profit motive. However, losses should not continue beyond a period that is customary for the profession.

The writing profession often requires considerable effort over an extended period before producing a profit. It is reasonable to assume, however, that as a writer's ability grows and publishers become more aware of that ability, losses will eventually give way to profits.

• **The amount of occasional profits, if any, that are earned.** An occasional small profit from an activity generating large losses, or an activity in which a writer makes a large investment, won't necessarily show the activity is for profit. Suppose you spend $5,000 on a computer and $2,000 on a printer but sell only two articles for $250. You may not be considered profit motivated.

However, a large profit, even if only occasional, will tend to show the writing activity is for profit where the investment or losses are comparatively small. For example, if you write on a typewriter worth

$95 and earn $2,700, you'd be considered in business.

Tax years that show an upward direction of profits are more likely to show a profit motive than those that stay stagnant.

• **Taxpayer's finances.** If the writer does not have large income or capital from sources other than the writing activity, it will help indicate that the writing is for profit.

Large income from sources other than writing (particularly if any losses from writing create substantial tax benefits) could indicate you are not writing for profit.

• **Elements of personal pleasure or recreation.** If you list personal or recreational expenses, the presence of personal motives in incurring those expenses may indicate the activity is not for profit. However, nothing in the Treasury Regulations states one should not enjoy or derive pleasure from the act of writing for profit.

These are the guidelines IRS auditors use to determine business or hobby status. Unfortunately, sometimes a writer's activities are not that clear. Thus, the IRS will usually presume your writing activity is for profit if you indeed show a profit in any three out of the previous five years. If this is true, it doesn't make any difference if overall losses exceed overall profits for those years.

Consider applying a reasonable person theory to help you determine your business status. If a reasonable person knew the facts and circumstances of how you conduct your writing activity, would he conclude you are running a business or merely playing at a hobby?

If you decide that your writing does constitute a business, there are two tests you should meet before deducting any expense.

• *Ordinary.* The expenses must be customary or usual for the field of business. For example, paragliding costs aren't typically an expense incurred in the writing business. But if you're writing an article on paragliding, the expense is now research—and an ordinary, deductible expense. Overall, there must be a relationship between the business deduction and the business.

• *Necessary.* This means the expense is appropriate and helpful in developing and maintaining your writing business. The expense does not have to be essential or vital. In fact, the courts have usually accepted the taxpayer's judgment as to what expenses are necessary. Suppose, for whatever reason, you consider your writing much more powerful if written on papyrus paper. Even though the rest of the world considers this nonessential, generally if you consider it necessary, the expense will be allowed.

If you're audited, and the auditor determines you are in a not-for-profit activity, your deductions may be disallowed. Your tax would be recalculated, and you might owe. Not only will this spoil your day, but it also will make it that much harder to claim business losses in future tax years. The time to plan for an audit is now.

Taking Stock of Yourself

BY GARY A. HENSLEY

Thanks to me, my brother is a corporation. You may know him as Dennis Hensley, a *Writer's Digest* correspondent and the author of several books. To me, he's Denehen, Inc., a one-man freelance writing and lecture business with a home office (in both senses of the phrase) in Fort Wayne, Indiana.

Becoming a one-person corporation may not be right for every (or even most) freelance writers, but it has significantly reduced my brother's taxes.

This article will help you decide if incorporation will benefit you as a professional writer.

DETERMINING FACTORS

Don't even consider incorporating unless, as an established writer your taxable income from all sources exceeds $24,000 if you're single or $40,100 if you're married and filing a joint return. If your taxable income from all sources exceeds these amounts, in 1996 you would have been taxed at more than 15 percent; however, if you were incorporated in 1996, your corporation could have net earnings (that is, all taxable income less all allowable business deductions) up to $50,000 before the corporation's tax bracket would exceed 15 percent. This gives you greater financial flexibility. Even in a good year, with proper tax planning, your corporate taxes should be little to nothing.

One of the factors that will influence your decision will be your "bottom line" business net income or loss. For example, if your total taxable income is more than the minimum cited above from all income sources but you have considerable business deductions—say, for travel, home office expenses, equipment or office furniture—which reduce your business income from writing to zero or less, there would be no tax advantage to incorporation. These and other allowed business expenses could be used to shelter your personal income sufficiently.

For writers earning a more substantial net business income that would place them in a 28 percent or greater personal tax bracket, however, incorporating can provide both lower total taxation and greater financial planning flexibility. For example, sole proprietor writers—which is what you're technically considered if you aren't incorporated—are locked into a calendar year for planning and financial reporting, and they must declare all income annually on Schedule C of their personal Form 1040. However, a one-person corporation can allocate a portion of his total corporate earnings to his personal return in the form of wages and dividends and retain the balance in the corporation. This gives the corporate writer significant control over his personal taxable income.

CORPORATE BENEFITS

Corporate fringe benefits are one of the main reasons a sole proprietor would choose to incorporate. Such fringe benefits as health insurance, a medical reimbursement plan, a company car, a travel expense account, an education reimbursement plan, group life and disability insurance, and more, convert what are considered personal expenses of a sole proprietor into tax deductions for his or her corporation.

"Flexible spending accounts" or "cafeteria plans" are fringe benefits the owner/employee can use to pay for medical expenses and day care costs with pretax earnings through payroll deductions or employer contributions.

Furthermore, an individual cannot deduct the cost of his life insurance premiums as a tax deduction, but a corporation can provide up to $50,000 of "group" coverage to the owner/employee as a tax free fringe benefit and deduct 100 percent of the premium cost. Medical and dental costs may be partially deductible by unincorporated writers—once these exceed 7½ percent of their adjusted gross income and they have sufficient amounts of other deductions to qualify for itemizing on Schedule A—but very few writers can scale these barriers. A corporation, however, can deduct all of such expenses. With regard to health insurance premiums, a self-employed individual is now allowed to deduct 30 percent of the annual premium on page 1 of Form 1040 (but only if his or her business net profit equals or exceeds this amount) and the balance is subject to the above percentage and itemization barriers. Again, a corporation would be allowed a 100 percent deduction.

In addition to corporate fringe benefits, you may borrow money from your corporation (instead of traditional sources) as long as the loans are well documented and a reasonable interest rate is charged. (I recommend that you prepare and file a written promissory note for each loan.)

RETIREMENT PLANS

Recent changes in tax structure mean many individuals have lost some or all of their Individual Retirement Account (IRA) deductibility. As a corporation, however, you can establish a Simplified Employee Pension (SEP) plan that can replace your "lost" deductible IRA or supplement your fully, partially or nondeductible IRA contributions. SEPs are also available to self-employed individuals, but the calculation is more favorable for "employees." The self-employed individual multiplies his net income by 13.0435 percent whereas the employee gets to multiply his wages by 15 percent to determine the maximum allowable contribution (not to exceed $30,000 per year in either case).

Perhaps the single greatest advantage of SEPs is their simplicity. They involve less paperwork. An employer can establish a SEP by filling in a few blanks on a one-page IRS form (5305-SEP). To avoid the administrative burdens of setting up a pension plan, an employer may set up a SEP plan and make IRA contributions on behalf of employees under much more favorable rules than those that apply to regular IRAs.

Following tax reform, a SEP can have a version of the 401(k) or salary deferral plan. This allows employees to designate a portion of their salary to the SEP before federal income tax withholding amounts are calculated. The $19,500 annual deferral limit on a regular 401(k) also applies to the SEP version. This salary deferral feature makes the SEP a good alternative for taxpayers who have lost their IRA deductions. They can have salary deferred into the SEP and get the same benefit as an IRA deduction. Depending on the salary amount involved, they might be able to contribute more to the SEP than to an IRA.

Remember: If you keep your modified adjusted gross income on your personal return below $25,000 if single or $40,000 if married filing jointly, you will be entitled to a $2,000 deductible IRA contribution in addition to your SEP plan retirement contributions. By incorporating, you can significantly control the amount of income that gets reported on your personal return each year. With proper tax planning, you can take advantage of many tax-deferral strategies.

One common strategy is to have your spouse and/or children perform necessary supporting services to the corporation and receive a wage in return. The corporation is allowed a deduction for the full amount of the wage paid and, if the amount is below $2,000 and your spouse/child deposits the full amount into his or her personal IRA, no taxable income will result on your personal return. Thus, a corporation allows you to distribute some of your writing profits among your family members and lower your total taxes.

GETTING STARTED

A writer should consider the extra cost of incorporation before converting from a sole proprietorship (for example, the cost of the necessary legal, accounting and tax preparation services). These expenses will vary from state to state. An attorney should always be used when incorporating a business to make sure all state regulations are met.

An attorney should charge no more than $1,000 for incorporation advice and filing assistance. Be sure to shop around: Call several, and determine the fees in advance.

For this money you should expect four services: one or two consultations with the attorney regarding incorporation procedures; full preparation by the attorney of your Articles of Incorporation; assistance with your initial stockholders' meeting after your corporate charter is received from the state, as well as help with your first Board of Directors' meeting wherein officers are elected; and the providing of a corporate minute book with appropriate stock certificates.

ACCOUNTING RECORDS

In addition to an attorney, you'll also need to hire a local accountant to set up your corporate accounting records and to instruct you on how to fill them out. Your corporation will need to keep a general ledger, a cash receipts journal, a cash disbursements journal and a payroll journal. After the start-up, a semiannual visit to your accountant will ensure that you're on track with your recordkeeping and that you're advised of any new laws or procedural changes the government has enacted. You should become familiar with payroll tax forms and either fill them out yourself or, preferably, have your accountant handle them.

Together, you and your accountant can make sure that you have properly paid federal and state withholding taxes, FICA (Social Security), FUTA (federal unemployment taxes), state unemployment taxes, state sales tax (if you direct market any of your books or other retail merchandise to customers) and that you complete the annual federal corporate income tax return (Form 1120).

This may seem like a lot of paperwork. It is. However, these tax payments (and the accountant's fees) are deductible expenses used in reducing your corporate taxable income.

One caution: Make sure that all of your writing assignments and agreements are between the client and your corporation, not you personally. Otherwise, the earnings could be subject to ordinary personal income tax rates. This is commonly referred to as the "PHC Trap" (wherein you are assumed to be an operator of a personal holding company). This area should be carefully reviewed with your attorney and accountant. The attorney should prepare a contract for you to use that avoids this pitfall. Remember—a client should not name you specifically in a contract, even though you actually will be doing the work.

With tax laws, regulations, interpretations and rates fluctuating annually, freelancers must be aware of every legal maneuver available for preserving income. Incorporating is an enticing option that can provide income protection for the established writer.

Freelance Opportunities

The Magazine Writer's Marketing Edge

BY JAY STULLER

The most critical factor in a magazine article proposal isn't your list of credentials. It isn't even the topic itself. It's how well your idea will appeal to a magazine's audience.

You may be a master prose stylist, but if you're writing on the fine art of cowpunching, the readers (and therefore, the editors) of *Urban Living* will pass you by.

That's why figuring out the common concerns, interests, age and income level of a publication's target audience is critical to selling your article ideas.

At times you'll start with an idea that's in need of a good home. For example, I'd long known that family automobile vacations were only slightly less stressful than being held hostage by terrorists. A piece on how to deal with such travails would be a perfect summer article for some magazine; my challenge was to discover which one. That meant finding the publication that draws the right audience.

I've read *Kiwanis* magazine for years, and noted its many pieces on raising children, gardening and other hobbies—topics that strongly appeal to middle-class, Middle Americans. They're the kind of folks who stuff the kids in the car and head for Yellowstone, the Grand Canyon or Wally World—and if they're like me, regret it about eighty-three miles later.

So I sent my idea to *Kiwanis*, and the editors purchased "Surviving the Great Family Vacation."

The process can also work in reverse: Analyze the magazine's audience *first*, then discover the ideas that speak to them.

For example, the readers of *Islands* magazine—by the very fact that they buy this particular publication—indicate a strong interest in exotic destinations and activities.

That fact led me to ponder alternative types of travel and the growing popularity of research expeditions in which the vacationer assists scientists in field biology, archaeology, geology and more. A little research revealed quite a few expeditions to island environments, which gave me the right slant for an idea for a magazine that is, after all, named *Islands*.

Sometimes it will be just that obvious. The titles *Fly Fisherman* and *Vegetarian Times* well define their readers' interests. *Woman's Day* is clearly aimed at women, and it's unlikely that many coal miners, cowboys and recent divorcées purchase subscriptions to *Bride's* and *Your New Home*.

Audiences aren't always to clearly defined, however. Coal miners, cowboys and divorcées *may* be among the readership of *Changing Times* and *Popular Science*. But even in those cases, it pays to remember that a magazine has target and secondary audiences. Editors need articles that will entertain and serve these readers' desires and needs. To provide such features, the freelance writer must decipher a readership's interests. It's possible, but it requires some thought, digging and analysis.

FOLLOW THE GUIDELINES

The first information source to which many writers turn is a magazine's editorial guidelines. Some are comprehensive. For example, *Chief Executive* magazine sends potential contributors a formidable packet that tells you everything you wanted to know and more: A journal of opinion written by and for corporate CEOs, *Chief Executive* serves readers with a median personal income of $221,200, investment portfolios of $703,000, and a median net worth of $1.8 million. (Clearly, a piece on budget travel wouldn't play here.) Its editors also send out a readership breakdown by business and industry.

Unfortunately, most writer's guidelines provide only a few clues to precisely what kind of person is a typical subscriber.

Readers of *Health*, for instance, are described as "predominantly college-educated women and men who, by reason of their intellectual curiosity or practical interest, want both a dependable source of health information and a perspective on the rapidly changing face of American health care." While its guidelines describe in detail the style and content required of articles, nothing else is said of demographics.

"I guess we think that if writers read the magazine and just think about it for awhile, they'll get a pretty good sense of our readers," says one-time *Health* editor Susan West. "The types of stories we run are important clues. Articles on health speak to readers who are increasingly concerned about it, for the most part people in their early- to mid-40s. It's also important to note what we don't publish, such as articles on fitness. These would appeal to the leotard and salad set, who tend to be in their 20s and early 30s. From just looking at the magazine, a writer should get an intuitive feel for the audience."

Well, there's the rub for many beginning writers; such intuition often comes from experience. But clues beyond the tips included in writer's guidelines are out there. They're in the magazine's editorial content, as West suggests. They can be found by noting a publication's advertising; by writing an editor, asking for answers to a few simple questions; or by talking with readers yourself.

THE AD ADVANTAGE

Advertisers know as much about a magazine's readership as do its editors. The products hawked in a magazine characterize its audience, says *Parenting* executive editor Bruce Raskin. "If you see a bunch of geriatric products," he says, "chances are it's an older readership."

Health's ads, agrees Susan West, say volumes about its readers. While most articles are gender neutral, the ads hint not only that more women than men read *Health*, but indicate the types of women who read the magazine.

"You see it in food ads because as much as we might not like to recognize this, women still do most of the grocery shopping," West explains. "Cosmetic ads are for more sophisticated, upscale products, rather than eyeliner. Again, that's a function of age, education and employment status. We've been getting a lot of auto ads, which means Detroit is recognizing that professional and managerial women buy new cars."

Such distinctions can clearly influence how you shape an idea and present it in a query.

"You won't find many ads for baby or young child products" in *Health*, says West. "Among readers who do have kids, most have children at least eight to ten years old. What this means to writers is that the magazine is unlikely to buy infant health articles."

But at *Parenting*, a two-page "The Joys of Kinder-Care" ad pitching the day care center chain makes it obvious that this audience includes working mothers. That alone might be enough to suggest that a proposal on some alternate form of day care—say, a local grandmother consortium of sitters—might have a chance at *Parenting*.

SURVEY INSIGHTS

If a magazine's guidelines lack good information about its audience, ask the editor a few questions about the readership in your next query letter. You'll want to know about income levels, median age and whether the readers have significant hobbies—all of which can be answered in one paragraph. Even better, request a copy of the basic subscriber demographics that magazines send to potential advertisers.

Some publishers consider this sensitive material. But I've requested and received survey results from several publications, and suggested to others that a condensed version be included with writer's guidelines.

A survey includes tidbits such as how often the readers travel, and whether by air, rail or boat. It can tell you how often they eat at fast-food restaurants and purchase discount clothing, and what percentage of the audience camps, takes photographs, attends the ballet or has graduated from college. The same information that helps advertisers sell products to the readers can help writers sell articles to the editors.

Magazine editors also use surveys and focus group studies to get a feel for their audience. As *Kiwanis* managing editor Chuck Jonak explains, "One of the first things an editor wants to determine is what other magazines the audience is reading, the social issues that concern them, their income levels, occupations and so on. Although we think we know our readers, we use surveys to refresh our minds about exactly what we ought to be publishing."

Recent surveys by *Kiwanis* show its audience (business and community leaders in their mid-50s) also reads *National Geographic, The Wall Street Journal* and *Business Week.* Jonak says, "Our readers' greatest interest in feature material is in financial planning, business and financial trends, followed by self-improvement and health and medical articles. But business and finance are at the top of the list."

Thus, writer Ted Rakstis had a natural when he pitched a piece on the impending leadership gap facing business in the 1990s. (As corporations restructured during the 1980s, many middle managers were let go. With the Old Guard now retiring, inexperienced Baby Boomers will have to step directly to the top.) Rakstis's article covered the need for improved training for these future leaders, making it a trend piece that also included useful advice for the audience.

My information base on *Kiwanis* shows that the Kiwanis organization has an international membership; there are now Kiwanis clubs in sixty-nine countries. That international slant has had a tremendous impact on the kinds of ideas I send Jonak, and how they are framed. For example, in recent years I've sold the magazine articles on the new global gold rush, a reexamination of the population bomb, the impact of solar storms, and how the lowly potato could save the world from starvation should the greenhouse effect wipe out other crops. Each of these could stand alone as a general interest feature, but each also contains anecdotes or information on a dozen or more nations. "Global" is a selling point at *Kiwanis*, because such a piece can speak directly to more of the magazine's far-flung audience.

The key in pitching any article, however, is describing how the subject might impact individual readers. In proposing the piece on geomagnetic solar storms, I explained that such events can knock out power systems, which could harm the computers of the small businessmen who heavily populate *Kiwanis*'s audience. When you show an editor that an idea has some direct value to the readership, he or she is more inclined to assign it.

READING THE READER

When I see people reading certain publications, I occasionally do my own "focus group" research. I ask what they like about the magazine and what sort of articles they might like to see.

For instance, after spotting a copy of *Oceans* (which has since folded) in a friend's office, I asked about the magazine. He said he'd like to see it run more articles on aquaculture. I'd just read a small newspaper item about mussels that were commercially harvested from the legs of offshore oil platforms, and *Oceans*' editors were just as interested as their reader.

CONTENT CLUES

The methods editors use to reach their target audience are often apparent from analyzing the magazine's content. As an example, let's consider a sale I made to the now-defunct *Ford Times*.

Early on, *Ford Times* had a folksy tone, and was aimed at readers in their fifties. Later, the magazine still spoke to Middle America, but with a tone that was a bit more hip and focused on a somewhat younger audience.

Ford Times ran a regular feature—called All American Classics— that profiled such things as the Louisville Slugger baseball bat, the Flexible Flyer sled and Crayola crayons. The magazine frequently recalls days gone by with such topics as a one-room schoolhouse that operates in the Pacific Northwest. It also featured stories on in-line skating, the comeback of miniature golf, and a revival of bowling with a rock and roll twist. You can see in these articles an interest in Americana and nostalgia, but with a slant toward today's cultural trends.

Knowing its editorial content, I thought of *Ford Times* when I found my father's old, leather World War II flight jacket, tattered but repairable, hanging in a closet at my mom's house. Replicas of such jackets are hot fashion items, but there's more to the story than clothing; many people who don't fly airplanes have a fascination with flight. They visit museums, buy books and videos on aviation history, and collect all kinds of flight memorabilia, including bomber jackets. Thus, I hit *FT* editors with a proposal on America's "Armchair Aviators."

They bought and ran the piece, which included the story about finding my dad's jacket, a healthy dose of nostalgia and facts on a trend that grew big in Middle America—all of which fit the *Ford Times* "formula" I'd recognized by studying the magazine's content.

YOUR EDGE ON SALES

Translating this information into article ideas requires mental processing. You must put yourself in the reader's frame of mind and use the clues you've assembled to find the right perspective on a potential topic.

When Whittle Communications published its *Special Reports* series of magazines, they had a core readership of 25- to 40-year-old mothers with one or two children. One of the *SR* series—the *On Living* edition—planned an issue on ethics. As I thought of that audience—which included a lot of baby boomers with kids approaching their teenage years—I realized I was living with an idea.

My then-fifteen-year-old daughter had grown up in the age of MADD, antismoking campaigns, animal rights and AIDS. She's a moral scold who often disapproves of my lifestyle, which includes cigarettes, an occasional drink and girlfriends. I figured a piece about our relationship might strike a chord with other baby boomers, who gained freedom from stern parents only to have their kids dish out daily lectures on ethical and moral behavior. *Special Reports* assigned and bought it.

Other times I've sold ideas by identifying a specific trait shared by the readers of a magazine, a trait I then use to bring readership and topic together.

Sometimes that trait is occupation. *Across the Board* magazine—

published by the New York-based Conference Board business research institution—is primarily read by senior corporate executives. Its generally weighty stories assist these managers in doing better— for themselves and their organizations.

When I pitched former editor Howard Muson on an idea about executive photography—the ins and outs of getting your picture taken— he seemed skeptical. But, I urged in a letter to Muson, a shot of a CEO can say volumes about the executive and the directions the company is taking. The CEO photo is one of the first things investors and securities analysts look at when opening an annual report. If an executive adopts a confidently aggressive posture, in a well-composed photo that shows a new factory going up behind him, the shot can carry a powerful message.

Muson agreed, and ran "The Camera-Ready CEO—What Your Portrait Says About Your Company and You," as a cover story.

In another instance, the common reader trait was age.

I'd read a news item on a recent medical finding that long-term overuse of acetaminophen, the active ingredient in a common, over-the-counter painkiller, could cause kidney damage. I already knew that many people aren't really aware of what's in nonprescription medications—for instance that certain indigestion potions contain aspirin, which for some people can irritate the stomach lining.

This probably wouldn't interest *Teen* or *Hot Rod*. But the mean age of *The American Legion Magazine*'s three million readers is fifty-seven—a stage in life when health problems start to arise.

In a letter to publisher/editor in chief Daniel Wheeler, I suggested a piece on misuse of nonprescription medications. Wheeler asked me to also include information on prescription pills, and how all these things interact with each other, an idea that became "The Hidden Dangers of Common Drugs."

To sell an idea to *Inside Sports*, I identified the readership's common trait as an unusually sophisticated understanding of pro sports.

I'd watched Manute Bol enter game after game for basketball's Golden State Warriors and immediately change the whole tempo of the contest. Bol runs slower than a wounded sloth, grabs rebounds mostly by accident and doesn't score points. But he blocks shots better than any other player in the game. When this reserve center appeared, opposing players started shooting wildly and the Warriors often took control.

So I wondered: Is there a correlation between blocked shots and winning games in the National Basketball Association? And what magazine's readers would be likewise interested in such a question? *Inside Sports*, of course.

Its editors agreed. I got my questions answered and shared those findings with *Inside Sports*'s like-minded readers. (And yes, blocked shots are a surprisingly large factor in games won.)

THE PERFECT FIT

Once a writer grows attuned to thinking about audience, the intuition that leads to salable ideas kicks into gear. I don't snow ski, but I'm certain that anyone who reads *Ski* is enthralled with the sport. I also know—from observing friends, co-workers and so on—that many skiers suffer serious knee injuries.

From playing basketball, I unfortunately know knee injuries all too well, and I know about the best braces to hold a bum one together. The brace that keeps me playing hoops, I figured, might help wounded skiers return to the slopes. With that analogy, I convinced the editor of *Ski* to commission and buy a piece that said: "Choosing the right brace may be the most important equipment decision you'll ever make."

Like the right brace, that idea was a perfect fit.

How to Survive When Magazine Markets Change

BY MARK HENRICKS

The news was bad. My first impulse was to rip the car radio from the dash. Instead I kept both hands on the wheel and listened, stunned, as the announcer repeated the awful bulletin: The magazine where I'd just filed a 3,000-word investigative story was ceasing publication.

Would my story ever be published? Would I ever be paid my fifteen hundred dollars? What would happen to the editor contact I'd so painstakingly developed?

If you've worked in the article writing business for long, this scene is familiar. If not, it's a coming attraction. The facts of freelancing are: Magazines die. Owners change. Editors get fired, quit or just move on.

With luck, you won't get the news at 65 mph. And with some instruction in how to administer last rites to a dying magazine, you need not lose your fees, your stories, your contacts or even very much sleep. Surviving the crisis is a matter of basics.

AN OUNCE OF PREVENTION

The best way to deal with a dying market, of course, is not to deal with it at all. You can avoid many problem situations by following a couple of commonsense business practices (although even the most careful freelancers will be caught occasionally).

First, know the magazines you submit to. Keep track of a publications health by reading market reports in *Writer's Digest*; publishing trade journals such as *Folio:*, *Adweek* and *Advertising Age*; and the business pages of newspapers. These can alert you to trouble long before it becomes a catastrophe.

If news of financial downturns, flagging ad sales, sizable layoffs or circulation declines pop up, consider redirecting your efforts toward more stable publications. Or make sure a floundering magazine pays for each article *before* you do more work.

Also analyze magazines from your own experience. A previously punctual pay schedule lapsing into tardiness might signal only a vacation in the accounting department—but it might also mean financial trouble. Sometimes you'll have a good enough relationship established with an editor to talk frankly about a magazine's health (this is touchy territory, however, and probably best left alone).

Having a contract is also key to avoiding problems. Doing business with a phone call and an oral promise seems friendly and easy—until the day you wish you had something on paper.

"With a contract in hand, if they simply stop publishing, you're in a pretty good position to come up with something," says Dennis Holder, a veteran freelance writer. "If you don't have it on paper, they can completely ignore you—and will. I never write a word until I have a contract and a publication that's going to pay me for that word."

Your contract—copies of which can be mailed to the publication—can keep you and new editors on track through the paper shuffle that usually accompanies staff turnovers. And, if a magazine goes under, your contract can still be used to prove—to either the accounting department or a court—that money is owed you.

A POUND OF CURE

When you're eventually caught in the middle of a magazine death or staff change, these six tips will see you through the crisis:

Ask for what you want. This is obvious but often overlooked advice. Industry practice says you get paid for writing a piece that wasn't published through no fault of your own; many writers, especially beginners or part-timers, are too intimidated to ask for what's theirs—or they envision a hassle greater than the worth of the work.

A simple, calm letter doesn't take much time and can produce results. If the editor who bought your piece leaves, write the new regime a letter asking if they'll still use your story and, if not, requesting a kill fee. (Of course, if your story's already been bought and a new staff decides not to use it, simply ask that the rights revert to you. You're then free to market your piece elsewhere.)

If a publication is struggling on a strapped budget, it's usually best to bypass your usual editorial contacts (they have worries of their own) and mail an invoice to someone whose job is paying bills.

"I just send a very official-looking statement right to the accounts payable department," says Elaine Liner, a Dallas freelancer. "And I always get the money."

Even a dead magazine might respond to a letter, either through a division set up to settle accounts or a parent company. Just don't forget to ask.

Control your outrage. When asking for what you want, respect the feelings of the people you're dealing with. It's not their fault they found new jobs, or had old ones fold under them. Here are two examples of polite but firm letters. Use them as models. The first might be written to check up on manuscripts caught in a magazine death.

Dear Pat:

I spoke with Jim Delancey today and got the grim forecast. Let's hope it's wrong and *Value* has many more years of success ahead.

In the meantime, here's my invoice 4199 for $46, covering phone expenses on the home infusion story. Including that one, *Value*'s account looked like this on June 1:

Invoice	Date	Subject	Amount
4152	1/25/89	Telecom story expenses	$ 95.25
4160	2/6/89	Expenses (misc.)	76.89
4164	4/3/89	Sports Town story expenses	21.62
4178	4/10/89	Home infusion therapy story	2,000.00
4199	6/6/89	Home infusion story expenses	46.00
Total			$2,239.75

Last month, I received a payment of $1,250 from *Value*. Thanks for getting me up to the front of the payment list. I'd greatly appreciate your help with the above as well.

If *Value* does cease publication, I look forward to working with you in your next position. Call with questions or if I can be of any assistance.

Best Regards,

This letter could be sent to a new editor to check up on previously submitted articles.

Dear Pat:

Nice talking to you today. I do, indeed, hope we'll be able to work together on many projects for *Value*.

As I said, I'm just dropping you a note to make sure the

manuscripts you have in-house (assigned by Jim Delancey) don't get lost in the shuffle.

You should have the first draft of my "Home Infusion Therapy" piece (billed on 4/10/89, $2,000) and the first draft on my "Telecom Scandals" piece—for which I've billed *Value* with invoice 4159 for $46, but haven't received payment yet. Could you see if that's in the pipeline?

I have a few other ideas for articles that seem right for *Value*; I'll drop you a query shortly. In the meantime, Pat, good luck with your new editorship. If you have any questions about either story—or if you need some quick writing done—give me a call.

Best regards,

Each letter politely checks on both the status of manuscripts sent to the publication, and miscellaneous payments.

Be willing to bargain. We write for money, but that's not the only medium of exchange. One freelancer accepted an answering machine in lieu of cash from a bankrupt publisher. Office supplies, equipment and even furnishings may be easier for a money-strapped operation to come by. This solution can be much quicker than dragging through legal proceedings to collect a few dollars.

Know when to step up the pace. If a turmoil-plagued publication doesn't respond to several letters and phone calls over a period of months, it's time to get serious.

If a new staff hasn't responded to your requests for payment, send a certified letter asking for a kill fee and stating that you are withdrawing the article from their consideration and marketing it elsewhere. If the kill fee never arrives, your options are limited. The fee usually isn't worth the time, trouble and money needed even to go to small claims court (more on that later). But you can submit the article elsewhere.

If a dying publication owes you money, however, do everything possible to collect the debt *before* it closes shop or declares bankruptcy. Freelancer Dennis Holder says a certified letter often works. "My approach," he says, "is not to let them forget me."

A step between the certified letter and going to court is hiring a lawyer to write an official-looking letter to the publisher. That will cost you a nominal fee, but usually produces results. I sometimes note on my letter that I'm informing my attorney (who happens to be my sister). A *cc:* to her has resulted in miracles and cost me no more than a modest dinner.

Small claims court is usually your last stop. But there are some problems here—in some cases, you must file where the court has jurisdiction over the publication (the city where the publication operates, usually). That can eliminate your local court.

The U.S. Postal Service mail fraud department is a long shot for help in matters such as this.

Be ready for bankruptcy. If you publisher files bankruptcy, matters have become truly complex. You'll have to marshal all your documentation and most of your patience.

First, file a claim to be added to the list of creditors. You don't need an attorney for this, but one could help you figure out in which court an out-of-town magazine filed its bankruptcy papers.

You'll get only a fraction of the amount you seek. And it may take months, so be patient.

"You're obviously not going to be a senior creditor," says Dennis Holder. "And you might get only ten cents on the dollar. But it'll be something."

Finally, look on the bright side. There really is one. When a periodical dies, the people who ran it move on to other jobs in publishing. If you left your former editors on a good note, they'll take your card with them when they go.

"I've learned to find out where the editors went and write them nice letters," says Elaine Liner. "They feel as if they owe you something."

HAPPY ENDINGS

After recovering from my highway shocker and swerving back onto the road, I called my editor and expressed condolences, talked to other employees of the floundering publication and passed out leads to freelancing sales.

My article was never published. But I was paid in full. The rights to the piece were returned (although, unfortunately, too late for its time-sensitive material to be of much value).

Best of all, the editors who survived the magazine's demise carried old address books to new jobs. Some had freelance budgets to spend and editorial space to fill. The phone started ringing. The news was good.

The Profitable Marriage of Words and Pictures

BY CARL AND ANN PURCELL

A young writer named Tom Block once interviewed us for a magazine story about our careers as travel journalists. During our discussions we offered to provide Tom with photos to illustrate the article. We told him to keep any payment he got for the pictures (reasoning that an article would be worth more to us in publicity than the photo payment).

Tom sold the package of article and photographs to the late *Ford Times*, which used the piece as a cover story. For the article, Tom was paid $500. For our photographs, he received $1,650.

Not surprisingly, our young friend has since developed an avid interest in photography.

Just how much top magazines and book publishers pay for photography often comes as a shock to writers who don't "do" photography. On the flip side, photographers are surprised at how much easier it is to sell a set of outstanding pictures when they are accompanied by interesting, readable text. Smart journalists are coming to the conclusion that it pays to have a working knowledge of *both* disciplines.

Editors think so, too. When faced by limited space and two submissions, they'll almost always choose the one that is accompanied by appropriate, timely, well-executed photographs. In fact, we credit a good part of our success as travel writers and photographers to our ability to provide editors with ready-to-print packages that contain both words and pictures.

YOU CAN DO IT

If you've hesitated to get involved in photography because you thought it too complex and too technical, it's time to reconsider. Modern cameras have become so automated that almost anyone who can frame a scene in the viewfinder and then press a button has the talent to get clear, sharp, *publishable* results.

Several special features on modern cameras allow even novice photographers to take near-professional photos. The most important are automatic (or programmed) exposure and autofocus.

Automatic exposure control has been around for quite a few years. Computer chips within the camera can read an almost infinite number of lighting situations and program the camera's exposure settings accordingly.

Autofocus came into wide use only about ten years ago, but is already used by most professional and nonprofessional photographers. Some cameras, using autofocus, can change focus more quickly and accurately than the human eye. The only drawback is that the camera focuses on a point in the center of the camera's viewfinder. If you're taking a photo of two people, the center of the screen falls between your subjects, and the camera focuses on some point behind them. But you can easily compensate for this. It doesn't take long to learn to focus on *one* of your subjects, push the shutter button halfway down to lock the focus, and then recompose your photo and shoot.

In addition to automatic exposure and auto focus, some cameras are equipped with zoom lenses. These lenses give beginning photographers the flexibility to select any view from moderate wide-angle (that is, a lens that takes in a wide view) to mild telephoto (or close-up) without changing lenses. Also, built-in motor drives advance your film rapidly, which means you are almost always ready to shoot.

The budget conscious writer may blanch, assuming that such sophistication will cost a bundle. Actually, these features are standard on most 35mm cameras with interchangeable lenses. Bottom-of-the-line models with a standard lens, automatic exposure, autofocus and motor drive start at about $300. You could easily recoup that amount on your first package sale.

In addition to the basic camera, you'll need three additional items: a lightweight tripod, a cable release and an electronic flash. These accessories allow you to take good pictures under marginal light conditions. You'll need the flash for close and medium-close pictures of people and things in dim light or darkness. The tripod and cable release allow for brief time exposures of cities at night or interiors of buildings. (Exposure and focus can still be automatic so that you don't have to try to guess how long the exposure should be.)

After your camera, the most essential piece of equipment is film.

It's best to always shoot with color slide film—preferably with an ISO film speed from about 64 to 100. We use Fujichrome 100 and Kodachrome 64 as our workhorses. These are the films of choice for color reproduction, and slides can also be used for making black-and-white or color prints. (Color can be converted to black-and-white, but you can't go the other way.) Black-and-white prints require the making of a transfer internegative, but if it's done at a good laboratory, it is impossible to detect that the original picture was shot in color. Most beginning photographers have their film processed at a dependable commercial lab, but use a local custom lab for black-and-white transfers.

PUTTING YOUR HARDWARE TO WORK

With a loaded camera in hand, you're ready to take the pictures that will illustrate your articles. It may surprise you, but this is where you, even if you're a novice shooter, hold an edge over professional photographers. Photos taken during your fact-finding and writing trips will be more relevant and specific to the article you're writing than those taken by someone else.

Let's say your article is an interview. You'll want to get a few pictures of your subject after the interview (don't try to photograph *and* interview at the same time). These are the easy pictures to take. We recommend shooting in daylight in open shade, or in soft light coming through a window (don't place your subject in front of the window, however, or you'll photograph a silhouette). Move in close for a shot of your subject's face, then back to include his head and shoulders, then back even further for a full upper-body pose. Ask your subject to avoid staring directly into the camera lens; have him look slightly up and off to one side.

Take at least three shots of each pose, "bracketing" to find the perfect exposure. You do this by varying the exposure dial from plus one, to zero, and to minus one. This should give you at least one perfect exposure.

You may want to try different sorts of shots, too. Never hesitate to experiment with your camera. Show your subject in conversation with another person, involved in his or her work, walking in the front yard, or even relaxing in a hammock. A picture editor is always pleased to have a choice, and the extra film is cheaper than your time would be if you were forced to come back for additional photos. Your goal is to let the editor know you can provide a variety of clear and interesting pictures to illustrate your article. Once this is established, that editor will be more receptive to future story ideas and may even seek you out for assignments.

Pictures for a personality profile are just one example of what you can do with your camera. Your article illustrations may be of a city, a day care center, a family reunion picnic or a special school program. The subjects can be as varied as your—the writer's—imagination. In all these instances, the camera becomes a professional tool, helping you to communicate with the readers and letting them see the places and the people about whom you are writing. This tool is more than a mechanical device. Properly used, it can convey the beauty of nature, a sense of place, moments of sadness or happiness, a look at the past and hope for the future.

In our work as travel journalists, we strive for images that establish the unique qualities of specific destinations. We invariably shoot an establishing picture—a view of a city or landscape that is distinctive to that culture and country. It may show misty minarets rising above the Bosphorus, thousands of migrating animals on the Serengeti or a caravan of camels in the Gobi Desert. We supplement this shot with many faces of local people, close-ups of animals, graphic colors or complex patterns, and details of architecture. We create a visual collage of a travel destination, trying to help our readers experience that place through our eyes. Our words guide them through this visual adventure, explaining and summarizing the total experience.

As you become more comfortable with your camera, your eyes will automatically look for good shots. Occasionally you will find a picture that gives you an idea for another story or angle you might have otherwise missed.

PUTTING YOUR PHOTOS TO WORK

Now that you can produce a package of words and pictures for an editor, what is the best way to market this product? The procedure is essentially the same as selling just an article to a publication. Obviously the subject and style must be appropriate to the magazine. As you study sample issues, research not only your target market's subjects and approaches, but the types of pictures it uses. Some travel and fashion magazines take a highly stylized approach with strong, graphic images. Others use pictures that are more photojournalistic or news oriented.

One of the best places to find out about the picture requirements of specific publications is *Writer's Market* (Writer's Digest Books). Many of its listings include a "Photos" paragraph that explains what a publication can or cannot use in the way of pictures. It may indicate that the editors prefer 35mm color slides or black-and-white prints. Some listings instruct you to state the availability of pictures in your query or cover letter; others encourage you to send slides or prints directly with your manuscript. We find that sending our pictures often helps to sell the article.

Never submit unsolicited pictures without also sending a self-addressed, stamped envelope (SASE) for their return. You cannot expect an editor to return unsolicited materials without an SASE. If you do not intend to send an SASE, it is wise for you to simply state that color slides or black-and-white glossies are available on request.

If your story and pictures have been specifically requested by the editor, you can send a submission form with your photographs, saying that there is a substantial fee if any original slides are lost or damaged (the American Society of Magazine Photographers has put a value of $1,500 on each original slide) and that there will be a holding fee if the editor does not return your slides within thirty days—or whatever period you have agreed on.

When submitting pictures, take great care in packaging and shipping. Insert slides in plastic sleeves (twenty slides to a sleeve) and place them between double cardboard stiffeners. Photographs should also be sandwiched between stiffeners. We recommend shipping via Federal Express, UPS or certified mail with a return receipt for the best security.

If you are making multiple color submissions, such as to a number of noncompeting newspapers, you may wish to have duplicate slides made. The quality of these "dupes" is important, so choose your lab carefully. You might want to test several labs with identical "practice" slides and compare results.

A more advanced photographer's tool is the model release. Though it's not usually needed for editorial use, it is still a good idea to get a signed model release for your people pictures. Releases are an efficient way to collect the information you may need to identify people when writing photo captions, and they make your photos usable for advertising (which will earn you much more money than any editorial use).

Before you start printing submission forms and model releases, however, you should refer to the American Society of Magazine Photographers' *Stock Photography Handbook.*

```
                                                    SUBJECT:

        DELIVERY MEMO


                                                    WORDS AND PICTURES
```

CLIENT   PHONE_____

ORDER FILLED BY_____   DATE_____
TOTAL SLIDES SENT_____
SHIPPED BY: _____UPS _____FEDERAL EXPRESS _____OTHER

The enclosed color slides have been submitted at your request. These slides are copyrighted and fully owned by the photographers of WORDS & PICTURES. Reproducing, duplicating, printing, or copying is prohibited without prior consent.

Please pre-edit and return any slides which you cannot use as soon as possible. With each return shipment include a copy of this submission form with a notation of the number returned and the number still being held.

These transparencies may NOT be projected.

Each original slide is submitted with the understanding that it has a value of $1200 IN CASE OF LOSS OR DAMAGE. If you choose to return the slides via Federal Express, your responsibility for the slides ends when they are picked up by the courier. With any other form of delivery, including regular mail, your responsibility for the slides continues until they are received by our office.

It is understood that this submission has a holding period of 30 days without charge. After that time has elapsed, there is a holding fee of $1.00 per slide per day unless prior arrangements have been made for a longer holding period.

If we do not receive objections to the conditions of this delivery memo within one week of its receipt, it is assumed that the client accepts all terms stated above.

PLEASE CHECK SLIDE COUNT   SUBMISSION #___206_____

A submission form (top) details what a publication may and may not do with slides and photos that you submit at the editor's request (don't send this form with unsolicited photos). A model release (right) is signed by the people you photograph, giving the photographer the right to sell the photo.

MODEL RELEASE

I hereby give photographers Carl and Ann Purcell, their legal representatives and assigns, the right and permission to publish, without charge, photographs of me, _____ taken at _____. These pictures may be used in publications, audio-visual presentations, promotional literature, advertising, calendars or in any other manner. I hereby warrant that I (or undersigned Parent/Guardian) am over eighteen (18) years of age, and am competent to contract in my own name so far as the above is concerned.

MODEL _____

ADDRESS _____   Signature of Model or Parent/Guardian   ___/___/___
                                                                              Date
CITY _____

WITNESSED BY _____ STATE _____ PHONE _____
                                                ZIP _____
                    Signature of Witness   ___/___/___
                                               Date

READY, AIM . . .

There is, of course, more to this sideline than we can fit into a single article. These are just down-and-dirty instructions for getting started in taking pictures. For more detail, we recommend these books:

- Our *Guide to Travel Writing and Photography* (Writer's Digest Books), which focuses on the type of writing and photography we enjoy most.
- *The Basic Book of Photography*, by Tom Grimm (NAL-Dutton), an instructional book on the theory and practice of photography.
- *Big Bucks Selling Your Photography*, by Cliff Hollenbeck (Amherst Media), which talks about marketing and promoting your pictures.

You may not believe that one photo is worth a thousand words, and we certainly haven't reached that stage where one photo is worth a thousand dollars. But as the writer who profiled us learned (to his delight), there are profits to be made when you add pictures to your words.

Getting Maximum Mileage from Your Writing

BY JOHN M. WILSON

W hen the movie *The Doors* was shooting on location, free-lance writer Pat H. Broeske filed a story on the film with the *Los Angeles Times*'s Sunday Calendar section. But she didn't stop there. Because she owned foreign rights to her article, she was able to sell essentially the same piece throughout Europe, where Doors lead singer Jim Morrison lived during the last years of his short life. Broeske also fashioned a much different piece for *Fame* magazine (now defunct) looking back at Morrison's dark side, spun off a brand new article on the revived interest in his poetry for a newspaper lifestyle section, and peddled several short *Doors*-related items to *Entertainment Weekly*. She even sold some of her notes to *People Weekly* for $750.

From an assignment that initially paid in the $1,000 range, Broeske generated several thousand dollars more, and she'll continue to milk new ideas—and additional income—from the same material in the months and years ahead.

There was nothing unethical about what she did, or even unusual. Reslanting for secondary markets is just smart business, Broeske says. "Every time you find a new market for your existing material, it's like finding an extra paycheck."

Broeske offers this advice for writing multiple sales from each idea you work on:

- Keep all your notes and research material, especially clippings from other publications.
- Maintain voluminous files by subject ("action heroes," "amusement parks," "women directors," etc.).
- Build relationships with editors.
- Network with other writers, who often suggest new markets or

introduce you to new editors (or maybe, God forbid, become editors themselves).

- Keep an eye on new and changing markets, as well as on trends or events that suggest new spins for previously published stories.

RESLANT IN ADVANCE

Three general rules will take you a long way in the multiple-markets game:

- Study the marketplace.
- Find individual publications that don't directly compete.
- Reslant carefully for those specific markets.

Here are thirteen specific tips to help you enjoy multiple successes:

Plan ahead. If you query on an angle within a general topic area, or receive an assignment, don't stop there. Try to come up with other hooks on the same general subject—*before* you begin your deeper research. Find noncompeting markets for those new angles. Here's an example:

Some years ago, a friend nailed down an assignment from a runner's magazine to cover the running segment of a triathlon in Hawaii. His fee was in the $2,000 range. He then queried an inflight magazine, focusing on business executives in the race and how triathlon training improved their career performance. The inflight guaranteed $1,000 or thereabouts, plus plane fare. My friend next pitched *TV Guide* on the difficult logistics of TV race coverage. *TV Guide* offered another $1,000, and picked up food and lodging expenses. The writer notched a fourth assignment with a women's sports magazine that wanted a profile of top women athletes in the race.

By knowing the marketplace and reslanting carefully for noncompeting markets, he landed four assignments—all *before* he boarded the plane.

Expand your research. Again, think ahead. When researching or interviewing, even at the preliminary stage for a query, broaden your scope. Ask questions that might generate quotes for spin-off pieces or queries. If possible, plan photos or illustrations for use in secondary markets. And, by all means, keep all your material.

Scan the categories. Run through *Writer's Market's* list of categories, from consumer publications on animals, art and architecture to trade journals on travel and veterinary, and the more than one hundred subject areas in between. Do these categories trigger new ideas, suggest appropriate ancillary markets, either for an assignment you're at work on now or for old material that may lie dormant in your files?

As I scan these categories, for example, all kinds of possibilities loom up from my files on wilderness travel: health and fitness, ecology, self-improvement, teen and young adult, camping, photography.

Brainstorm. Jot a list of every conceivable angle you might wring from your broad topic; discard the ones you don't really want to do or feel might fall beyond your scope.

Now find markets for the new hooks you do want to develop. Or work the other way, glancing over individual markets to see what new angles they suggest; scan those tables of contents, particularly the departments, and watch marketable ideas spring to mind.

Think article types. Concentrate on each article type—profile, roundup, travel, historical, nostalgia, personal experience, essay, investigative, how-to, service and so on. What new possibilities do they suggest?

Think short. As you study potential spin-off markets, be aware of magazines and newspapers that use shorter items. Sometimes a pithy quote or two from the right person, a useful anecdote or factoid, can be enough for a brief item.

You can also work the other way. A friend recently sold a 500-word item on an unusual new movie to a leading entertainment magazine, yet his interviews and research provided enough to fashion a profile of the director for another market, as well as the beginnings of a trend piece on film for a third publication.

Update. Look over your files or published articles. Can you find a current take for a topic, perhaps updating a subject with only a few phone calls and some new research?

James Joseph writes prolifically on engineering and related matters for publications like *Popular Science.* Bicycles, which are popular around the world, are one of his favored topics; each time there's a new development in the industry—mountain biking, for example— he's able to spin off a new piece. He reslants, does new research and meticulously repackages and sells these articles worldwide.

Think topically or seasonally. Do upcoming dates, holidays and special events suggest ways to rejuvenate or stretch your material? Be aware of trends, because they tend to be cyclical, making old material useful again.

Broeske, for instance, first profiled actor John Travolta for the *Los Angeles Times*, focusing on his career decline, when he was making the film, *Look Who's Talking*. When the movie became a hit, Broeske reworked her material for an *Us* piece on his career *comeback*. When the picture was released abroad, she allowed a syndicate to sell an updated Travolta profile in overseas markets. She even resurrected her material when the sequel, *Look Who's Talking Too*, came out nearly two years later. She estimates her overall take from the topic at close to $10,000.

Change viewpoint. If you've completed an article for a target readership, can you flip the viewpoint for a contrasting audience? Gender bend an angle for the women's market into one for a men's magazine? Retool a piece aimed at one age group for another? For example, if you've written a self-help piece for a senior's magazine about communicating with grandchildren, can the viewpoint be switched for a teen publication?

Think regionally. Start locally and expand your market survey outward, from city to regional to national publications. What new markets does this suggest? Does your regional peg suggest a piece with national scope? Or, conversely, can you localize a national topic?

Using a national peg, Broeske sold a survey piece on America's top ten amusement parks to several Sunday supplements around the country. She went historical for a look at turn-of-the-century amusement parks for *Minnesota Motorist* (now *Home & Away*). Then she used a regional angle for the inflight *Air California*, examining the Golden State's top thrill rides.

I took a similar approach with an assignment for the lifestyle section of the *Los Angeles Times* to profile the ecology-minded National Outdoor Leadership School (NOLS), based in Lander, Wyoming. I angled the piece on how the organization's rigorous backpacking expeditions help young people develop character. Next, I fashioned an article for *Western's World*, the inflight of the old Western Airlines, on a NOLS kayaking trip in the Alaskan wilderness, designed for professionals (Alaska was on the airline's route). Using the same material, I reslanted for *Alaska Outdoors*, focusing on NOLS setting up a new branch in Anchorage.

Remember that in most cases it's necessary to create a completely different article, especially if you're selling to higher paying markets that don't purchase second rights. They generally expect something *new*—meaning a new slant, written in a different way. This often requires a completely different *focus*, and plenty of new or additional information (fresh quotes, interview sources, statistics, etc.). Don't try to just change your title and lead—unless you're selling second rights, it's illegal.

Reader response. Was there a reaction to your published article that suggests new spins on the same subject? New leads, contacts, sources?

Keep in touch. Maintain communication with subjects, publicists, related organizations and the like. Not only can they keep you current, they'll often have ideas for stretching your material into other markets.

Extract and re-mix. Are you able to take bits and pieces—quotations, anecdotes, statistics, other details—from a number of your existing articles, find a new theme and create a new piece?

A few years ago, I got to reminiscing about the handful of celebrity interviews I'd done over the years that had ended in kill fees for one reason or another. From that throwaway material, I put together an anecdotal humor piece for the *Los Angeles Times* about a freelance writer dealing with rejection and frustration.

Making money off rejections? Now, *that's* maximum mileage.

Simple Steps to Multiple Marketing

BY DENNIS E. HENSLEY

F reelancers must sell each piece they write as many times as possible. I do this by marketing my articles from the smallest local publications to the largest circulation periodicals in this sequence of steps:

local newspapers (pay $5-$25)
county papers (pay $5-$25)
statewide periodicals (pay $50-$400)
regional publications (pay $30-$400)
specialty magazines (pay $75-650)
national magazines (pay $100-$1,500)
international publications (pay varies)

Most editors don't mind buying a feature that you've already sold elsewhere when it meets these four requirements:

The previous appearance should not overlap too much with the reprint market's readership. For example, when I sold a tourism article to the *Detroit Free Press* on the Calumet Theater of Michigan's Upper Peninsula, I later sold it to *The Fort Wayne News-Sentinel*, because people in Indiana don't read Detroit newspapers.

Provide the new editor with different photos. In this way, even if *some* readers have seen a version of the article before, they'll at least get a different visual perspective of it the second time. Of course, if you can't provide new photos, submitting your old ones is preferred to sending none at all.

Rewrite the article in the style of the new publication. For instance, some publications refer to people by last names only, whereas others insist on titles, such as *Dr., Mrs., Senator,* etc. Some publications want just the facts—who, what, when, where, why and how—

whereas others want background, anecdotes or humor. Study back issues to determine the necessary tone and slant.

Insert news items that are pertinent to the readers of each new periodical. I used this technique when writing about Pete Schlatter, a childhood polio victim who grew up to invent the world's first workable two-wheel automobile. I focused on Schlatter's life in Francisville, Indiana, when I did the article for the local paper. When I rewrote the article for the Sunday supplement magazine of *The Indianapolis Star* (a statewide newspaper), I dropped the hometown recollections and, instead, inserted a list of all the auto shows across the state where Pete's car would be shown that year.

Remember, in order to do this sort of multiple marketing, you must retain the rights to your material. Be sure to read your contract carefully. Avoid selling all rights to your articles. Selling one-time rights only is your goal.

SEVEN STEPS TO MULTIPLE SALES

Let's walk through my seven-step process for multiple marketing, using as an example the first article I "multiple marketed." I began the process in October 1977 with a profile of nineteen-year-old Ben Timmons.

Timmons was a fascinating young man for several reasons. Deaf from birth, Timmons attended a public high school and made excellent grades. He was a member of the school wrestling team and took statewide honors in his weight division.

After graduation, Timmons became a mobile blacksmith. He put a fiberglass cab over the top of a flatbed pickup truck, mounted a forge, anvil, hammers and horseshoes inside, and drove around the county servicing farms and stables. Here's how I sold his story:

• **Local.** My first article on Timmons appeared in *The Muncie Star* as a home-town-boy-does-well story. I earned $15.

• **County.** My second article ran in *The Muncie Weekly News*, a countywide tabloid. I expanded the article to include some history on blacksmithing, told who trained Timmons to be a blacksmith and explained how he'd decided to become mobilized. I earned $10, which I gave to a photographer for prints of six photos he had taken of Timmons and his truck.

• **Statewide.** My third article sold to the Glimpses section of the Sunday magazine of *The Indianapolis Star*, I received $75 for 300 words and one photo. The editor wasn't concerned that the article had appeared twice in the Muncie area, for the *Star* circulated throughout Indiana.

• **Regional.** My next four sales were regional, to farming sections of newspapers in Louisville, Kentucky; Dayton, Ohio; Lansing, Michigan; and Peoria, Illinois. These are all farming communities in neighboring states, and a feature on a new approach to blacksmithing appealed to them. Average pay was about $45 for a feature of about 700 words with two photos.

• **Specialty.** I made five sales at this level: one to a Lutheran periodical, since Timmons was of that faith ($35); one to a magazine for disabled people, because Timmons was deaf ($85); one to a teen magazine, as Timmons was a teenager ($100); one to *Auto News* about how Timmons had converted the truck ($60); and one to *Indiana Sportsman* about Timmons's background in wrestling ($50). (Remember that these payment rates were for 1977 to 1982 and were good for that era.)

• **National** and **International.** In the U.S., I sold two photos and a 350-word article to *Grit* ($100); and internationally, I sold a filler to *Canadian Farm* for about $17 and a 500-word article with one photo to *World View* of Australia for about $62.

I earned nearly $800 on fourteen sales, with expenses of about $30 (postage was cheaper back then). I've had even greater success with an article on effective listening. I wrote it in 1978, and since then I've sold it thirty-four times for a total of $7,950! And I'm *still* sending it out.

Obviously, it may take years to work your way through all seven steps. To keep track of my submissions, I put a copy of the typed manuscript into a file folder, label the folder, and then staple a piece of paper that lists where I've sent the manuscript.

Each time I sell the article, I put a copy of the published version into the file. The collection of tearsheets gives me credibility as an expert source should I ever want to approach a publisher with the idea of writing a book on that same subject. I also keep my original interview notes and spare photos and negatives in that file, as well as any new information on that topic that could provide additional data for my future revisions.

It pays to remember this simple dictum for achieving financial success through multiple marketing: It's not how many articles you write, it's how many times you sell each one.

Your Passport to Worldwide Sales

BY MICHAEL H. SEDGE

H ow well do your words travel? Are you as popular with editors in London, Sydney and Tokyo as you are in your hometown?

As an experienced writer selling articles around the world, I know that most American writers miss out on the potential wealth of marketing to publications outside their own country. It's a costly omission: Magazines overseas regularly purchase foreign-language rights or slightly rewritten versions of articles already published in the U.S. and Canada. For instance, I collected $1,000 by selling Norwegian rights to a scuba diving article that I'd already sold to *Oceans* in the U.S.

To prepare your words for travel and to be successful at foreign sales doesn't require much special knowledge beyond *thinking internationally.* You must learn to put yourself in the shoes of Germans, Australians and Japanese, for instance, as you decide which of your articles can travel to these countries.

Luckily, foreign readers are often interested in the same subjects as U.S. audiences. Modern communications have shrunk the globe, and everyone watches the U.S. closely. Foreign news broadcasts regularly cover Washington and U.S. affairs. As a result, U.S. business and politics are hot topics for many foreign periodicals and newspapers.

Because many foreign television networks purchase their programs from the U.S., celebrity articles or anything dealing with *Roseanne, Murphy Brown, General Hospital* and other well-known series are always in demand. Movie, music and (to a lesser degree) book personality pieces also fall into this most-wanted category. I once collected $1,100 by selling a feature on Stephen King to magazines in West Germany, Italy, India and Sweden.

Travel magazines feature American destinations. And inflight magazines are as lucrative a market elsewhere as they are in North America. I've sold general interest pieces covering topics ranging from jellyfish to macro photography in this market.

Magazines for women reflect similar problems, dreams and desires, whether they're published in New Zealand or Singapore or New York. Medicine, family problems, cosmetics and fashions are among the common topics.

And as the popularity of American sports spreads, so does the demand for good interviews and general sports articles. That goes for almost all sports—from football, baseball and basketball to tennis, boxing, auto racing, gymnastics, track and field, and golf.

Not all topics that sell in the U.S. or Canada will sell equally well overseas, of course. A topic that appeals to New Yorkers, for example, may be taboo in Arab nations. This is when it's helpful for you to know about the histories, habits, cultures and governments of the countries you wish to sell in.

I learned this the hard way. I had sold "The Smoke of Kings" in the U.S., and I considered this feature on the world's finest tobacco products an easy foreign sale. To my amazement, most of my proposals came back rejected. Two editors explained that government regulations in their countries forbid the promotion of tobacco products in any way. Obviously, I did not know my markets as well as I thought.

One way to become a quick expert on any country is to read the "Background Notes" published by the U.S. Department of State. These short fact sheets cover every nation of the world, are updated annually, and are available in many major libraries. Or write the Superintendent of Documents (U.S. Printing Office, Washington, DC 20402) for subscription information.

In preparing to sell your work to foreign magazines, you'll also need to become an expert on the foreign marketplace. While *Writer's Market* lists a few overseas publications, you'll find more extensive information in *Willing's Press Guide* (Thomas Skinner Directories, Windsor Court, East Grinstead House, East Grinstead, West Sussex RH19 1ZE, England). It lists more than twenty-one thousand publications worldwide and is unrivaled in its coverage of United Kingdom markets.

TRAVEL ARRANGEMENTS

Even though your article has sold in North America, you must treat it as a fresh idea when pitching it to foreign markets. And that means producing new query letters for the article. (You should send only a clip with a cover letter telling what rights you are offering if the article was originally published in a prestigious, "name" periodical, or if an editor asks for clips.) As always, you'll want to study back issues of target magazines and write your query letters with each magazine's readers in mind.

And you'll want to ask yourself, "What makes me—an American writer—the right person for this assignment?" In your letter, answer the question in a way that will convince foreign editors—who'll be asking the same question.

A common mistake among writers approaching international markets for the first time is sending queries and manuscripts that say *America*. Take, for instance, a query containing the words *color, flavor* and *catalog*. If your potential market is in the United Kingdom, these words might better be spelled as the English do: *colour, flavour* and *catalogue*.

Picky? Perhaps. In fact, minor spelling differences will not usually block an assignment for an article that otherwise fits the magazine's needs. But for borderline proposals, "proper" spelling can make a difference.

A greater cause for rejection is the use of Americanized language. No matter how common a piece of slang or jargon is in the United States, there's no room for it in a query or article ticketed for overseas. "There is a very American flavour to the writing in your script," read a London literary agent's recent letter to me, "which I take to be your deliberately slangy approach. But this makes it inaccessible to British readers."

As you revise your articles for foreign readers, also be wary of using U.S. statistics and authorities. Authoritative information obtained from people or agencies known to the magazine's audience is often a strong selling point and should be emphasized in your query. For my article on top retirement Edens of the world, I included quotes from Italian businesspeople, German expatriates, Australian government officials and foreign and American retirees. The piece sold to the Swedish inflight *Scanorama* and to *The Robb Report* in the U.S.

Once you receive the green light from a foreign editor, submit a smooth, clean copy of your manuscript—not a clip of the previously published article. Remember, you must treat each article as if it were an original sale.

You'll also want to include with your submission a self-addressed envelope and enough International Reply Coupons to cover return postage. (IRCs are available at your post office. One IRC covers the postage for a one-ounce package at surface mail rates.) Always use air mail to send your submissions, as surface mail can take months to arrive. (Once I establish a working relationship with an editor, I cut postage costs by using airgrams—letter-envelope combinations designed for air mail—for queries and correspondence.)

Pay rates and other contract arrangements vary as widely in foreign markets as they do here. Editors may ask writers unknown to them to work on speculation at first; previously published articles may earn less than original work; and payment time may be on acceptance or on publication. As when dealing with North American editors, clarify such matters *before* submitting your manuscript. (I often include an invoice for the agreed-on fee with my manuscript.) When your check arrives, it will likely be payable in the currency of the magazine's home country and not U.S. dollars. In most cases, this won't be a problem as long as you deposit it into your bank account. The bank may charge a fee for handling foreign checks, the check may take longer to clear, and few banks will cash the check on the spot.

RIGHTS OF PASSAGE

One of the nicest aspects of selling articles internationally is that you can approach many markets at once. Unless you query more than one magazine in the same country, you are technically not submitting multiple queries—despite the fact that you might have ten queries out on the same subject at the same time. The key to making the most of your foreign sales is to avoid approaching competing markets and to judiciously parcel out the rights to each article.

Successfully reselling your work in foreign markets depends on retaining as many rights to your work as possible. That begins with your first sale in North America; by selling only first North American serial rights (that is, the right of first magazine publication in North America), you keep the opportunity to sell the work overseas (as well as to market book rights and reprint rights in North America). Pursue a similar policy in international sales, offering first or English-language rights in the magazine's geographic area—such as first English-language rights in Germany or Australian serial rights. When selling to high paying markets, the added income may justify the publication's request for all rights in a given country—such as all France rights. A similar request often comes from inflight magazines, which seek first rights in their geographic locations, as well as exclusive rights to the inflight market.

Another opportunity for sales is dividing rights by language. Let's say, for example, that you query a Spanish-language magazine in Argentina. If you offer first Spanish-language Argentine rights, you are still free to offer the same piece to an English-language publication in Argentina. (And there are English-language magazines nearly everywhere.) Be open with editors in all your dealings. But if they object to your retaining individual language rights, their purchase price should be higher.

Translations should always be the periodical's responsibility, and most magazines that deal with foreign-language materials retain translation agencies and at least one editor who reads submissions in English. If you prefer to work only with English-language publications, you might consider sending clips to a foreign syndication agent and asking him to sell foreign language rights only.

Just how well-traveled your articles become is limited only by the universality of your ideas and your marketing skills. Take those articles lying fallow since their North American sales, and pack them off to editors abroad. Offer first European rights, first Asian rights, first rights to individual countries, exclusive rights to a particular market, reprint rights, and any other rights you can think of—and that are yours to sell. Don't overlook any paying market. If an editor offers $800 for first rights in England, take it. If someone else offers $25 for reprint rights, take that, too. This so-called "free money" can add up to thousands of dollars a year, more than enough to support your own travels.

Winning on
Publishers Row

BY RUSSELL GALEN

W hen I was a teenager, I had a part-time job in New York City and delivered a package to the hallowed old Scribner Building on Fifth Avenue. I was awed, realizing that through these doors had walked Hemingway, Fitzgerald, Wolfe and their editor, Max Perkins. I swore that one day I'd walk through those doors as a big shot.

As Herodotus says, "No man can enter the same river twice, for the second time, it is not the same river and he is not the same man." I was certainly not the same man: when I finally returned, it was as an experienced literary agent.

But the river had changed just as much. By the time I grew up and made it in publishing, the Scribner's I'd vowed to conquer, and the entire publishing civilization it represented, no longer existed.

Scribner's, one of the last of the old, cozy, privately owned houses, was fighting a losing battle to compete with the rising communications conglomerates. They'd recently merged with another privately held house, Atheneum, becoming a kind of baby conglomerate themselves. Not long after that Scribner's/Atheneum gave up the struggle altogether and sold to a Fortune 500 company, Macmillan (which was itself later swallowed up by giant Simon & Schuster).

Today, with only a few exceptions, major publishers of books for the general public are tiny parts of vastly larger organizations. From this fact derives every conclusion you'll make, good or bad, about publishers, editors and agents today—and how you'll work with them to further your career as a writer.

THE BIG-BOOK TRICKLE-DOWN THEORY
Big-business conglomerate publishing has *not* resulted in a disastrous homogenization of books being published, or even—despite what's

often said—vastly fewer books of modest expectations. That's because there's still no way to run a publishing company or find books to publish without editors, and at heart editors haven't changed. Just as baseball players, no matter how big-business and profit-oriented the game may become, are still born out of sandlots and playgrounds, so editors are still grown-up versions of dreamy kids who read too much and worship the splendor and variety of books. Censor them, inhibit them too much, take away their right to take chances, and before you know it they're working for your rival.

As in every age past, the big profits and losses tend to come from the top 15 percent or so of a publishing list. That means that the remaining 85 percent has less impact on the bottom line by which conglomerates allegedly keep tabs on their employees. If you have two huge bestsellers in a season, you're going to have a good year and no one's going to blame you for publishing a few literary novels or *pro bono* nonfiction books.

But those big books are much, much bigger than of old, because the new giants have far larger resources to put behind them. Therefore, authors expect bigger advances, making bigger advertising budgets and first printings necessary to generate the sales needed to earn back those advances. This influx of money has had a distorting effect that has trickled down to affect the entire industry.

Now that big books can be so big that one can make the difference between a good year and a bad year for a publisher, up-and-coming writers are rushed along before they're ready for the big time. The hunger to receive a big budget can warp writers into writing books for which they're really not suited, for audiences that don't really exist. Bookstores, having learned that one thousand copies of a much-hyped novel will sell faster and more consistently than fifty copies each of twenty different books, sweep aside the other nineteen to make room for stacks and stacks of that season's blockbuster. Publishers sometimes feel that the book everyone likes but no one is willing to die for is not worth publishing. (Though the book that editors *will* die for, no matter how risky or modest commercially, will usually find an editor sufficiently devoted to it to get it acquired somehow.) But it's a mistake to think of conglomerate publishers as evil privateers who brought this situation about with their greed. Agents (and by extension the people who employ and authorize them, the writers themselves) can't cluck their tongues.

I remember a negotiation with the late Judy-Lynn del Rey, a

publisher who had little truck with the hype and bombast of modern publishing. "My client's last book earned $379,000," I said to her, "and therefore we want an advance of $400,000 for her new one." "Wait a minute," said del Rey. "An advance isn't supposed to be a prepayment of everything the book is going to earn in its entire life. It's just to get the author started, and then if the book succeeds, there'll be plenty of royalties." Well, yes, in the days when publishers just didn't have the money to prepay it all. But del Rey's house, Ballantine, which is part of Random House (then owned by RCA, now by the Newhouse book/magazine/newspaper conglomerate), did. Faced with the choice of paying up or seeing my client go to another house, she came across. (Well, she got me to come down a little.) It was a negotiation I wouldn't have initiated, much less concluded successfully, at a house that didn't have access to vast amounts of cash. As a result of that advance, though, Ballantine couldn't publish the book carefully and prudently in the hope that it would find its audience as my client's previous book had. If the book had been less than a huge success, Ballantine stood to lose hundreds of thousands of dollars. They had to be sure from the start that the book would earn back its advance, which involved further huge expenditures in publicity, advertising and the size of the first printing. With many other big-ticket items under contract, Ballantine's plans to publish other books for which it had paid only $5,000 had to be affected. So, was it giant RCA, or the author and her spokesman who set this "blockbuster syndrome" in motion in this case? Neither: It was the coming together of means, motive and opportunity on both sides.

BIG OPPORTUNITIES IN SMALL PLACES

In some important and unexpected ways, the giants actually have made it possible for there to be *more* independent, risk-taking publishing. There always will be editors who simply can't stand the world of big business. Some of them are our brightest people, and a well-run conglomerate knows that it can't let them escape. Thus, we've seen an increasing number of imprints: Large publishers creating a house-within-a-house run by a well-regarded editor with little or no interference from headquarters. Dealing with these imprints can be a delight. Through the parent company they have all the money you could possibly demand, but the atmosphere is small, informal and dominated by the individual taste of a publisher who sees his list as his own personal baby.

The fear and dislike of large organizations felt by many literary people also has led to an explosion in the number of small houses outside New York. One of the biggest publishing stories of the eighties has been the bestsellers produced by tiny houses, from the Naval Institute Press (Tom Clancy's *The Hunt for Red October*) to North Point Press (Evan S. Connell's *Son of the Morning Star*). These houses attract brilliant editors who don't want eight levels of bureaucracy between them and the person who makes the final decision, and who want to buy books that leave the larger houses cold. The editors in turn attract brilliant authors. Suddenly, New York isn't the only answer, not just for those who want to get published, but even for those who want to make a lot of money.

You'll find these imprints and small publishers as you browse the bookstores and conduct your market research. *Publishers Weekly*, the publishing industry's trade magazine, reports on the creation and progress of new publishers. You'll also find them listed in the Markets section of *Writer's Digest, Writer's Market* and *Literary Market Place*.

THE FINE ART OF TREND-HOPPING

Despite the "blockbuster syndrome," the biggest houses continue to publish mixed lists containing healthy amounts of serious fiction and nonfiction. What protects us against homogeneity is the plain fact that no one has any real idea of what's going to succeed or fail. If you follow a bestselling high-tech thriller with nothing but more thrillers, you still don't know which thriller will succeed, and you'll be wrong twice as often as you're right. For all you know, more thrillers may be the last thing the public wants and you'll make all your money with the lone adolescent comedy on your list. To protect their profits, conglomerates have no choice but to hire intelligent editors and let them publish according to their best mixture of commercial and literary instincts.

The gloomy side of this is that there is less tolerance at conglomerates than at some privately held houses for books that have *no* chance to make money. Mr. Jones of Jones Books is going to damn well keep on publishing poetry, no matter the losses, if poetry is the love that led him into publishing. No such luck at today's big houses, where poetry is perceived as something that simply *can't* make money (except for a few writers established in an earlier era). A couple of major New York houses occasionally introduce new poets; the rest have abandoned the form.

Here, though, big houses are more led than leading. A few years ago I would have included short story collections in the above paragraph; the only way to sell such a book in New York was to make it a condition of simultaneously acquiring a promising novel by the same author. Then, out of the blue, several collections by new writers hit the big time commercially. So short story collections were in demand like they hadn't been in years. Publishers offered serious money for these books in many cases, the superheated sales earned even more money for the authors, and by the time the young author was ready to start his first novel, he was in a position to demand a six-figure advance. While that cycle has run its course now, it could happen again. And if the American public should find a few young poets that it likes, and if the public should buy, say thirty thousand or forty thousand of their books, you'd see the New York houses clamoring for poetry in half a minute and poets driving Mercedes the following years.

Directing enormous sums of money overnight at any particular group of writers is something new in publishing and has changed the whole climate. Merely writing the best possible book, hoping to sell it, and hoping it does well once published, is from another age. Today, the commercial writer must be versatile, ready to zoom in and out of rising and falling fields. For those who aren't so flexible, life can be a transition from begging the spotlight to fall on you, to dancing like mad when it does, to pining away for its return. The public determines the fads, but publishers throw gasoline on the fires until all is consumed in a brief, intense season; then publishers turn their backs and move on to something else. The idea of studying trends is itself a new trend; editors—and more important, writers—are learning to see themselves not just as champions of literature, but as cultural seismographers who must know what's shaking and what's not. When a field suddenly goes cold, there's too much money to be lost not to abandon it quickly; when something seems to be getting hot, you must seize it, help *make* it hot.

A PROSPEROUS BUSINESS ENVIRONMENT

All this may sound a lot like the declining movie and television industries, but there are important differences. The movies lost their exalted position as one of the nation's biggest businesses with the rise of the television networks. The networks are seeing their audiences splinter among cable and independent stations and VCRs. But books have no real competition. There's no evidence that people watching movies and TV would have spent those same hours reading had those media never been invented; the overwhelming bulk of readers still find that nothing replaces reading, and we mix it in with the other forms of entertainment and information. You don't hear laments within the book industry about declining audience; sales continue to rise over the long run, and the sales of the biggest books are way, way up.

The overall mood in the industry is one of optimism and health. There are long-term concerns, of course, such as steeply rising retail prices caused by increases in the cost of raw materials; the industry experienced less growth in the past decade than it could have, particularly in paperbacks, because high prices scared would-be buyers away. But this era of ultra-bestsellers has made it possible for one book to be *so* profitable that it can turn a whole year around and make up for scores of screwed-up distribution plans, overprintings, bad reviews and other disasters that afflict the rest of the list. (Remember that to sell one million copies of one book is vastly more profitable than to sell one hundred thousand copies of ten books, both because the one book had a tenth the start-up and development costs of the ten, and because printers' per-copy rates drop as the print order for a single book increases.) For those houses that can't afford the big budgets necessary for the ultra-bestsellers, the horizon looks bleak; but for the majority of conglomerate-backed biggies, things look good. (Though it must be pointed out that privately held houses occasionally publish ultras, too. As long as these houses continue to attract authors through the tender loving care they can offer, they will be around.)

Perhaps it's a little like six strong people and six weak people marooned in a lifeboat with only enough food for ten. If the strong throw the weak overboard, there's suddenly more than enough food to go around. By absorbing and eliminating their competitors, the surviving giant houses have created a prosperous business environment for themselves.

It's a prosperity that gives rise to greater prosperity, because the giants are capable of a wholly new kind of publishing. Listening to Bantam Books' marketing people, for instance, talk about their campaign for *Iacocca*, you felt as if Dwight Eisenhower was describing his strategy for D-Day; no small house has access to the troops and money necessary to bring off such a massive effort. The fantastic profits that resulted from *Iacocca's* sales of more than two million hardcover copies were in large part plowed back into new Bantam books: a multitude of seven-figure advances and titanic marketing efforts that generated new windfalls. With the rich getting richer in this way, publishing's new order becomes self-perpetuating.

THE BEST-SELLER AS CAREER-ALTERING DRUG

As in any successful, invulnerable system, attitudes begin to change. Young editors talk half-jokingly of having been "corrupted" by the system. They came into publishing wanting to change the world and foster great writing, but as soon as they get lucky and have one blockbuster, they can't wait to experience that feeling again. It's not that they lose the desire to work on great books, it's that great books simply aren't enough. While there's something enormously satisfying about working on a good book and seeing it get good reviews and sell twenty thousand copies where only six thousand had been expected, it really can't hold a candle to calling up an agent and saying, "Our offer is one million, five hundred thousand dollars." *My God*, you find yourself thinking. *I'm a person who offers one and a half million for things!*

What's evil about this isn't that the truly good books no longer get done. That a facile, oversimplified conclusion created by those who've received one rejection slip too many. What's evil is that a caste system has been created.

To those authors in the lower castes—profitability being the dividing line—becoming a part of the publishing world isn't what it used to be. When an author is depending on an on-signing check to feed his family, his view of the industry, and of being an author, comes down to one painful criterion: How soon can I get my check? The big houses will tell you, "Well we've got to have seventeen bureaucrats approve the check request, then it gets sent out to our accounting division in New Jersey, then eighteen more have to OK the check before it's mailed. So be patient." But that same house can get a $500,000 check out overnight because it has priority. A minor point to make about publishing at the present time? Perhaps. But not if the delayed $3,000 check is yours; not if being treated with indifference poisons your entire experience of being an author.

More serious is the instant-gratification mentality that results when an editor's life revolves around getting that next best-seller. Editors still want to publish bright young authors; how else can you be sure of being able to publish the stars of tomorrow? Every time an editor takes a chance on a manuscript from an unknown he pats himself on the back because he hasn't been truly corrupted. The problem is that if that book fails, and a chance is taken on the author's second book and that one fails too, the editor—denied his fix—feels the author has blown his shot. This doesn't mean the author's career is over; it just means that he has to find a new publisher. Thus, authors who need some time to develop and grow move from house to house.

When authors shun the large houses it's usually out of distaste for this caste system, no matter what level of it they occupy. It isn't that big houses don't want their work. Or that the smaller houses don't care about commerce (*every* publisher has to make a profit, and a few bad years at a small house cause even more panic than at a big house because there's less cushion). It's because the smaller, private houses are less addicted to thinking in terms of millions and therefore less likely to treat authors like untouchables. A $10,000 book, even a $300,000 book, is simply more important at a Farrar, Straus & Giroux than it is at Simon & Schuster.

THE WEAKENING EDITOR-AUTHOR RELATIONSHIP . . .

This shreds any old-fashioned idea authors or editors might have about mutual loyalty. The problem is exacerbated by editors constantly switching jobs; big houses don't foster the loyalty that used to keep editors in place. When a rival house offers a raise, few editors resist. Out of every one hundred books I sell, perhaps thirty-five are actually published under the aegis of the acquiring editor; the rest are orphaned and go through the publication process handled by an editor who wasn't responsible for bringing the book into the house, who gets no credit if it succeeds, and therefore doesn't much care what happens to the book.

On the big-money levels, of course, publishers fight to keep authors for book after book; if the old editor leaves, the new one will care about anyone who has a million dollars of his employer's money. But even on this level, old-fashioned publisher-author loyalty, and editor-author rapport, is hard to find. The money is just too distorting. Because the money at stake on one book can set an author for life, and one disaster can destroy an editor's career, authors and editors approach each other warily. The editor is a customer, the author a golden-egg-laying goose. The author probably chose his editor merely because the editor's house was the top bidder in an auction. Even if a bond could develop, why bother, since the editor will probably be at another house in a year? The editor must be ever-so-careful about what he says to his new star acquisition; one too-honest word and the author, who's always looking over the fence at greener pastures anyway, could bolt and take his next book to another house.

There are exceptions: James Michener's long history with Random House, or Danielle Steel's with Delacorte. But that kind of relationship used to be the norm; today scarcely a week goes by without news of a bestselling writer auctioning his new book to the highest bidder.

. . . AND THE STRENGTHENING AGENT-AUTHOR RELATIONSHIP

While most authors have something like five different editors per decade, chances are they've had only one agent during that time. Many agents are self-employed, and even those who work for large shops are autonomous, or close to it, in choosing their projects. This freedom, combined with the fact that a successful agent's commissions can bring in many times what even top editors earn, means that an agent rarely leaves his job.

Authors do leave their agents, of course, if they become dissatisfied for any of a thousand reasons, but they do so far less often than they switch publishers. Perhaps it's because, with editors jumping houses right and left, the author wants to preserve the agent relationship as the one stable thing in his professional life. Or it may be because agents treat their authors better because they want to make sure they're still handling that author when his big break finally comes. And, of course, when an agent gets a great deal for his client, he tends to paint it in bloody colors: The cheap publisher kept saying *no*, but the brave and aggressive agent kept pushing until he turned that into a *yes*.

Whatever the reason, suddenly authors, who are still the source of all money and power, are more loyal to their agents than ever before. This puts unprecedented power into the hands of agents—an *editorial* power. When an author assumes that his agent cares about him and that his editor cares only about his employer, he's going to follow that agent's advice about what he ought to write, and how and when he ought to write it. Despite my obvious bias on this subject, I think agents and not editors today decree what will be published in America. Editors have the final choice, of course, but they can choose only from what agents have selected for them.

Agents themselves have worked to increase this power, taking advantage of the distorting power of big money. With millions at stake it's essential that what an author proposes to an editor be the right project presented in the right way. A wrong step could cost a fortune.

Gone, therefore, are the days when authors and editors engaged in long bull sessions to talk about the author's ideas and plans. Agents won't allow their authors to do this, for fear that presenting an editor with a swarm of half-formed ideas gives the impression that the author doesn't know what he wants or where he's going. Instead, the agent sits down alone to face that chaos, helping the author draw out the material that has the best chance of persuading an editor, and helping to put it in the most persuasive possible form. The editor may now say only yea or nay, making him a passive observer of the process of conceptualizing a book, not the midwife he once was.

This has both helped and hurt the state of literature. On the negative side, agents are even more profit-oriented than editors and will usually encourage a client to do his most commercial work. But with their long-term view, agents can *afford* to put their time into an uncommercial book if it's dear to the author, and wait for a more commercial book. An editor might have to reject that book as simply being unprofitable; but the agent can live with the modest commission from a modest sale, and thus deepen the author's loyalty. Thus you'll see agents going to bat for some strange things and getting them published by hook or crook, motivated not so much by that book as by the author's potential.

It all comes down to the fact that guessing wrong on a book can be a catastrophe for a publishing house, but agents, who risk their time but hardly any money on even the biggest projects, can afford to fool around.

Agents also influence publishing because editors let them call so many shots. A generation ago it was unheard of for an agent to submit a manuscript to more than one house at a time. This put all the power into the hands of publishers; if the agent thought a book was worth twice the offer, it was often too risky to walk away hoping that the next editor might be more generous. But today editors will put up with just about anything to satisfy the ever-present lust for blockbusters— including book auctions. This technique is so advantageous to the author that agents have made it virtually the norm for all but the most modest books. Auctions make any retreat from the big-money orientation impossible because the house that decides to hold prices down is simply going to be outbid for the most commercial projects and soon will go under. Auctions have become a self-fulfilling prophecy; in many cases a book's entire future is determined not in a publisher's strategy meeting, but in the moment an agent decides to conduct an auction. If the editors in the auction agree, or can be hyped into agreeing, that the book is indeed a big one, the result will be a mega-deal and a book that can't be published successfully without huge additional amounts of money. By deciding *not* to auction a book, the agent also sends a message: This is a book available for modest money and that you'll want to publish modestly.

Getting the right support for your book is one of the reasons most writers benefit from having an agent. Some successful writers do very well without one, but you're in a better position to deal with publishers if an agent conducts the negotiations. *Literary Market Place* lists literary agents, and *Guide to Literary Agents* offers information on the types of writers represented by specific agents.

THE POWER OF THE PEOPLE . . . AND YOU

Fortunately, the public doesn't pay attention to any of these behind-the-scenes decisions. They're constantly ignoring books that the industry says ought to be big, and seeking out the ones the professionals perceived as modest. "Damfino" is a word you hear a lot on Publishers Row, as in "Damned if I know why this book is selling so well or that book has become such a failure." This is the one thing that can never change about the publishing industry: All of its attempts to influence the public have only a small effect.

Readers make their own decisions and are influenced more by their friends' opinions than by any weapon in the publishers' public relations and advertising arsenals. When a publisher decides to push a certain book, he can guarantee only that the public will *notice* it; he can make sure this is the one out of one thousand books that doesn't sink like a stone the week of publication. Often, though, this simply means that when the big houses fail, they fail spectacularly.

While they can't guarantee successes, the giant companies have two great assurances: When they do succeed they succeed in a big way, and when they fail they can afford to take the loss and move on. When readers like a book and start moving it out of the stores, the big houses react quickly. By rushing out massive new printings and directing their dollars to bolster the books with momentum, the big publishers can take an already big book and make it gigantic. While tiny Naval Institute Press sold hundreds of thousands of copies of Tom Clancy's first novel on a budget of practically zero, it was the huge Putnam Publishing Group that got Clancy's sales into seven figures (in hardcover!) on subsequent books by putting its limitless resources behind Clancy's momentum.

The conglomerates have, in the final analysis, not changed the basic nature of publishing so much as they've widened its extremes. It's a bad industry to be in if you want to exercise real power. IBM can decide to spend a few billion and change the computer industry; today's rich publishers can only spend money and hope the public goes along. The author working alone in the boondocks on a new kind of book, one the publishers will look on with suspicion but that happens to be right for the public at that moment in history, has the only real power in publishing. In that sense nothing has changed since the day a crowd of ancient Greeks cried, "Homer is the guy we want to hear; tell the other guy to sit down."

Writing the Copy

BY LINDA BRODSKY

W hen I first started writing advertising copy, I tried hard to write sentences that were grammatically correct. One day, my boss said to me, "Linda, in advertising copy, grammar ain't got nothin' to do with it." So after years of learning how to write correctly, I had to force myself to write incomplete sentences. I soon found that it really wasn't necessary—or even desirable—to write grammatically correct prose (but I must admit, it did take a while to feel comfortable about not doing so).

When writing any form of advertising, whether it's print ads, brochures or TV or radio commercials, the consumer's first impression is all-important. In TV and radio commercials, it's the first few seconds that count; in print, it's the headline; in brochures, it's the headline and lead paragraph.

When I sit down to write an ad, I first gather up all the information I've received from the client. I look at the product or service and determine what sets it apart from its competitors. When the public is already familiar with the product or service category, the writing is much easier; you simply stress how this particular one is better than the others.

When the product or service is new to the public, however, you'll have to do more work. You must first convince consumers that this new product/service is *necessary* to their lives and will benefit them. Then you must sell the *client's* product.

As I read through the material supplied by the client, I use my highlighting pen (always do this on photocopies, in case the client wants the information returned) and mark anything that stands out. It may be a testimonial from a reputable business magazine praising the company or product, or maybe it's important facts and information regarding the president, company or product. The president may have been in this type of business since it was first introduced. Or maybe the company has been at the same location for more than eighty years. Facts like these build trust in the company and its product or service. After highlighting, I weed out any unimportant facts. Then I brainstorm and create a list of key words that best describe that product or service.

I once had to write an ad describing a new process for packaging valuable, fragile art and antiques before shipment. The market wasn't aware of this type of service, but art and antique owners *were* concerned about their valuables arriving at their destinations safely. With that in mind, I built this word list:

New
Revolutionary
State-of-the-art
Method
Protects
Surrounds
Art/Antiques
Valuables
Delicate items
Packaging
Experts
Custom
Techniques
Arrive
Safely

I then used the list to write this headline:

NOBODY APPRECIATES YOUR ART & ANTIQUES
LIKE PACKAGING PLUS.

When creating a headline, keep these tips in mind:

• Mention the product and company name.
• Promise something.
• Avoid negatives (instead of writing "no cholesterol," write "100 percent cholesterol-free").
• Don't use gimmicks or old advertising tricks. They may be funny, but they don't sell products.
• Try to use the words *you* and/or *your*.

When writing the body copy, hook the readers with the first few sentences. If you don't, they'll never read to the middle and end. The first line of my packaging ad read:

Trust the <u>experts</u> at Packaging Plus to pack and ship your <u>valuables</u>. Our <u>state-of-the-art custom packaging techniques</u> and materials allow us to ship <u>safely</u> and confidently, <u>protecting</u> the most <u>delicate</u> items.

Notice the underlined words; these came from my word list.

Use short, snappy sentences; long ones tire and confuse readers. Also, be specific and get straight to the point.

Instead of using *however*, use *but*; instead of *at this moment*, use *now*. You can find lists of substitute words in many English handbooks and books on writing business letters. Remember, you're trying to communicate with people, not impress them with your vocabulary skills. Always write to your readers' vocabulary level. If you're writing a print ad for a trade magazine, for example, you'll build credibility if you incorporate some industry jargon.

There are several types of ad copy. One common kind is straight, factual copy that lists a product's benefits by setting them off with bullets (the typographical term for this: ●). In my packaging ad, bulleted copy might look like this:

- Lightweight Material for Lower Shipping Costs
- State-of-the-art Packaging Technique
- Valuables Arrive Safely
- Expertly Packed by Packaging Engineers

Another type of copy is the emotional, "we care about and understand your needs" copy. I once wrote an ad for a company that shipped Christmas gifts. It started: "We know the packages you send are as precious as the people receiving them." The ad's illustration featured two small children opening gifts on Christmas morning. The ad generated a considerable amount of new business.

After the headline and body copy, the last thing you must include is a call for action. You've told the reader, "Okay, here's my product, and what it can do for you." Now you must tell him where he can purchase your product or how he can request more information about it. Include phone numbers, addresses, names of businesses where the product can be purchased, a business-reply card and other such devices.

If you've written a clever, attention grabbing beginning, backed that up with relevant facts and information that show the product's benefits for readers, and stated how the reader can go about getting the product, you've done your job. Your client will sell products—and you will sell your client on future jobs.

Big Bucks in
Business Writing

BY ROBERT W. BLY

J ohn Frances Tighe, a softspoken, bearded gentleman, modestly
refers to himself as "the world's second-most successful freelance direct mail copywriter."
John's fee for writing a direct mail package? $15,000.
But that's peanuts compared to the $40,000 Henry Cowen charges.
Cowen's fees are the highest of any writer listed in *Who's Mailing
What!*, a newsletter covering the direct mail industry, and he may very
well be the highest paid freelance copywriter in the world. (According
to *Direct Marketing* magazine, Cowen's income for writing the
Publishers' Clearing House mailing—for which he receives a royalty—
was $900,000 in a recent year.)

Next to the movies, TV and bestselling novels, direct mail is one of
the highest paying markets for freelance writers. Although it's a market surprisingly easy to break into, most freelancers don't even know
about it, and direct mail copywriting is dominated by a few dozen writers who earn six-figure incomes. But you, too, can enter this exciting
market and get high paying direct mail copywriting assignments from
commercial clients.

How much, specifically, can you earn? One writer, in just her second
year as a direct mail freelancer, confided that she bills clients approximately $7,000 a month for her services. Many others earn annual in-
comes of $120,000 or more. A few superstars even top the $200,000 a
year mark, though this is rare. As a beginner, you can realistically
expect to make $50,000 a year or more as a freelance direct mail writer,
and an annual income in six figures is not unreasonable.

Direct mail is unsolicited advertising or promotional material (that
is, material the recipient has not requested) sent to an individual or
company through the mail. The general public and press call it *junk
mail*, although professionals in the industry abhor that term.

For proof that direct mail is big business, just look in your mailbox. If you're like most people, you're getting more unsolicited advertising materials in the mail than ever before.

Other facts that demonstrate direct mail's fast growth:

- According to *DM News*, direct mail has become the leading medium among national advertisers. It accounts for 29.2 percent of all advertising expenditures (versus 26.6 percent for television).
- Direct mail now generates more than $120 billion in direct sales revenue, accounts for 15 percent of U.S. consumer purchases.
- Mail order is growing at twice the rate of retail sales. Nearly half of the adults in this country buy products through the mail.

A LOOK AT THE MARKET

Who hires direct mail writers? Any company that promotes its products or services by mail. One way to build a list of prospects is to track the names and addresses of companies that send *you* direct mail. Often the person whose signature appears at the bottom of the sales letter is the one who hires freelance direct mail writers.

Here are some of the types of companies that hire freelance direct mail writers:

Publishers. Magazine publishers use direct mail to gain new subscribers, renew current subscribers and get bills paid. Because their income so depends on the success of their mailings, magazine and newsletter publishers pay top dollar for direct mail copy, with fees for a single package ranging from $3,000 to $15,000 and up. Some publishers will even pay the writer a commission or royalty for a successful mailing, although this is rare. Book publishers also need direct mail packages and direct response ads to sell their products, although fees here can be lower, since book publishing is generally not as profitable as magazine publishing.

Financial services. According to the Maxwell Sroge Co., insurance is the leading mail order product in the U.S. For this reason, advertising managers at insurance companies constantly look for new writers who can sell insurance by mail. Other financial service organizations, especially banks, also do a lot of direct mail promotion. Contact the advertising manager and offer your services.

Fund-raising. Nonprofit organizations depend on mail-generated contributions to stay afloat, and so creating a successful mailing is of key concern to them. Although fund raising doesn't pay as well as commercial assignments, you can still get $2,000 or more to write a fund-raising direct mail package. And these packages are usually shorter and less complex than the packages used to sell insurance or magazine subscriptions.

Mail order products. There are many other products sold through direct mail packages, catalogs and mail order advertising. These include home furnishings, housewares, gifts, clothing, collectibles, sporting goods, crafts, foods, records and tapes. And the companies selling these products need writers to create mailings for them.

Lead generators. In addition to generating direct sales, direct mail can be used to generate sales leads for follow-up by mail, telephone or personal call. Companies that use direct mail to generate inquiries rather than mail order sales include industrial manufacturers, high-tech companies, and service firms such as PR agencies, accountants and management consultants.

Although lead-generating direct mail writers command lower fees ($500 to $1,500 for a letter and $1,500 to $4,000 for a package are typical), the mailings are simpler, and this area of direct mail is easier to break into. Plus, the use of direct mail by "nontraditional mailers" (companies that don't use a lot of direct mail or sell through mail order) is perhaps the fastest growing segment of the direct mail industry.

Ad agencies. These agencies—both general ad agencies and those specializing in direct mail—are a big market for freelance copywriting services. You will find more than 4,400 ad agencies listed in *The Standard Directory of Advertising Agencies*. Also known as the *Red Book*, this directory is available in the reference areas of most good local libraries.

GET DIRECTLY TO WORK

To get started:

Get a feel for the form and style of direct mail. Pay attention to the "junk mail" you receive this week and next. Instead of throwing it away, read it. Study this mail as carefully as you would analyze an article in a magazine in which you want to publish. Which mailings grab your attention? Which turn you off? Collect samples of direct mail packages that interest you and save them in a "swipe file." You'll turn to this swipe file for inspiration and ideas when writing direct mail for your clients. One hint: Any mailing you receive repeatedly is probably a winner (if it wasn't successful, the advertiser wouldn't keep mailing it).

Take a course. Much of my own involvement in direct mail came about as a result of taking Milt Pierce's Direct Response Copywriting Workshop at New York University, and I strongly urge you to take a course in direct mail copywriting at a local college or university. Not only will you learn the basics of direct mail and build your writing skills, but you'll also make contact with a working direct mail professional—the teacher—who can introduce you to the right people in the local direct mail industry. (Before signing up for the course, make sure the teacher is a professional freelance direct mail copywriter and not an academician.)

While a book on direct mail writing can't offer the personal interaction of a classroom, there are several that can teach you the basics—and more. Five of the best are:

- *Direct Mail Profits*, by Bob Bly (Asher-Gallant Press). A primer on direct mail. Covers strategy, planning, copy, design, list selection, production, postal regulations and testing.
- *Direct Mail Copy That Sells*, by Herschell Gordon Lewis (Prentice Hall). The title tells it. An entertaining book on how to write direct mail copy.
- *Mail Order*, by Eugene Schwartz (Boardroom Books). Direct-mail copywriters must understand all aspects of mail order, not just copy. This book will teach you all those basics.
- *Successful Direct Marketing Methods*, by Bob Stone (Crain Books). The classic book on direct mail marketing. Comprehensive.
- *Money in Your Mailbox: How to Start and Operate a Mail-Order Business*, by L. Perry Wilbur (John Wiley & Sons). A folksy, friendly primer on how to get started in mail order. Fun and easy to read, and informative.

Find a mentor. The direct mail industry is fairly close-knit, and a lot of business comes from referrals, contacts, friends and word-of-mouth. Try to establish a relationship with an experienced direct mail writer or other professional who can serve as your guru and guide you through the field.

"Try to find a mentor, or, at least, someone with more experience than you—someone who likes you, is willing to be helpful and believes in your ability," advises direct mail writer Suzanne Becker Ramos. "Stay away from naysayers—you need self-confidence and a bit of brashness in this business."

Become more involved in direct marketing. Join a local direct mail club or association. Attend meetings. Talk with as many people as you can. And become involved in the organization. You might volunteer to serve on a committee, for example.

Subscribe to one or more magazines covering the direct-marketing field. *Direct Marketing, DM News* and *Target Marketing* are all excellent. If you see an article that interests you, start up a correspondence with the author. You never know where it may lead.

Then, once you've familiarized yourself with the field:

Volunteer. "Volunteer to write whatever you can," says Ramos. "Do fundraising letters for local good causes or sales letters for your uncle's store." Writing copy for friends, relatives or worthy causes is an excellent way to build a portfolio of real-life direct mail letters that have been tested in the mail.

Start small, and keep it simple. I'd rather see you start with a simple one-page lead-generating sales letter than a big, complex mail order package. As a novice, you'll find writing a mailing with just two elements (letter and reply card) less intimidating than a job with many different inserts, brochures, letters and forms. Once you're comfortable with the format, you can experiment and get more elaborate.

Do the best you can. Don't worry about how long the job takes to complete (but don't miss your deadline, of course). Your first letters will take longer because you're learning direct mail as you go along. Once you become comfortable with the format, future assignments will go much faster.

Right now, concentrate on doing the best job possible and don't worry about how much you're earning per hour. You want to write a letter that gets good sales results for your client, because this generates repeat business for you and builds your reputation as a writer whose copy is successful in the marketplace.

Write simple sales letters for local clients. For example, you can write a letter for a new restaurant inviting people to a grand opening. Or perhaps a small consulting firm will hire you to write a letter to generate interest in its services. Established, big-volume users of direct mail—magazine publishers, insurance companies, mail order houses—usually won't hire a beginner and prefer a writer who can show samples of previous packages written for other big name clients. Small companies, on the other hand, have no such prejudices. Indeed, they may not even think of the letter you're writing for them as "direct mail." To them, it's just a letter. Yet, by writing these simple sales letters, you gain valuable experience and samples for your portfolio.

Eventually, you show these proven successful letters (try to find out sales results, if you can) to larger firms, and one will surely try you out on a mailing package. You do the package, add it to your sample portfolio, and build your business from there.

Offer your direct mail services to current clients. Maybe you're doing press releases for the local animal shelter or an ad campaign for a high-tech software publisher. Suggest to these clients that direct mail is another effective way to promote their cause of generating more sales. Then write the letter for them.

Offer to work on spec. A major publisher or other big mail order firm might hire an unknown writer on a spec basis. In this arrangement, you tell the client: "Let me write a direct mail package for you. Pay me only if you like it." You may find some takers for this offer. And even if they don't use your package, you've created a sample you can send to other potential clients.

DIRECT MAIL COPYWRITING TECHNIQUES

These nine basic copywriting techniques can dramatically improve the effectiveness of the direct mail copy you write:

1. **Do your homework.** Don't write off the top of your head. First, gather and read all you can about the client's product or services. Ask for copies of previous letters, ads, brochures, press releases, and catalog descriptions of the product. Read this material carefully and take notes. If you're missing a key fact or don't understand something, call the client and get the information.

2. **Write person to person.** Pretend your prospect—the person your direct mail package is aimed to sell to—is sitting across the table from you. What would you say to convince him to buy your product or request more information on your client's services? This sales pitch, put into writing, becomes the basis of your letter.

3. **Start with the prospect—not the product.** Your prospects' primary concern is not with the product *per se* but with what the product can do for them. Direct mail experts are fond of saying that people don't buy products; they buy solutions to problems. So instead of beginning your sales letter with "Our telecommunications system," start with "Your telecommunications needs" or "Is your current phone system obsolete?" Start with the prospects and their concerns—not with the product. Tell your customer about his lawn—not your grass seed.

4. **Stress the importance of the offer.** The offer is what you send

the prospect when he responds to your mailing. In a mail order package, the offer consists of the product, the price, the payment terms, the guarantee and any premiums (gifts) included with the product.

The offer—and how it is phrased—can make a dramatic difference in direct mail results. In one test, three identical packages were mailed, the only difference being the phrasing of the offer.

The three offers were:

A. Half price!

B. Buy one—get one free!

C. 50 percent off!

Each statement conveys the same offer, but B generated 40 percent more orders than A or C. Apparently, people would rather get something free than get something for half price or 50 percent off.

Always try to use the word *free* in your offer. If you can't, at least stress money savings and discounts. And always offer a thirty-day money-back guarantee with all products sold through the mail.

5. If the client doesn't have an enticing offer, create one for him. In lead-generating mailings, where the purpose is to generate an inquiry rather than a mail order sale, a common mistake is to have a weak offer or no offer. Many such mailings start strong but end with a lame, "So, we would be delighted to do business with you and hope for a mutual relationship soon"—or some other such nonsense. A lead-generating mailing needs a strong call to action. It must tell the reader what to do next, and then give him a reason to do it.

One effective technique is to offer a free booklet, report, article reprint or some other useful information that (a) relates to the service you are offering and (b) would be of genuine interest to the reader. For example, freelance direct mail writer Richard Armstrong offers prospects a free booklet, "6 Questions to Ask *Before* You Hire a Freelance Copywriter—and One Good Answer to Each."

In many lead-generating campaigns, the goal is to set up a sales meeting with the prospective client. If this is the case, why not think of this event as a *consultation*, not a sales meeting—which it is. Then stress this offer in your letter. For example:

> Want to improve the effectiveness of your trade show displays? Call us right now to arrange a free, no-obligation analysis of your exhibit needs, including a FREE design sketch of a new MOD-TEK display that highlights your products as no other exhibit can.

6. **Ask a provocative question.** Questions, if phrased correctly, can be a powerful opening technique for grabbing attention and arousing curiosity. The most effective question openings deal with a timely, important or controversial issue or ask something to which the reader genuinely wants the answer. Some examples:

- What do Japanese managers have that American managers sometimes lack? (Economics Press)
- If you were to find out today that you had only a short time to live, would you feel comfortable with the amount of life insurance that you have provided your family? (United Omaha)

An example of a typically *ineffective* question lead is:

- Do you know what XYZ Company is up to these days?
  Remember, the reader is interested primarily in his own needs, not in your company or your product.

7. **Be specific.** Write copy that is factual, concrete and specific. As in article writing, vagueness and generalities make for weak direct mail copy.

For example, instead of, "Our new wealth building plan can make you RICH!", say, "Now you can earn $5,498 a day in the seminar business!" In one mailing I received, which offered a business opportunity, the brochure featured a photo of the writer holding up a check. The copy said, "I'll send you a check for $4,154.65 for selling just one order!" This is what I mean about being specific.

8. **Narrow the focus.** Always encourage clients to pursue narrow market niches whenever possible. The more you can identify the specific needs of your target reader, the better you can address those needs in your copy.

One of my clients creates customized computer systems for small businesses. He had been using, without much success, a mailing whose theme was, "A system tailored to your specific business needs." Our new mailings, which were much more successful, targeted certain groups of businesses that represented good prospects for him—lawyers, accountants, liquor stores. In these mailings, we could promise specific solutions to the problems law firms, accountants and liquor stores had in managing their businesses.

9. **Use a provocative teaser.** A teaser is copy printed on the outer envelope. Its purpose is to get the reader to open the envelope by creating an interest in the information inside. This is done by arousing curiosity or promising a reward. Some examples:

- 1996 SURVEY ON DIET AND CANCER—Important: The enclosed survey is reserved in your name. You are requested to complete and return your survey.
- CAN 193,750 MILLIONAIRES BE WRONG?
- CHEMLAWN HAS A $10 GIFT FOR YOU.
- Your telephone bill refund is coming.

Another effective technique is to use a blank white outer envelope with no teaser, logo or company name. By making the package resemble a personal letter, you ensure that the reader will at least open the envelope.

SETTING YOUR FEES

Here are typical fees for the various assignments you are likely to handle as a freelance direct mail writer. Note the wide range, especially in fees charged for mail order packages. As freelancer Sig Rosenblum puts it, "Fees are all over the lot." Also note that prices depend on the size of the client company, the size of the market (number of pieces being mailed), the profit potential of the product and the experience of the writer.

As a beginner, you might charge at or below the low end of the fee ranges listed here. For a sales letter, for example, a fee of $300 to $750 is reasonable. For a magazine publisher's mail order package, a beginner might charge $1,500 to $3,000.

My feeling is that, at the beginning, it's more important to get prestigious clients and plum assignments than it is to charge big fees. Once you build a client list and a track record of having written successful direct mail packages, you can increase your fees according to what the market will bear.

- *Direct mail package, mail order, subscription consumer: $3,000 to $12,000+.* For major magazine subscription promotions or other consumer products sold in high volume. Includes outer envelope teaser, four-page letter, brochure, order form, reply envelope and any other additional inserts (such as a lift letter or buck slip).
- *Direct mail package, mail order, business-to-business/smaller markets: $2,000 to $5,000.* For business-to-business products, books and other smaller volume mailings to limited or specialized audiences. Contains the same elements as the package described above.
- *Direct mail package, lead-generating: $750-$4,000.* Designed to bring back inquiries rather than direct sales. Consists of a one- or

two-page letter, brochure and business reply card.

• *Sales letter: $750-$1,500.* Business letter designed to generate sales leads, clean/update mailing lists, get appointments for sales-people, or produce requests for sales literature. Usually one or two pages long.

• *Postcard: $400-$650.* Postcard for direct response card deck *or* a magazine bind-in or blow-out card. Copy fits on one side of a 3×5 postcard.

• *Self-mailer, 8½×11: $750-$2,000.* Piece of 8½×11 paper folded twice to form six panels. Third panel is designed as a reply card with a tear-off perforation. Used to generate leads.

• *Self-mailer, 11×17: $1,200-$2,500.* An 11×17 sheet folded once to form four panels. Frequently used to sell business seminars.

• *Television commercial, direct response: $700-$1,500.* TV commercial designed to sell products via mail order by encouraging viewers to call a toll-free number. Usually two minutes long. Often seen late at night, during the daytime on weekdays, and Saturday and Sunday morning.

• *Space advertisement, direct response, full page: $1,000-$3,000.* Magazine or newspaper ad designed to sell a mail order product. Usually includes a coupon and/or toll-free phone number. Writing a "fractional" ad—one smaller than a full page—will pay $350 to $600.

• *Catalog copy: $75 to $150 per item; $400 to $600 per page.* Product descriptions for items featured in mail order catalogs. Usually written from specifications sheets or other materials provided by the client.

Among the self-promotion techniques used by freelance direct mail writers to get new business is—not surprisingly—direct mail. Freelancer Bob Schulte told me his self-promotion mailing package generated $15,000 in new business in a short time. I have created a simple one-page letter and reply card offering more information on my free-lance services, and this mailing generates a 7 to 10 percent response whenever mailed.

My friend Milt Pierce gets a lot of business through networking, personal meetings, lunches with potential clients and participation in various direct mail activities and clubs including the Direct Marketing Club of New York. Freelancer Don Hauptman prefers to use publicity—giving talks and lectures to various advertising and marketing groups.

I've been successful with small classified and display ads in various direct mail and general advertising magazines, both local and national. And I've gained visibility by publishing how-to articles in writing magazines—something I urge you to do, too.

But do keep in mind that this article was written to help *you*, not me. Here's hoping you put it to good use.

Scripting the Company Line

BY MANDY MATSON

W hen people at parties find out I'm a scriptwriter, they inevitably ask, "Oh, what show do you write for?" I suspect my answer often disappoints them because I don't write crash-and-burn car chases or sizzling sex scenes. My market is corporate communications. And *that* revelation is usually followed by a muttered "how interesting" as my acquaintance edges toward the cheese dip.

But corporate scriptwriting is a living—and a good one at that. There's a ready market for what I write, my programs reach thousands of people, and the messages I deliver run the gamut from pure fluff to life-or-death instruction. My goal is that of most serious writers: to entertain while I inform.

BREAKING INTO THE MARKET

Businesses and industries use television for training, marketing, in-house organs, developing footage for the news media, etc. And someone must script every program a company produces.

I got into nonbroadcast television after a few years in the technical end of broadcast TV and the creative end of advertising. That experience probably enhances my marketability, but you don't *need* a television background to write scripts. A Fortune 500 company isn't likely to hire you without a track record, however, so you'll have to start small—and work for less—before you can charge big clients the going rate.

A typical corporate video is five to twenty-five minutes long and takes from two weeks to two months to write, for which you can expect to make between $500 and $5,000. You and your client may decide that you'll be paid on a project basis, an hourly rate, a page rate or by the screen minute (meaning that you would be paid, say, $100 to $200 per minute of produced video). Rates vary according to the writer's experience and negotiating skills, the project's importance, the region of the country and the depth of a client's pocket. Local scriptwriters may be willing to suggest guidelines to use when negotiating with your client.

Many universities, technical schools and special interest groups offer classes in corporate scriptwriting; taking one is a good first step. If you'd rather just jump in and give it a try, though, the easiest way to gain experience (and build a file of sample scripts) is to volunteer your services to your employer, an existing client or a nonprofit agency. (Even a company with an in-house production facility and writers on staff might welcome an interested employee's help with overloads or low-priority projects.)

If you already do freelance advertising or PR work for corporate clients, those firms could provide your first script assignments. Initiate the opportunity by offering to do audiovisual projects for a low fee or on speculation.

Nonprofit organizations often need volunteers to write scripts. If you're involved with such a group, make your interest in scriptwriting known; otherwise, call several organizations in your area—at least one will probably be delighted to put you to work.

To find out who's producing nonbroadcast programs in your area, you must do some research. Start with the yellow pages. Call some companies listed under "video production services," and ask if they hire freelance writers. Talk to people in the communications and training departments of area corporations, and instructors at technical schools and colleges that offer television production courses.

Finally, there are two organizations with members who use or produce video: the International Television Association (ITVA) and the International Association of Business Communicators (IABC). By attending meetings of these groups, you can network with people who may be interested in your services. To find a local chapter, send a self-addressed, stamped envelope to ITVA, Suite 230, 6311 N. O'Connor Rd., Irving, TX 75039; or IABC, Suite 600, One Hallidie Plaza, San Francisco, CA 94102.

Potential clients will want to see samples of your work. Some ask for videotapes; other like to see scripts alone. I generally send two or three entire scripts and, if the client is insistent, one tape. I feel that since I'm selling my writing services, scripts are more relevant to the negotiations than tapes.

DO YOUR RESEARCH

Panic may set in once you've got an assignment. If you have a lot to learn about scriptwriting and the subject matter is also alien to you, the whole process may seem overwhelming. Stay calm; make an appointment with your content expert (probably assigned by the company), the producer and the client (one person may wear more than one of these hats); and get answers to at least the following questions:

- What's my deadline for the first draft? The final draft? (Plan on two revisions.)
- Why have you chosen video over other means of communication? (Some people haven't given it much thought beyond, "Well, the other guy is using it.")
- How will the video be viewed (one-on-one, large groups, part of a training workshop, with accompanying literature)?
- How do you envision this program? (If a client has definite ideas, pay close attention, but don't assume those ideas can't be changed.)
- Have you seen any videotapes on a similar topic that you like or don't like? (Ask for copies and specific comments.)
- Have you decided on a budget? (The producer will have to determine whether an idea is within budget constraints.)
- What information do you already have on hand about the subject, and where can I obtain more?
- Whom should I call when I have questions, and how available is that person?
- Do you want to use only employees, or can we use actors for narration and role-playing scenes?
- What script style do you prefer: two-column or screenplay? (Ask for samples of programs the producer has worked on and study them.)

Finally, learn everything you can about the subject, and ask questions when you don't understand something, including jargon specific to the industry. Don't be afraid to show your ignorance; most people enjoy explaining the nuances of their business to an interested outsider.

CHOOSING A FRAMEWORK

As with any writing assignment, one of the most difficult aspects of creating a script is deciding how to present the subject matter. Unless your client or the producer has a specific program concept in mind, do your research before you decide on one.

There are many script frameworks from which to choose, and most programs incorporate more than one of them:

Narration can explain a product, a process or a message that visuals alone can't convey. Narrators also introduce programs or provide transitions.

Generally, narration works best if used sparingly. Beginning scriptwriters often write narration that carries the entire message; that is, the narrator's text reads like material meant for a print medium, and the visuals seem to have been plugged in after the narration was written. Good scriptwriters minimize narration by letting dialogue, sound effects, music and visuals help tell the story.

You can use narrators on- or off-screen. If you choose an on-screen narrator, try to tie him into the setting. I once watched a program set mostly on a construction site. Some unidentified man in a suit kept appearing and disappearing without much rhyme or reason. A co-worker and I stopped listening to his message and began placing bets on who he was supposed to be, and when he'd make his next appearance. I doubt that was the scriptwriter's intention.

I was once asked to write a script designed to teach job procedures to new power plant workers. The program required a lot of narration, so I decided to create a narrator who'd sound like "one of the guys." The actor played the role so convincingly that several employees asked if he was still working at that site.

Roundups consist of short clips of people talking, interspersed with one or more other elements, usually narration or dramatic vignettes. When done well, they're very persuasive because the audience sees real people expressing their own feelings.

The roundup is a good choice for a marketing or sales program (who can better convince a prospective customer than an existing one who's satisfied?); for any type of "team spirit" effort (employees generally love to see their co-workers on TV); and for clients whose budgets are not large enough to pay professional talent (sure, employee "actors" are free, but keep in mind that acting abilities are usually commensurate with the pay). Because the roundup structure is such a versatile option, I provide a more complete explanation in the sidebar article on page 199.

News style mimics a news program, complete with anchor people, reporters and short segments. It's overused in corporate television and is best reserved for a company's in-house news programs. (Many large corporations produce monthly or quarterly shows for their employees.)

Entertainment frameworks can be serious or silly. Either way, I wouldn't recommend this type of script for your first effort. Both drama and comedy can and do communicate effectively—if they are done well. Dramatizations of real or "typical" situations require professional, believable dialogue and convincing actors. Comedy is even riskier; if it's done poorly, it's usually more memorable for having missed the mark than for having made a point.

Do some on-site research before you try to write dialogue. If your action is set in a hospital laboratory, ask lab workers to acquaint you with their jargon. I frequently select members of my target audience to work with me as "dialogue consultants," and they see all drafts of the script to ensure their peers won't jeer at unrealistic language or behavior.

And this cautionary advice doesn't just apply to drama. Every work group has its own inside jokes; I often use humorous suggestions supplied by my consultants, and scan office walls for cartoons or slogans that can be incorporated into my programs.

Satirizing popular shows, commercials or music videos can be very effective if you have the talent (and experience) to pull it off. Otherwise, these scripts can be disasters. Generally, a good satire requires paid talent and a hefty budget. More important, there has to be a reason to imitate something. A *Tonight Show* take-off could be fun, but don't struggle to make this concept fit the project just because it's your favorite show.

Animation can be helpful to illustrate how your client's product works or to enliven graphic displays. Many production studios (including in-house corporate facilities) offer computer animation, but seemingly simple effects can be surprisingly expensive to produce. Few budgets allow for a program that's heavily animated.

If you feel that your concept lends itself to some animated effects, talk with the producer to determine whether her budget will support that luxury. Then ask to see a sample animation reel from the facility that will produce the program to familiarize yourself with what's "doable." Watching how others have used animation can also trigger ideas that might work for your own program.

WRITING THE TREATMENT

A treatment is simply a script outline. Some are very specific, describing every scene and element the writer intends to include; others are little more than a page or two of ideas. The more detail you provide up front, however, the closer you and your client will come to a shared understanding of your ideas.

I usually start my treatment with a cover page listing facts: client, writer, project, intended audience, proposed length, projected shelf life (that is, the length of time the completed tape should be usable) and the deadline for the completed script. The rest of the treatment is devoted to describing what the audience will see and hear, including settings, action, visual effects and music. For particularly detailed treatments, I may use subheads that break the program into parts.

SCRIPTING YOUR IDEA

Once you and your client have haggled over details and he's approved the treatment, you'll start work on your script. If you're working on a two-column script format, in which one side of the page describes the "VIDEO" components and the other the "AUDIO," the temptation to first write all of your audio—especially the dialogue—will be strong. Resist.

The strength of video presentations is the visual component: "Show, don't tell" your viewers as much as you can. That means you must think carefully about what you can communicate without words. Some of the best scripts I've seen go on for pages describing action, music and sound effects, and not a word is spoken.

I gave up the two-column format a few years ago, and believe a modified screenplay format has helped me create better scripts. This format forces me to concentrate more on visuals and their relationship to the audio, rather than considering these components separately. (See the sample on page 196 for an example of modified screenplay format.)

Scripting dialogue is an art unto itself, and to write it convincingly, you must really listen to speech patterns. Beginning scriptwriters tend to overburden their actors with speeches and have them talk in complete, grammatically correct and utterly unnatural sentences.

Often you can get your point across more quickly and convincingly with short sentences or phrases, action, strategic shot planning and sound effects.

Burroughs Wellcome/American Social Health Association
"ASHA HOTLINES"

1. BLACK

Fade up to:

ANONYMOUS CALLERS
In the following scenes, the audience never sees any of the callers' faces. Shots are from behind; in quarter-profile; only of a hand; or backlit, so the features are indistinguishable.

2. INT. HOUSE, A SITTING ROOM

A woman's finger is punching the hotline's number into a touch-tone phone. She wears an expensive ring and watch. Her hand and voice suggest she is in her 50s. As she talks, her fingers nervously drum on the antique table on which the phone rests.

> SFX: THE SOUND OF THE LAST TWO DIGITS OF THE HOTLINE NUMBER BEING PUNCHED INTO A TOUCH-TONE PHONE, AND A CONNECTION BEING MADE. THE VOICE QUALITY SUGGESTS EACH CALLER IS ON THE PHONE.
>
> HOTLINE COUNSELOR (Voice Over):
> National AIDS Hotline. May I help you?
>
> CALLER #1:
> I just found out I shared a hot tub with someone who has AIDS. Can you get it that way?

Cut to:

3. INT. HOUSE, A SUNNY KTCHEN

A woman talking on a wall phone. She's casually dressed, and seems to be in her thirties. Nearby, several pictures—apparently drawn by grade-school children—are attached to a refrigerator with magnets.

> CALLER #2:
> There's a girl in my son's class who's HIV positive. How can I protect him?

If you want the audience to understand how your character feels, she doesn't need to turn to someone else and say, "God, I'm so nervous!" Think about the range of possibilities open to you: She could bite her nails, chew on her lip, or systematically destroy a paper napkin.

When you describe action, don't worry about planning every shot; that's the director's job. But do include enough information to let everyone know what the viewer should see. If your character is moving from one place to another, explain how. Is he walking briskly, dancing or gliding in his wheeled office chair? And don't forget prop details like safety equipment, tools and clothing. Describe each actor's "business"—details like finger-drumming, paper-shuffling, typing. Include business to avoid dialogue between talking heads. If one secretary is telling another about a terrific new incentive program, don't let her just sit at her desk. Make her file while she talks, answer the phone and smile at employees dropping work on her desk.

UNEXPECTED REWARDS

Corporate scriptwriting sounds second rate to many writers. Granted, some projects focus on topics so mundane that you'll wonder if there's any way to hold an audience's interest. (I used to feel that way about programs explaining employee benefits until I was on a panel that judged one as the most entertaining and informative show in a regional competition.)

Several years ago I was assigned to write a script encouraging employees to donate to United Way. I decided the viewers needed to understand how United Way programs affect their co-workers, so I designed a roundup. A narrator introduced employees who volunteered time to, or received services from, United Way funded programs; then each told his own story. A moving musical score provided transitions and worked well with visual montages.

In one segment, for instance, the narrator explained that Rick works with the Special Olympics every year. As they listened to the narrator, viewers saw Rick working with the kids at several events. Then Rick talked about what he gains from the experience. Part of the time he was on-camera while he spoke, enabling the viewer to watch his expressions; but "talking heads" get boring very quickly, so most of his comments were spoken over more video (called *cutaways*) of the kids.

I spent weeks laboring over my rough draft, pre-interviews, transcriptions, on-camera interviews, script revisions, production and the final edit. As the project took shape, I began to realize the power of people's candid thoughts and emotions. But would the viewers feel it, too?

Anonymously, I watched the audience watch my program. I was amazed at how intently they listened. The room was silent until a different employee appeared; then there would be a hum of conversation as viewers identified someone they knew. The comments the audience members made to one another as they left the room reinforced my feelings about the impact the show would have on them.

The people in the program "sold" United Way to their co-workers; donations that year reached record levels, and employees found creative ways to serve their communities. One group organized itself into teams and renovated a United Way sponsored day care center for handicapped children. I'm more proud of what those eighty people felt inspired to do after seeing the show than I am of the two awards it won.

Of course, there are plenty of mediocre corporate programs. But many of them are boring because the writers didn't use enough imagination. (Then again, some clients aren't open to imaginative work.) Good scriptwriting takes skill, creativity and detailed planning. If you're the curious sort (and what writer isn't?), creating scripts for corporate clients will enable you to learn about everything from phone systems to convenience store procedures. And if you'd like to earn a reasonable living (and what writer wouldn't?), becoming part of a company's stable of scriptwriters can keep you in video assignments lucrative enough to be downright addictive.

ROUNDUP SCRIPTS: THE MOST VERSATILE FRAMEWORK

The format I use most often when writing corporate scripts is the roundup—several short clips of interviews interspersed with narration, dramatic vignettes or some other structural element.

But a good roundup script is more than a collection of random interviews. The questions you ask must be crafted to elicit comments that can be incorporated into a carefully structured program. The first step in developing the script is pre-interviewing the people who will eventually be in the program. Talk to twice as many as you expect to use; some won't speak well enough to be videotaped, and others will fail to offer any new information.

When you call a subject for a pre-interview, describe the project and explain why the person has been chosen. Make sure he understands that a number of people won't make it to the final program so he won't be angry if cut. If the subject doesn't want to be videotaped, call the next person. Phrase your pre-interview questions in an open-ended manner: "What do you like best about working for Wilberry Widgets?"

As you're putting the rough draft together, refer to the notes you've gathered from your pre-interviews. You'll have to work the rest of the script around your subjects' comments, so it's tempting to quote an engineer who says, "The thing I like best about working for Wilberry Widgets is the people. We're just one big, happy family here."

But people don't usually say the same thing twice. And since your client will approve a script based on words he expects to hear, when shooting begins the director may have to struggle to put specific words into the interviewee's mouth.

There's a safer approach that avoids this problem. Use the comments you've gathered to *suggest* what each subject will talk about, and keep the description general:

(AN ENGINEER)
(Talks about how much he enjoys
the people with whom he works.)

This gives you some flexibility and forces you to focus on the important aspect of what someone has expressed, which should help you organize the material in your script.

Roundup programs are best taped in two phases. The first phase consists of interviews, and the second phase includes the rest of the program material. Although the producer may be used to handling the interviews on her shoots, ask if she would allow you to accompany the crew and handle this part yourself. You know the sorts of comments you need to elicit from the interview subjects; having done the interviews will make finding the right cuts a lot easier when you're transcribing the tapes, and the experience will help you understand how a program is put together. (Ask both the client and the producer about conducting the interviews as early as possible. Then, if the producer won't relinquish the interviewing task to you, ask to go along as an unpaid observer.)

After you've finished all the on-camera interviews, you need to transcribe them. It's tedious, but necessary. As you transcribe you can judge whether the inflection is right and the video looks good. You'll also know the transcription is accurate.

The payoff is the fun of piecing everything together. With highlighted transcriptions by your side, you can plug words into different parts of the script and decide what feels best. Sometimes you'll discover that an interview subject gave you just the right transition to the next point, and you can scrap a section of narration; other times you'll have to add narration or other transitional devices to fill gaps you couldn't have anticipated.

When you're satisfied with the results, pass the script by your client for a final approval. It's best to read it aloud to him, emulating the inflections your subjects used to help him understand their meaning. If he has problems with your new version, offer to show him some footage or go over some of the other options in your transcribed notes before you try another draft. Once he's approved the final script revision, the production crew can shoot and edit the rest of the program.

The Ghostwriting Gold Mine

BY LARRY CHAMBERS

I n my second year as a full-time business writer, my gross income averaged more than $10,000 a month.

Just three years before, I was a stockbroker. Each morning, as I fought the traffic, I would dream of being a full-time writer. I wanted to quit my job, retreat to a mountain cabin and write. But I had a wife and two children to support. I had to have a continuous source of income. I couldn't see how anyone could survive by simply writing magazine articles while trying to sell a first novel.

I shared my problem with a friend, a marketing representative for a major money management firm. "Why don't you get corporations instead of magazines to pay you for writing articles?" he asked. "You'd make more money."

He went on to explain that he had once hired a local writer to write articles on his behalf, with his byline, and then to submit them to small trade journals and magazines. After the articles appeared, he sent reprints to his sales reps in the company's offices across the country. For this, he paid the writer $3,500.

The idea hit me like the stock market crash of 1987. I would stay in my industry, write about investment firms and get paid well for my efforts. I wouldn't have to ask an editor what he pays. I could even "sell" my articles for free! The corporations would pay me more than most magazines paid *all* their freelancers in any given month.

I started by writing a basic article about how investment management could help businesspeople. I called a local trade magazine and, to my surprise, the editor liked the story and printed it the following month. After getting his permission, I reprinted the article and sent it to firms I wanted as clients, along with an introductory letter and a price list. Before going to my job in the morning, I would call on these firms. To my astonishment, their only questions concerned cost and how soon I could get an article in a magazine.

Apparently, they realized that hiring me to write an article for a reputable trade magazine was far cheaper than taking out a $10,000 full-page ad in the same publication. My initial $500 fee seemed high to me—but my customers considered it a steal.

I quit my job and averaged $6,000 per month writing articles for more than ten different clients in my first year.

HOW TO GET STARTED

If you have a business background, the first step is to call on your business acquaintances. In many cases, just a phone call can land you a writing assignment. You'll be surprised how receptive most will be. Most businesspeople have no idea how to go about finding a writer who understands their field. A writer with a little expertise in a particular industry can be of tremendous value.

If you don't have any business contacts, just go to the library. The reference section will be full of books listing the names and address of thousands of businesses that can use your services. Another readily available source is the yellow pages. Look up the type of business you want to write for, then call some companies and ask for the person in charge of marketing. Explain that you have a writing service that can keep their name in front of customers, giving their company an edge over competing businesses. Then ask to meet with them to discuss your ghostwriting services.

Once you get an audience with a marketing director, start your presentation by explaining how articles published in trade journals and business magazines can help him or her build a bridge to the customer, establish credibility and contribute to a positive professional image. Then explain how reprints of those articles can be used in sales presentations, as visual aids to enhance company credibility or as handouts to explain business processes.

Be sure to give each potential client a professional presentation package, which should include a bio, writing samples and a simple contract outlining your services.

Or, you can get businesses to come to *you*. I call this the "drip method." I have a list of potential clients that I want to write for. Each month I send everyone on my list my most recently published article. It's just like a leaky faucet; eventually they'll notice me. And clients are often more open to hearing new ideas if they're the ones who initiate the contact.

HOW TO WRITE ARTICLES MAGAZINES WILL PUBLISH

When I started, I had one skeleton of an article that I would insert information into each time a new client hired me. I used that one variation of the same article successfully twenty times, circulating it to different magaiznes. But today I try to create at least two new articles a month—which gives me a library to draw on when I can't come up with new ideas or when I need a chapter for a book.

Once you have a basic article, often you can simply give it a new title, slant it toward a different industry or company, and send it to a new magazine. By changing the focus from, say, the medical community to manufacturing, I can effectively create a new article.

By designing articles to explain the complexities of a certain business or a problem in an industry, you increase your chances of getting published. My goal is always to create a feeling within the readers that they have discovered something new.

In most cases, my articles carry my byline. In other cases, they carry my client's name. In all of my stories, I mention my client's name as an example of a service, or quote him or her directly as an authority.

Don't write self-serving articles; if your article sounds like you're trying to sell something or be manipulative, you are! Instead, try to address a problem or explain an opportunity. Begin with a brief introduction of only a sentence or two, and then get right into the "how to" of the article. Educate, solve a problem or reveal an advantageous situation. Success sells success—and highly educated professionals are always looking for timely information that will increase their wealth of knowledge.

An example: In an article for a financial planning journal, I described how one of my clients attracted more than two thousand new customers by conducting seminar workshops promoted by local radio personalities. My client wanted to attract more financial advisors to represent his firm in different cities. By writing a story explaining how successful the seminar programs have been, I subtly conveyed that my client was successful, too. I designed the article as a how-to piece, taking readers step by step through the seminar planning process so that they would know how to run them, too. The magazine editor liked the story so much he slated it for the next issue. He called me and requested that we expand the story, which made my client even happier. And I developed a continuing relationship with that editor.

Once you've secured a writing assignment, contact editors of pertinent publications to see if they'd be interested in a how-to article written by an expert in the field.

Finding these magazines is easy. *Writer's Market* is full of trade and business magazine names. Every industry has reference books, available in the library, listing trade magazines. I also ask my clients which publications their prospects read. Many are devotees of obscure trade magazines, such as *Bank Investment Representative, American Fire Journal, Public Accountant Magazine* and *Cemetery Management Magazine*. In addition, most trade associations have their own magazines, and these are relatively easy to break into.

If an editor responds positively, submit your article. After he or she agrees to use your piece, secure permission to copy the article or to order reprints directly from the magazine. This assures your client of rights to reprint the article so that it can be sent to his or her clients or salespeople.

Don't ask for money from these magazines. Trade magazines usually have small budgets and can't pay much anyway. Remember, you're being paid by the business, not the magazine. Most editors appreciate ghostwritten articles. They know the article will be professionally written and will require less editing.

HOW TO WORK WITH CLIENTS

If you're writing about an industry you're already familiar with, one interview with your client should be sufficient to write a story. If you're writing about an industry you're not familiar with, spend some time in the library, read trade magazines and interview someone in that industry.

After you've written the article, send it to your client for revisions. Clients will always have revisions—probably more than you'd like—and you simply have to get used to it. If you continuously seek your client's input, however, you'll find that after a while a level of trust will develop, and the number of revisions will decrease.

I keep experimenting with my fees. I started charging businesses $500 an article, and now I'm up to $5,000 for a package of two. I actually have two fee schedules: One is an all-inclusive flat monthly fee of $5,000 for two 1,500-word articles, including placement, plus travel expenses; the other is $3,500 for one article and placement. I always explain that placement is not guaranteed; it's on a best-effort basis.

Each month I send my clients a formal progress report. It reminds them of our goal and shows where our articles were sent that month, which magazines accepted them and when each is scheduled for publication. Businesspeople are used to progress reports; in fact, they expect them—especially if an article won't be published until six months after it's accepted.

To remind my clients of how cost-effective my services are, I've started including in my progress reports the advertising rates of magazines in which my articles appear. One of the magazines I write for charges $9,500 for a full-page ad; my client pays me $3,000 for a full-page article in the same magazine. Reminding him of this makes him appreciate my services more—and makes him more inclined to use me again.

FROM ARTICLES TO BOOKS

Even more valuable than articles are books. A book with your client's name bylined on the cover becomes more than a marketing piece. It establishes his or her expertise, gives him or her added creditiblity—and does wonders for his or her ego.

Accordingly, clients are willing to pay more for them. I charge $30,000 to ghostwrite a 250- to 400-page book: $3,000 to start and $3,000 each month after that, for the next nine months. I produce a set number of chapters each month.

(An even easier sell are booklets or books for trade associations. Most businesspeople belong to at least one trade association, many of which print books to sell to members. I've been able to charge such associations $3,000 for ghostwriting a single 20-page handbook. Find a subject that an organization has an interest in, and offer to write something it can send to members.)

When I get a contract to write a book for a client, the first thing I do is try to find a publisher. I write a synopsis of the book, a table of contents, a brief profile of my client and myself, etc. But then I go one step further: I tell the publishers how my client will market the book. I explain that I'm ghostwriting this book, and that my client is interested in buying two thousand or more copies to distribute to his or her own clients. Since publishers know they can recover their costs by selling the book back to my clients, they have very little risk. I get the publisher and the client together at this point so there's no misunderstanding.

This method also allows me to forgo asking for an advance from the publishing company. I explain that I'm being paid by my client, so I ask for a higher royalty instead.

I try to line up a publisher in my first month of work on a book project. This way, my client risks only the first payment. If we can't find a publisher, I simply sell the chapter as an article with my client's byline.

If we do secure a commitment from a publisher, and I've already ghostwritten some articles for the client, I can often use many of those articles as chapters. At the end of each month, I send first draft chapters to my clients for rewrite. I've found my clients often add to these chapters; this makes them feel like they're making real contributions and gives them more confidence in their books. As a result, they promote the books with greater enthusiasm—and I make more money.

My most lucrative book assignments have come when I've convinced clients to "write" books explaining their side of a controversial or misunderstood business topic. This has helped me land three book deals worth, in total, more than $90,000.

One of these was about an investment product called a "wrap account" (a method of bundling various investment management services into one product and paying one fee). At the time, financial writers were blasting these as not being a good investment. They were saying the fees were too high and comparing them to no-load mutual funds. I disagreed with this argument and felt the comparison was unfair and biased.

I approached one of my clients who sells wrap accounts and told him that he should write a book about their benefits. He told me if I could write it and get it published, he could buy more than two thousand copies for his clients and trade association members. He wanted to use the book to combat all the negative press and tell the other side of the story.

After lining up a publisher, I sent my client an agreement outlining each of our responsiblities. I wanted to co-author the book because I felt so strongly about the topic and the possibility of writing other books.

The promotion worked. My client lined up a number of book signing engagements and distributed a copy of the book to CPAs and attorneys in his town. And I earned more than my fee because of the satisfaction of writing about something I believe in.

Virtually any writer can break into article ghostwriting, and the market is enormous. With the same effort you'd spend selling your articles and books to editors, you could be selling your talents to businesses—with far more lucrative awards.

This Pen for Hire

BY LAWRENCE BLOCK

W rite your own novel. Tell your own story. To thine own self be true. Hunt the buffalo, and let the chips fall where they may. In the long run, every writer best achieves his goals by following his own star.

In the short run, however, it sometimes profits us to take a detour. A great many of us, at one or another point in our careers, find it worthwhile to write someone else's book, to do some sort of ghost-writing or work-for-hire.

In the world of nonfiction, the spectral presence of ghostwriters is assumed, if not always visible. The public more or less takes it for granted that the autobiographies of prominent persons are collaborative enterprises, with the celebrity supplying memories and the writer putting them into words and arranging the words in some sort of order upon the page. Sometimes the ghostwriter gets a joint byline, sometimes a credit on the copyright page, sometimes an earnest note in the acknowledgments. Sometimes the ghost gets no credit at all, and the purported author goes on the talk shows and assures Jay and David and Oprah that he or she wrote every word of it, and gosh, writing is sure hard work. Some viewers believe the celebrity wrote all the words, just as some people believe that the planet Jupiter is actually a hollow sphere, and that all the survivors of the lost continent of Atlantis live on the inside of it. (And, let it be said, every once in a while some celebrity *does* write a book himself. It happens.)

The general public is rather less aware that ghostwriters function in the world of fiction, too. In recent years, novels have appeared by people prominent in other fields. In many if not all cases, the celebrity has had virtually nothing to do with the production of the book. A writer, generally unsung, has written the book. The celebrity has furnished a name for the cover, a photograph for the back, and has gone

on the tube to flog the thing. Sometimes the purported author acknowl-
edges the writer for "creative assistance" or "editorial help." More
often the celebrity takes all the credit, and the real writer has to content
himself with half the cash.

The celebrity novel is becoming increasingly common, and it's not
hard to see why. The books sell rather well. They're easy to promote
for a couple of reasons. First of all, the celebrity author has name
value. The name's fun to drop in-house, at editorial meetings and sales
conferences. Publishers' sales reps recognize the name right away,
and so do the people they sell to. Just as important, it's a cinch to get
the book plenty of ink and air. Gossip columnists take note of a novel
by a celebrity while they would overlook the same book by a nonentity,
or even by an established novelist. Celebrities are naturals for the talk-
show circuit because, unlike professional novelists, they don't have to
sit up there and talk about the book. They can talk instead about life
in the fast lane, or about their career in Washington or Hollywood. Or
they can just look beautiful.

Finally, readers figure the celebrity author brings some real expertise to the novel. He or she really knows where the bodies are buried.
And the reader already has a relationship with the celebrity, already
feels as though they know each other, so it's not like buying a book
by a faceless stranger.

In the past two months, my agent called me twice to relay feelers
from publishers. First he mentioned a rather prominent actor best
known for his work in suspense films. "They think he should write a
novel," he said.

"Perhaps he should," I agreed.

"But of course they don't want him to write it," he went on. "They
think you would be the perfect person to write it. They thought it might
have a Hollywood setting, and he'd help out with that, and possibly
furnish some ideas. I told them I didn't think you were interested."

"How well you know me," I said.

A few weeks later he reported that a forensic medicine expert, already the published author of two works of nonfiction, was ready to
turn his talents to the novel. He didn't actually want to *write* a novel,
but he could supply a few ideas, and of course he'd furnish the medical
expertise. The proposition was not entirely unattractive—I had met
the gentleman in question, found him pleasant company, knew him as
a tireless and enthusiastic promoter of his earlier books, and could
believe that he would indeed contribute useful background material

for the novel, and that the venture would be financially profitable for all concerned. Nevertheless, I said I wasn't interested.

THE GHOST AND MR. FICTION

Before I explain why, let's look at some other opportunities for fictional ghosts. The series provides frequent employment for spectral novelists. The paperback racks overflow with endless series of category fiction featuring the same lead character or characters over and over again, all ostensibly by the same writer. (All the books in a given series are supposedly by the same writer, that is. Not all the books in all the series.)

Sometimes one writer does indeed write all the books in a lengthy series. But sometimes a particular writer will do the first three or six or twelve books about a gunfighter in the old West, or an ex-mercenary going up against the mob, or five Marines winning World War II a battle at a time, and will understandably tire of the sport. Because the series is profitable for all concerned, ghostwriters will be brought in to keep it alive. The original writer may furnish outlines, may vet manuscripts before they go to the publisher, or may do nothing but collect a piece of the action.

Sometimes there is no original writer. On such occasions a packager dreams up the idea for a series, gets a proposal written, cuts a deal with a publisher, and finds writers to produce the various volumes. The packager may supply his writers with fully developed outlines or he may leave them largely on their own.

Occasionally an established writer simply leases out his byline. Thirty-five years ago, a series of paperback originals appeared carrying one of the most respected names in American mystery fiction. Some people probably wondered why the author, who had previously always published in hardcover, was now writing paperback originals. As it happened, his sole connection with the books was monetary; he was in ill health and bad financial straits, and his agent managed to set up a deal wherein lesser writers supplied the books and the Big Name took a cut. And all the royalties and subrights.

Film novelizations and tie-in novels are not necessarily ghostwriting—one more often than not uses one's own name, or one's own pen name—but I mention them because, once again, the writer winds up writing someone else's book rather than his own. The novelization is what the name implies; one takes an original screenplay and turns it into a novel, which is published at approximately the same time the film is released. A tie-in is a little different; it's a novel based on the characters in a TV show, with the plot devised by the book writer. Outside the *Star Trek* universe, there haven't been many tie-ins lately, but some years ago they were common, and tie-ins based on *The Man From U.N.C.L.E.* and *The Partridge Family* were quite successful.

Novelizations and tie-ins are successful because the publicity generated by the film or TV show creates a ready-made audience for the book. Movie and TV people like them because their presence on the newsstand helps to promote the show or movie, and because they get a licensing fee and royalty on copies sold. As far as the writer is concerned, both are generally considered a rather low form of hackwork, which is curious when one considers that the process of turning a screenplay into a novel is not philosophically different from that of turning a novel into a screenplay.

I did a couple of tie-ins thirty-five years ago; one of them, curiously, was republished twenty-five years later by Foul Play Press, retitled *You Could Call It Murder*. My publisher thinks it's good enough to merit reissuing, although I have my doubts. I had never done a novelization, and was counting on that distinction to get me into heaven at a later date, but that same year I did indeed do one—of which more later.

GHOSTLY GREEN

Is this sort of writing a good deal for the writer?

Well, it depends. It depends on the deal, of course, and it depends on the stage one is in in one's career. And, to be sure, it depends how badly you need the money.

Most of the writers I know have done some sort of ghosting or writing-for-hire early in their careers. Most of us, when we're starting out, are not capable of writing our own books out of our own inner selves and supporting ourselves in the process. Sometimes we have to learn how to write before we can manage more ambitious books, and various forms of hackwork (if you want to call it that) provide a paid apprenticeship. Anyone capable of learning in the first place will unquestionably learn a great deal by writing a book from someone else's outline, or with characters supplied by another. Similarly, sooner or later one will no longer be learning much by writing these books, and persisting in their production will hinder one's growth rather than contribute to it. The trick is knowing when to stop; as with most forms of self-destructive behavior, one generally stops a little later than one should have, and some people never stop at all.

Suppose one is past one's apprenticeship. Can one then justify writing books for a packager, or ghosting novels for an actor or politician?

It depends what sort of justification works for you. There is a series of mystery novels set in Washington that has consistently hit the bestseller list and has made their actual author a considerable amount of money, more than he ever made off books for which he received full credit. Has he made a mistake?

Only he could tell you. Only he could guess what he might have written, under his own name and out of his own self, if he hadn't been writing these books instead.

I know a writer who eked out a living for years in several areas of category fiction before he began writing an extended series of paperback historical novels for a book packager. The packager developed plotlines and set up a deal with a publisher and took, as I understand it, half the income from the books; the writer undertook laborious research and wrote the books for the other 50 percent. And made a fortune, and broke through to bestsellerdom, and turned out to find himself as a writer in these books as he never had previously.

And why did I turn down the two ghosting jobs I was recently offered?

Not because I don't think they might have been lucrative. I'm sure either of them would have paid me as much in front as I normally receive for a novel, and either of them could have done very well, possibly achieving bestseller status. From a dollars-and-cents standpoint, it would seem that both books offered me great potential and no real risk.

On the other hand, this kind of writing doesn't do much for one's career. It is anonymous. There is no glory in it, and the people won't rush out to buy your other books because they won't know who you are. It would take me at least as much time and energy to write a book under the actor's name, or under the doctor's name, as it would to write a book of my own. And it would add nothing to my body of work.

And, because I have a limited amount of time and energy and creative ideas available, to write either of these books would mean to forego writing a book of my own. I'm not sure just what books of my own I'll wind up writing, or just how I'll employ that time and energy, but at this stage I'm unwilling to spend it on someone else's book.

Why, then, did I do the novelization?

Good question. It was a sort of special case, in that the publisher thought I was just the person to turn this particular screenplay into a novel, and was willing to back up this conviction with a much higher advance than one generally gets for a novelization, and a generous royalty on top of it. (The writers of novelizations do not routinely get royalty contracts.) Furthermore, I read the screenplay and liked the story and characters. Finally, the publisher wanted a real novel, with my own creativity brought to bear and the whole book to be something of substance, on which I would put my own name. (As it turned out, the author of the original screenplay had the legal right to bar the publication of the book and he exercised it; thus, although I was paid in full, the book will never be published.)

Before I knew of the book's fate, however, I had decided two things—that I was glad to have written it, and that I would never want to undertake another novelization. Explaining this to my agent, I cited the story of Voltaire, who once accompanied a friend to a specialized Parisian bordello and enjoyed himself. A week or so later, the friend invited him to go again, and Voltaire declined emphatically.

"I am surprised," the friend said. "You seemed to have such a good time."

"I did," said Voltaire, "but I should not care to repeat it. Once, a philosopher. Twice, a pervert."

Switching Sides

BY SANDY MACDONALD

I f you were the person your college roommates turned to for last-
minute edits of their term papers, you may not have to wait tables
while drafting your Great American Novel. Anyone with a knack
for spelling, punctuation and grammar has a good shot at secur-
ing freelance editorial work—if not at a prestigious publishing house
halfway across the country, then perhaps at the little start-up business
down the block.

"People shouldn't feel limited by their geographical region, with all
the faxes and overnight mail services around," says George Milite,
former co-executive director of the Editorial Freelancers Association
(EFA), a nonprofit educational organization and clearinghouse based
in New York City. Then again, he notes, building a local following
first is a good way to acquire the necessary skills, confidence and all-
important references.

"You'll be in a better position with a book publisher if you have a
couple of people who'll speak glowingly of your work," says Laura
Fillmore, founder of Editorial, Inc., in Rockport, Massachusetts. Once
a freelancer herself, Fillmore found she enjoyed "bragging about other
people's work" even more than doing her own. In the past decade, her
agency has almost cornered the market for freelance editorial work in
the Boston area, matching hundreds of professionals with scores of
media and corporate clients, and offering services ranging from computer composition to book packaging.

The slot she finds hardest to fill? Ironically, it's proofreading—the
most essential editorial task, and one with many hidden challenges.
"It's intellectual work, but also mechanical," Fillmore explains. "Your
attention cannot waver for a second."

THE PROOF IS IN THE PROOFING

Many years ago, I finessed my first proofreading assignment—obtained through sheer braggadocio—by relying on the crib sheet I found in a dictionary (it's still there, under *proofreader's marks*). Luckily, I was dealing with a straightforward block of text, and I sailed through with no one the wiser about my inexperience.

It was only when I parlayed that minor success into an in-house position as copyeditor that I ran into trouble—or more specifically, the agonizing punctilios of the University of Chicago Press's *A Manual of Style*—widely referred to as "the copyeditor's Bible." For all I knew at the time, it might as well have been written in ancient Mesopotamian.

The woman training me to take her place (she was eager to move on to content editing, where you get to wrestle with ideas, not just semicolons) was at once impatient and enormously helpful. "It's just jargon," she reassured me, "a way for copyeditors to maintain their mystique as specialists." And she was right: Once I'd mastered the precepts of the book—referring constantly to the glossary at the back—it didn't seem so impenetrably dense.

There's an answer for every question, no matter how picky, between the orange covers of this hefty tome. Should quotation marks go inside or outside the period? (Usually outside, with some key exceptions.) Why should *Communists* be capitalized and *communism* not? Should a restrictive appositive—e.g., "my son the doctor"—get a comma? (Not unless he's your one and only son.) The peculiar habits of the lowly comma rate a good ten pages.

Presumably, mere proofreaders need not be responsible for such arcana. Their job is usually restricted to reading against copy—making sure the typesetter has set what's on the manuscript page and carried out the author's, copyeditor's and designer's instructions.

On scrutiny, you may find the author to be a semiliterate windbag, and you may have all sorts of brilliant suggestions for improving his or her text. However, any comment on content or style at this stage of the game is out of bounds and tantamount to professional suicide: You're permitted, at most, an occasional, painstakingly polite marginal note to the copyeditor, flagging what might perhaps be a slight technical oversight. There are definite boundaries to be observed. As the EFA's handy *Tips for Successful Freelancing* pamphlet puts it: "Do the work you're asked to do. . . . If you're asked to proofread, don't edit."

Proofreading needn't be purely passive, though, if you treat it as an educational endeavor. After all, this is your chance not only to analyze an author's style up close (if the work's being published, it must have *some* quality worth emulating), but to start familiarizing yourself with the copyeditor's domain. Study every mark and choice; soon it will be your turn to make those decisions.

On some jobs, it may be the art director's duty to make sure that the *specs* (type specifications) have been handled correctly, but increasingly that function is falling to proofreaders. The Chicago *Manual* is relatively closemouthed on the topic of checking type specs, perhaps because it's much easier to demonstrate in person than on the page. Fillmore suggests that those not yet proficient with picas, points and the like limit themselves to "typologically simple" projects, such as novels, at the beginning. Once you've proved your usefulness, your contact at the publishing house will probably be happy to coach you a bit and help you branch out.

HOW TO GET HIRED—AGAIN AND AGAIN

The typical entrée at a publishing house begins with a brief letter of inquiry (with references) to the managing editor or chief copyeditor. (Names, titles and addresses can be found in *Literary Market Place*, a directory available at most libraries.) With any luck, this letter will earn you an invitation to take a test—in-house, if you're close enough, or at home on the honor system. And it doesn't pay to cheat: Whether a time limit is imposed or you report the time it took you, they'll expect your first assignment completed just as quickly, and an excess of billable hours will reflect poorly on your performance.

Neophytes afraid to take the plunge can avail themselves of the proofreading and copyediting courses available at many community colleges and extension schools, and through such organizations as the EFA (71 W. Twenty-third St., New York, NY 10010). Local branches of the National Writer's Union and the American Society of Journalists and Authors often sponsor seminars, as well.

Whatever your level of expertise, George Milite says the continuing education that regular contact with peers provides is absolutely essential. Word of mouth is often the passkey in this volatile profession: "For every person who says, 'I can't make a living at it,'" he reports, "there's another saying, 'I can't keep up with the work available!'" Busy freelancers often subcontract, or at the very least pass along referrals. You also need to network like crazy, and maybe take a few none-too-thrilling jobs, to keep your name in the mix. "Once you have a reputation," Milite promises, "you'll be able to pick and choose."

BEYOND PROOFREADING

What if, after investigating the field, you find that polishing copy till it's letter-perfect isn't your forte after all? Not to worry—there are plenty of other editorial subspecialties you can pursue.

If you're a born logician with a fanatical regard for details, you might look into indexing—which can also be learned at courses readily available at most colleges. If indexing classes aren't convenient, Fillmore suggests an unusual approach: Check bookstores for the kinds of material you might like to work on, contact the indexer through the publisher, and see if you can work out some sort of apprenticeship deal. "There's a lot of clerical, menial-type work that goes with indexing," she points out, and an experienced indexer might be willing to trade valuable pointers for a helping hand.

Those fluent in an extra language or two (or more) might try translation. Literary translation, alas, has traditionally tended to pay less than straight typing, but if you can afford the low fees and find a text you admire, it's a wonderful way to get into an author's head—it's a bit like writing, with the inspiration provided! Technical proficiency in the source language isn't as crucial as facility in the target language (English).

Other services that publishers regularly need include research (for both text and photos), fact checking, tape transcription, and typing or word processing. The latter can be particularly interesting if you're working directly with an author, and many publishers keep typists' names on file to match up with writers who need help.

Beyond the rarefied world of literary endeavors, there's another whole universe of corporate editorial work—a realm that pays, on the average, about 50 percent more for precisely the same services. EFA publishes a biannual rate survey drawn from its members: It's available to nonmembers for $20 and worth perusing to get an idea not only of the going rates (roughly $10 to $25 an hour, depending on the task), but of the *range* of contract work available. EFA also maintains a telephone job line (212) 929-5411.

To get back to that little shop on the corner: AT&T may not be quite ready to hand over its copywriting concession, but that new pet store or copy center down the block might let you have a stab at spiffing up its promotional brochure—particularly if, as both Milite and Fillmore recommend, you initially volunteer your services. It's from such humble beginnings that mighty client bases are built.

YOU'RE THE BOSS

In my own checkered past (with résumé to match), I've been happily at play in the fields of the word, even if the financial rewards have sometimes been less than staggering. I once spent two years, for instance, translating two thick nonfiction books for a fee of $2,000—it worked out to about 50 cents an hour. Actually, some of the work I'm proudest of I did for free, for *Aphra*, a feminist literary magazine of the early seventies that, for a time and in its own small way, helped make history. I managed, somewhere along the line, to pick up the skills that today enable me to ask—and get—perfectly respectable fees for what is an entirely pleasurable pastime. I remember remarking to friends, when I first started freelancing, "It's as though they're *paying* me to go to my room and read a good book." Twenty-odd years later, I still feel as if I'm getting away with something every time I start an intriguing new project.

The rollercoaster cycles of freelance work do have their downsides, of course. When the stress level gets too high and I start craving job security, I'll leap at the chance to take temporary shelter in a salaried position in publishing—another option for which my catch-as-catch-can training has prepared me well.

As a writer, I also find it very helpful to work as—and think like—an editor. Whenever colleagues kvetch at the arbitrary treatment given their flawless prose, I tend to sympathize (silently!) with the thankless editor forced to mediate between the effect the writer was after and the actual result. It makes me easier to deal with (I hope) when *my* work gets blue-penciled.

Of all the benefits, however, the best has surely been the ever-evolving opportunity to work with others equally besotted by words.

Even You Can Be a (Newsletter) Publisher

BY LORIANN HOFF OBERLIN

They greet us on our desks and in our mailboxes. They tell us when the next meeting will be, what interest rates might do or what the minister has to say. In today's information age, newsletters appear almost everywhere and come from nearly everyone.

In any given month, my church sends my family the latest news regarding special events, births and deaths; my financial planner advises us where to put our money; even the real estate agent we once used sends us monthly tips to help us decorate our home and accent the yard. More newsletters come from my travel agent, dentist, favorite charities and companies whose products I've used. Someone has to plan, write and put together all of this information. Why not you?

You probably already *have* many of the skills needed to turn newsletter writing into a profitable venture. You just need to know how to get started—I can tell you.

THE DESKTOP REVOLUTION

The great majority of newsletters published today are created using desktop publishing (DTP). Paul Brainerd, president and founder of Aldus Corp., coined this phrase in the early eighties, envisioning computer systems that could perform the functions previously accomplished by expensive typesetting and layout equipment. With the advent of DTP, writers became instant newsletter publishers, combining text and graphics on camera-ready pages with the click of the mouse.

I have only a cursory knowledge of graphic arts. But with my Macintosh, I can take advantage of clip art and other illustrations available on diskette. I can even import a client's logo into my documents, tying the newsletter's design to the design of the client's stationery, brochures and other materials.

Purchasing a DTP system is easier than you might think. Most personal computers have enough memory to operate the popular page-layout programs, like PageMaker or QuarkXPress. If you can't afford the latest system on the market, try buying a used one. The necessary software may cost you several hundred dollars, but the investment will last throughout your writing career. Look for the latest versions of these packages. Finally, you'll need a laser printer to print camera-ready pages. If you can't afford a laser printer, check your yellow pages for a printer or "service bureau" that supplies laser printers to professionals who don't own their own. Just copy your data onto a disk (along with the program you're using), head for the print shop and let the folks there output your files.

Of course, you don't *have* to have a computer to make money from newsletters. You can still gather information, plan each issue, write and edit your stories and the contributions of others, and select clip art from catalogs. But someone else will have to do the typesetting, and possibly the paste-up, before you can take the camera-ready artwork to the printer. And all of this will drive up your costs.

LAYING THE GROUNDWORK

It's essential that you know how you'll tackle a newsletter before you can sell the idea to prospective clients. After all, you've got to convince them to spend money on a new product. If a particular organization already has a newsletter, what can you offer to make it better? An attractive format? A more sophisticated look? Better content? A crisper writing style?

If the organization doesn't have a newsletter, you should emphasize the importance of keeping employees, clients or members informed. Done correctly, newsletters can be wonderful public relations vehicles.

Once the client agrees to the newsletter, you need to establish a few basics. Not the least among these is pay. Though it will vary depending on where you live, whether you work with nonprofit groups or money-makers and whether you have much competition, newsletter writing and production can gross you anywhere from $25 to $2,500 an issue.

In setting your rates, estimate the time it will take to write, edit, revise, layout and work with the printer. Then add at least two hours to your bid. First issues and start-ups always take longer, and you'll want to be compensated for all the design time it takes to strike a final format. If possible, charge separately for the setup.

Finally, always ask printers, paper suppliers and other vendors to bill their services directly to your client. Nonprofit organizations are often tax-exempt, so direct billing is in their best interest.

Next, determine how often you will publish your newsletter—weekly, semi-monthly, monthly, bimonthly, quarterly, semiannually or annually. Most newsletters require at least a quarterly frequency to establish the comfort level necessary for readers to recognize and expect it.

At the same time, don't promise more than you can deliver. I once was contracted to start a weekly employee newsletter from scratch. We found "reporters" in each department and got the executive director to write a regular column. We had more than enough material to fill the first several issues. But once the initial excitement wore off, it got to be one more chore each week. So we decided to publish semimonthly—a decision we should have made in the beginning.

Be consistent with whatever decisions you make. We're all drawn to our favorite sections in newspapers and magazines because we know exactly what to expect from them. But move the funnies from the entertainment page to the sports section, and you could seriously ruin someone's evening. The key here is comfort. Give your readers the consistency that earns their trust, and they'll keep your newsletter, devour it, clip it, post it and love it.

NAMING YOUR NEWSLETTER

Starting a newsletter from scratch means selecting a name. Choose a word or phrase that quickly and clearly identifies the newsletter and its content. It should be easy to pronounce and remember. In trying to be lively, however, avoid titles that sound too cute. Aim for something with impact, a powerful word or two to make just the right impression.

This is especially important if you're publishing a newsletter for self-employed consultants or other professionals who want to turn dormant clients into active ones or to attract media exposure. In this case, consider using that individual's name in the title.

Many newsletter names build on words that convey a sense of communication—words like *almanac, briefing, digest, forecast, outlook, notes, spotlight* and *update*. Newsletters I've produced have used the words *connection, direction, reporter* and *quarterly* in their titles. If you need more than one or two words to convey your message, consider using a subtitle. I publish a subscription newsletter for communicators, students and working professionals called *Perspectives*. But that title alone wouldn't do the job, so I use the subtitle "concepts for a career in communications" to explain what the publication is about.

LESS IS MORE

When deciding on your newsletter's format, keep in mind that two or more columns look most professional; one column of text looks like a typewritten letter. Use white space to make a page look uncluttered; consider boxes or tool lines, photographs, clip art and pull quotes to graphically break up text.

Using reversed type and screens is acceptable, but use them sparingly. If there's one rule in layout, especially when it comes to desktop publishing, it's that less is more. Put a novice with little graphics expertise in front of a computer, and watch his eyes light up at all the possibilities. Give this person fifty fonts, and he'll use them—all in the same document. The result will look amateurish.

The same rule goes for content. A newsletter's format is tight and capsulized, allowing for timely information or trustworthy commentary. Tell readers everything they need to know in as few words as possible. As in news writing, structure your stories in inverted pyramid form, with the most important details—who, what, when, where, why and how—in your lead paragraph. Then, if you must trim the copy to fit the space, you can chop the bottom without sacrificing important details. Of course, always provide a lead, a strong middle and a satisfying conclusion, but in a more concise form.

Use the active voice to convey a sense of immediacy, and edit yourself once you've written a first draft. Do your words evoke images? Can your readers visualize what you are writing about? Have you eliminated unnecessary words? Have you provided good transitions? Are there enough paragraphs? Are your sentences diverse enough, or are they subject, verb, subject, verb? Finally, read your copy aloud to determine whether it's conversational in tone. Remember, you're aiming for comfort.

SOME ADDITIONAL POINTERS

If you don't use desktop publishing, you'll need a few inexpensive supplies. A light table (at least a small portable one) helps, though a drawing board or flat surface will work in a pinch. You'll need artboard for laying out graphics, or simple white paper if you only need to paste up an occasional piece of art. Apply acetate over the blocks where photos will go. Glue down everything with rubber cement, checking for proper placement with a T-square and triangle. Apply a fixative to avoid smudges, and use tissue overlays to write notes to the printer.

To make production as easy as possible, I develop newsletter stationery with the title, subscription information (if there is any) and standard tool lines. I print several months' worth of sheets in a particular color ink on a grade of paper that allows no show-though. In my case, this is PMS 287 on antique gray classic laid. Tell your printer if you plan to feed your paper stock through a photocopy machine or laser printer. It will make a difference in the type of paper and ink used. I always allow for this flexibility, ordering laser finish stock so that I can print extra copies myself if I need to. By printing stationery ahead, you can just plug in the items that change each month, usually in black ink. These include the date, the volume, the issue number and, of course, the text.

As for the writing, here are some tips for catering to specific audiences:

• When working with church groups or community organizations, the value is in content, not in slick design or expensive paper. If you're at a loss for ideas, try a brief tease for the next sermon or speaker, a calendar of events, birth announcements and obituaries, profiles, financial information or excerpted material (with permission, of course).

• For employee publications, remember that a newsletter may be the only communications link between management and staff. Use your newsletter to build morale, concentrating on the positive while reporting the facts as they are. Avoid selling the management line and becoming too preachy.

• For the marketing newsletter, provide readers with practical information they can use. And while your goal is to report on the product or service, you can write about other subjects, too. The real estate newsletter I receive provides occasional recipes and tips for household safety.

• When producing a subscription newsletter, remember that readers are paying for information, not fluff. Keep graphics and artwork to a minimum or don't use them at all. In *Perspectives*, I focus on ways my readers can get ahead in their careers and make money—universal objectives for just about everyone in my diverse audience.

Indeed, newsletter writing can be lucrative. It can keep the income flowing when other writing payments are slow in coming or when writer's block gets you down. And turning your attention to another kind of writing can recharge your batteries for other projects.

To learn more about newsletter publishing, consult these sources:

• *Editing Your Newsletter*, by Mark Beach (Coast to Coast Books, distributed by Writer's Digest Books, 1507 Dana Ave., Cincinnati, OH 45207, (800) 289-0963). A complete guide for the writer who wants to produce a newsletter from scratch. Good advice for setting goals, naming a newsletter, writing copy and working with graphics and printers.

• *Newsletters From the Desktop*, by Roger C. Parker (Ventana Communications Group, Box 2468, Chapel Hill, NC 27515, (919) 942-0220). Tips for planning a newsletter, designing a nameplate, working with type and creating an attractive layout. Includes sections on choosing hardware and software and obtaining technical support.

• The Newsletter Publisher's Association, a nonprofit association of newsletter publishers, provides information and the book *Success in Newsletter Publishing*, by Frederick D. Goss (The Newsletter Publisher's Association, Suite 207, 1401 Wilson Blvd., Arlington, VA 22209, (703) 527-2333). An excellent resource detailing the business side of publishing and managing newsletters. Special "Publishers Profiles" interspersed throughout add a personal dimension to the facts.

Freelancer as Publisher

BY ART SPIKOL

I remember the delight I felt when I wrote my first magazine article long, long ago. I was working for an advertising agency. We had as a client a real estate developer who was rehabbing a downtown Philadelphia office building, attempting to return it to its former glory (and make a barrel of money in the process). The client was going to run a full-page ad in a local magazine; the magazine, hungry for business, promised in return to write an article about the building. I ended up getting the assignment to write that article. (I also learned a little about how business is done in publishing's bargain basement.)

I wrote an OK article. It was probably better, in the final analysis, than the building. It wasn't *real*, and I knew it, but that byline in print was really nice. It was to be my first and last taste of magazine writing for a decade, until I finally broke into the real world of magazine journalism. I jumped in with both feet. Loved it. Still do.

But since then, like many article writers, I have taken one foot out and put it into various other arenas. It has turned out to be the busier foot, with adventures in everything from scriptwriting to fiction to advertising. That other foot spends most of its time in the corporate environment—a lot of it with newsletters. And every time I've spoken to a group of writers, I've found that many or most of them do the same—they're involved in newsletters and other corporate publications.

Newsletters seem to be today's hot means of communication, with thousands of them in circulation. People create them to sell their own products or services, build credibility, make a name widely known, attract new customers. Sometimes the newsletter itself is the product—there are many that go, by subscription only, to various kinds of business and professional environments with tips on how to run better organizations. As a communications medium, newsletters cover the waterfront, ranging from naively written and poorly designed to ultra-sophisticated in both areas; quite often, they are written by people who, like you, write magazine articles. There is a tremendous amount of cross-fertilization going on here: what is an interesting story for a corporate newsletter is quite likely to be an interesting story for, say, a business magazine.

I spend a good bit of my non-magazine time helping corporations improve their publications (and much of it producing publications for them), and some of you may have considered producing a newsletter for a corporation. For the rest of you, let me point out that one bi-monthly newsletter—just one—can be worth more to you in one year than you can expect to earn in your best *two* years of article writing, present or future, no matter how good you are.

Now that you're interested in being a producer of newsletters, let me pass along some tips I've learned.

Look at the competition. See what else is out there. Do some research. Chances are your workplace—assuming you are em-ployed—gets several of the publications that will be your competitors.

Team up with a good graphic designer. I do my own design, but I have a lot of experience in design and illustration. If you don't, find somebody who does. Graphic design is a lot more than deciding how the pages will break and where certain articles will appear; it's creating an attractive and appropriate organization of matter, a sensible use of type; it's having a sophisticated eye for photographs and illustration.

For that reason, I have to tell you to avoid anyone right out of art school—new graduates should not get their experience at your ex-pense, and certainly not when they have the power to make executive decisions. Find someone with the maturity and experience to look at the product as both a creative entity and a business, someone who knows a lot about printing and typesetting and what things cost and what people buy.

Remember, you're not necessarily looking for a partner. The essen-tial thing is the information, so there's no point in giving away half the profits to an artist. Ask your friendly neighborhood graphic designer for a quote—then get a competitive quote or two—and make your decision based on the available talent, bucks and chemistry. Paying is cheaper (and easier) than sharing.

Use color sparingly, and not in headlines. Headlines in color are like people who shout: they lose credibility. Color can be used to call attention to a particular area, but it shouldn't compete with the message. Put it to work as backgrounds for illustrations, the masthead, screens over sidebars, and wherever the way things look is more important than what they say.

And be appropriate. I remember a bank client showing me a newsletter that used a muddy green for its second color (on a two-color printing job, black is known as the "first color"). The bank felt that there was a metaphorical basis for using green, the color of money, but it was ugly. The attractiveness of the newsletter was being sacrificed for a metaphor, and I suggested changing it. Another client, whose name was, let's say, Brown, had been producing a newsletter on brown paper. Clever, no? No. Because the publication was as dull as October earth after a thunderstorm. And it didn't brighten up until we changed our stock color to white.

Figure on a two-color newsletter, probably black (or another very dark color, dark enough to support the body copy) and a compatible accent color.

Also figure on a four-page product. Some newsletters contain eight pages, but I haven't seen a corporation that couldn't tell its story more effectively in four. Four pages—we're talking about an 11×17 sheet folded to $8\frac{1}{2} \times 11$—is generally enough for a monthly or even a bimonthly. The first issue is easy: There'll surely be enough material for eight pages. But by the second or third issue, you may hit the wall. Don't bite off too much. How much can the average recipient read at a time, anyway? Four pages are enough to start.

Use the front page wisely. Many corporations squander newsletter front pages on the "story of the month." It's understandable. But the problem is, if you happen not to be interested in that one story, you might never get to page two.

I like to use the front page in a more newspaperly fashion: two or three significant stories beginning there and jumping to the inside. Use page 1 to create some excitement, give it a "breaking news" look. And watch out for the "tombstone" effect: headlines, side by side, competing for attention because they're of equal weight. Let there be no doubt in the reader's mind which story you think is most important, which is second, which is third. That's one reason why you need a good designer.

I have a pretty good rule of thumb for a newsletter's front page: It consists of three stories. One story reflects a message you want to get across. One may not have much to do with your company but will hold a great deal of interest for your readers, particularly the media

(I remember running a piece about smoking in the workplace—it didn't have much to do with my client, but it was the best read story in that issue—and it doesn't make a lot of difference which story is read first, as long as the reader opens the publication and goes to work on it). And finally, one "must-include" story, if there is one, that simply needs exposure in terms of dovetailing with corporate goals.

Keep the media in mind. The newspapers and television stations in your corporate client's geographical area are usually your primary audience, because if you can influence them, you influence everybody—and make believers out of readers you might never otherwise reach. But the media are sophisticated in the ways of newsletters; they can spot a phony story a mile away. So don't allow a client to use a newsletter for puffery. Every good business has worthwhile *true* stories to tell; it's your job to ferret them out.

Why bother? Because you want to make the company one of the experts in the field, the one that everyone calls first for information, quotations, etc. That's how newsletter articles can lead to spinoffs in national publications.

Be aware of your publication's "geography." One thing that endears publications (magazines, newspapers, whatever) to readers is a sense of geography—knowing where they can find their favorite departments or sections. In *Writer's Digest* for instance, readers know precisely where to find Letters and The Writing Life and Chronicle. That sense of geography is just as important to a newsletter, enabling readers to quickly get involved with their favorite areas and to develop a familiarity with them.

Hold down the photos of people's faces—"head shots," as they're known. The fewer of these, the better, and don't use them on the front page unless they're special—or can be made special by the use of some outstanding quotation. Also avoid grip-and-grin photos, where a couple of people are shaking hands and smiling into the camera. There has to be a better way. There is.

Avoid the first person. A lot of "we" and "us" and "our" in a newsletter diminishes credibility: you're talking about yourself. You can easily alter this perception by having the publication sound like it's written *about* the company instead of *by* the company. In other words, a third-person news style sounds more believable than the first-person style many newsletters employ. The closer a publication gets to sounding like it's being written objectively, the more credibility it obtains.

Be subdued in headlines. Two caveats: avoid superlatives, and make sure the company name doesn't appear in large print more than 25 percent of the time. Newsletters are one-sided publications; the less noticeable that one-sidedness is, the more impact the newsletter will have on its various audiences.

Don't be afraid of injecting a national perspective. Your newsletter may be for a predominantly local corporation, but what happens in the world has an impact on what happens locally. Quoting a company spokesman on a national or international situation, and allowing the company to take a strong position on the issues involved, can make the company seem to be more of a major player.

Maintain diversity. Unfortunately, most newsletters restrict themselves to subject matter about the companies that produce them. Logical but boring. I always shoot for diversity, and I wouldn't dream of not including a column of bite-sized fillers—interesting events/comments from *The Wall Street Journal,* trade publications, etc. This not only entertains your audience; it also says that you have your ear to the ground, that you're national, that you're part of the world of your readers.

Now, how does one get started? That's the hard part—getting the corporation to allow you to create a newsletter or to make an established newsletter better. You probably won't be able to just walk in and do that, but you can become the kind of freelance writer that corporations turn to. Once you're established, introducing the newsletter concept is easy.

The Freelancer's Lifestyle

How to Make Time to Write

BY ROBYN CARR

It's getting worse, this time thing. Our entire society is hooked up to beepers, cellular phones, answering machines and services, faxes and computerized appointment calendars. We are expected to be productive every waking moment, to get by on little sleep. Everyone works overtime and in addition to that, we have to eat fiber, exercise, meditate, volunteer, and make sure our kids get in the gifted program.

When the heck are we going to relax, much less write?

There are a lot of reasons why people who want to write don't, and amazingly, only one of them is time. People don't write today because they won't have time to continue tomorrow. Some people, and I've been one, won't start on Monday if they have to go out of town on Thursday because that means they'll have to pack and clean house on Wednesday and that leaves only two days—better to just wait until next Monday. People don't write because they aren't ready—whatever idea is simmering in the skull isn't ready for the page yet and sitting before the computer will be too unproductive. And people don't write because they're scared that when they do write it won't be good enough. People don't write because they only have an hour. . . . Or they work all day to get all their "obligations" taken care of so they can finally write guilt free, only to find themselves exhausted and brainless. People don't write because someone is going to interrupt them any second, or they don't write because everyone in the family has helped them clear the time and now the pressure is too intense.

Not only are there plenty of reasons not to write, there are lots of different kinds of writers.

There is the *all-or-nothing writer,* so compulsive when the ideas strike that everything else in his life goes to ruin. No wonder his wife begins to harangue him when he heads for the computer. No wonder he avoids starting again; when he starts, he'll be consumed.

There is the *scheduled writer*, who has courageously allotted herself certain hours of the day during which to create . . . and God help the story if the idea isn't there on time.

There is the *catch-as-catch can writer* who's always working on and off, grabbing paragraphs between carpooling, business meetings, cooking, cleaning, sales calls or whatever.

And there is *SuperWriter,* who writes in lieu of sleep and food, late after the household has gone to sleep or early, before the newspaper comes, so no one from spouse to boss should be inconvenienced.

It is possible to carve writing time out of hectic schedules filled with day jobs and family responsibilities even if you aren't the kind of person who can live on four hours of sleep. The first thing to do is find out where the time *is.* When do you knit, read, watch TV, golf, gossip on the phone, paint, build, needlepoint, restore classic cars, etc.? Are there hours before work in which you're fresh and snappy that you use to slowly browse through the paper and consume five cups of coffee? Do you stay up for late-night TV?

If you find there is no time during your day or week that isn't committed to essential responsibilities, consider a fundamental change in *values*; a conscious decision to stop the frenetic pace of the reeling world. Just have the courage to say *Hold Everything!* while you reassess how you'll spend your time. This could be a change as minor as getting an answering machine or refusing to make every meal a gourmet event, to something as major as a residence or job change. Perhaps you need to refocus your approach to life—the time is essentially yours. You don't have to be bullied into this cultural obsessiveness to do everything and be everything by filling up every minute. More is less.

Next, give writing some kind of priority in your life. Unless you've chosen writing over the rest of life (in which case you're off writing and aren't reading this article), this is not as simple as it seems. Yes, writing is important, but not more important than your marriage. Not more important than your job, which brings in the money on which you live. Not more important than the children, who will see the psychiatrist for years if you're slack in parenting. So, list the relationships, commitments, obligations and expectations in your life. Now, study each one. Have discussions with people involved in this issue, if it seems appropriate. No, you wouldn't want to neglect the ties that bind, but do you work on your marriage twenty-four hours a day? Maybe you'd better protect that weekly movie and dinner out, but *must* you watch television together to keep your marriage healthy? Do you parent twenty-four hours a day? No; you're *available* to parent twenty-four hours a day no matter where you're working, but it is seldom the case that a parent's every free moment is spent playing, cuddling, caring for and nurturing. The lovely thing about children is that the small ones go to bed early and the big ones want to stay out late. The job? Many writers make career or job choices based on the fact that they need time to write; some people write while on the job; some schedule work hours (nights, evenings, half-time, long vacation breaks) to provide time to write in off-hours. A friend of mine takes his own computer disk to work, arrives an hour early, eats and writes at his desk during lunch, and stays an hour late.

Once you've decided exactly what priority your writing has in your life, it's time to let some things go. It isn't easy, but it's critical. You've determined that writing is less important than cooking dinner for your husband, but more important than watching television with him. Now, where does your desire to write fit in with that long visit you get every morning from your neighbor? Or babysitting your sister's kids? Can you trim down the time spent on the phone? Can you give up bowling? Golf? Poker? Long lunches? Do you have to serve chicken *cordon bleu*, or will nuked frozen lasagna do? The family vacation is essential, but do you have to watch weekend football? Not only can't you do it all, you can't have it all.

You may have to take your writing hours from something else. Sometimes this has to be negotiated. Maybe its time for you to stop coaching soccer and start merely attending your child's games. Maybe that board of directors position for the church or school is too much— you have a few hours to spare, but not every spare hour to give. I used to sew; I don't anymore. I used to pore over cookbooks looking for new dinner ideas; now I rely mostly on the quick and easy. I've been working on the same needlepoint for eight years, I'd love to make a quilt but can't, I rarely go to lunch with friends, and gardening lures me but it's out of the question right now.

There are trade-offs that can be made; trade-offs that are imminently reasonable and probably necessary. Can you hire a sitter sometimes? Can you get the kid down the block to cut the grass? Can you convince your best friend that you can only spare half the time for play? Can you get a little help with the chores from other family members? Where is it written that your list has to be that long? I mean, everyone is entitled to a dream now and them, huh? And a little time to pursue it? Just don't expect anyone to find you the time. It's up to you.

Another helpful hint is to alter the *way* you do things. One way is *fast*. I don't mean learn how to deal with people fast—though that bears considering. When I was a young mother, I bought a how-to book. In bold type it said "Your baby will want to nurse every two hours." Underneath were tips on how to sail through the housework in record time. I learned to wipe out a bathroom sink with a dirty T-shirt while collecting laundry, to clear surfaces by gathering clutter (from shoes to papers) into one box to dispense with later, and so on. These were tricks; books, magazines and friends are full of them. I have a cookbook called *Excellent Meals in 30 Minutes*. It's the only one with worn pages. But by far the most important trick for efficiency I've ever learned is *Get someone else to do it*. I found a neighborhood restaurant that sells pies, cookies and muffins as cheaply as I can make them. There's a dry cleaner who only charges $6 to hem a skirt or pair of pants, and I never buy anything that has to be ironed, ever! A very successful writer I know who also raised four children said, "See a child, give it a chore." You don't have to be rich to be clever; there are lots of things you can "get done" for very little money—and what's your time worth? I taught my kids how to do their own laundry when they were ten . . . my sister-in-law is still laundering for college students.

Organize. Become an efficiency expert. Set up a plan for yourself with the goal of setting off *blocks* of time for your writing. Make appointments for the vet, the hairdresser, the doctor, the dentist, the lube job, the carpet cleaner, the accountant, etc., on one day of the week only. Or mornings only. If there's a lot of stuff that regularly pops up, make it two days. You have to wait a whole extra six days to get your teeth cleaned? You'll live. Do your running around town for errands all at once. When you start stacking appointments on top of errands on top of work on top of everything else, you can find yourself too busy, which makes that hour you have left for writing not enough to bother with. If it means making menu plans and shopping lists, do it, but be sure you're doing it once rather than all the time. Train your family to participate—if Junior is going to run out of peanut butter and Cheerios, he'd better jot it down because you're no longer making extra trips. What writers really need is a *clear* calendar, not a carefully choreographed one.

By all means, have a family conference. Express yourself honestly about your desire to spend some significant time writing. Ask your spouse and kids for help. For some people this extends to other family members—moms, dads, brothers, sisters. Rather than cutting them off, aggravated, tell them what you want. *Need.* Hey, that kid has soccer in addition to school. Can you have a little writing in addition to work? There must be a way. Make sure that if anyone is threatened by this time you seek, you have an opportunity to work it out with them.

Warning: Don't try to do everything and be everything to everyone. You'll fizzle like a bad firecracker. Be reasonable. If there's already more on your plate than one adult can manage, you've got a problem that needs to be handled. No one can do it all! Everyone needs a little leisure time to be healthy, to be sane. If you choose to use your leisure time on writing rather than needlepoint, so be it and good luck. But if you try to find a way to *add* writing to an already beleaguering lifestyle, something's going to crack and who knows what it will be. You? Your relationships? Your job? Think seriously about this. Human beings need a few things, and Maslow listed them. They need food, shelter, safety and love. Then they need an opportunity to actualize their true *selves.* Some of us have found that writing is the way we can best pursue that. It is a matter of choice, change, compromise, negotiation and *balance.*

There are hardly any writers, outside of the federal penitentiary, who got started because they had time to kill. Successful writers usually claim to have made huge sacrifices to write. Take a deep and honest look at why you haven't *already* found the time to write. Are you scared? Is fear that you can't do it causing you to procrastinate? It's risky to give up your hobbies and pastimes to write, only to find out you aren't very good at it. There's terror involved in asking your family to pick up the slack for you and then, when they've given you this extra time, you don't perform. Well, let me tell you something— writing is hard, it takes a long time to learn to do well, and you simply won't know until you try.

Are you allowing yourself to be victimized? Are people using you? Do you find that the happiness of other people—their needs, which only you can fulfill—take precedence over your own? Whether you're pursuing a writing career or not, you'd better learn to take care of yourself; to say *no* when you're getting overwhelmed. Does the saying "You can't get blood from a turnip," mean anything to you?

And, finally, after examining your schedule, your priorities and obligations, is there simply *no time left*? Is there nothing to trade off, except sleep? Is there nothing about the way you do things that can be changed or compromised or eliminated? You're simply booked up, from morning till night? If so, then I submit to you that you haven't quite decided that writing is terribly important to you. And trust me on this one—if it isn't all that important, you'll be wasting your time. Writing is one of those things you have to want . . . and you have to want it bad.

Home Is Where the Office Is

BY NORMAN SCHREIBER

T he fable goes like this: A Hollywood studio hired William Faulkner to write screenplays, and brought the future Nobel laureate to California. After a decent interval, Faulkner asked if he could write at home. When permission was granted, Faulkner promptly went home—to Oxford, Mississippi. This delightful apocrypha illustrates a point. Writers have long known what millions of other Americans have begun to discover—working at home can be wonderful.

And better than just working at home is working in a home office. Without a patch of space designated for your work, you are a nomad in your own house. Before you can begin each day's work, you must erect your tent. At the end of the session, you must break camp.

Joyce Baldwin, a Long Island-based freelance writer who specializes in health and science, remembers the years of working at home without an office.

"I always had to clean up after working," Baldwin explains. "Sometimes I misplaced something and then spent a lot of time looking for it when I needed it. I did my interviewing on the kitchen telephone. This meant I had to get the kitchen organized for each interview."

Three years ago, Baldwin shanghaied her unfinished basement, polished it up and set up shop. Her cluttered desk is now a proud symbol of a permanent office that helps her work. Baldwin had been daylighting as a schoolteacher. Perhaps it's a coincidence, but recently she was able to resign her teaching position and spend more time on her rapidly growing writer career.

"I think," says Baldwin, "that setting up the office forced me to take myself much more seriously as a writer."

The home office is a tool. It won't double your talent or triple your inspiration, but it might increase your productivity. Even that, however, is a minor perk compared to the really big plus. Your home office lets you take full advantage of your most basic natural resource—you. Whether your home office is a sliver of a room or the west wing of Tara, it is where you go to think and create. You design it so that it stimulates *you*. You organize it so that *you* can work most effectively. It is yours.

Two basic steps lead to the home office.

- Identify and confiscate the space where you will work.
- Fill the space with stuff.

SPACE EXPLORATION

One key question will guide you in your office search: Is this an area where I can work in comfort? It's a fertile question that spawns other queries such as "Is there room for everything I need in the space," and "Can I plug my electrical equipment in here." Other concerns of this ilk are:

How much distraction can you stand? Do you need an ivory tower or are you adept at playing in traffic? Does gazing through a window drive you on or slow you down?

Just what will you put into your office: How much room will you require?

Then there's the big question—What space is most ripe for liberation?

Many writers, like Joyce Baldwin, already have an area in waiting. Home offices blossom not only in basements, but in attics, garages, dens, guest rooms and the kid-is-finally-gone bedrooms. I use the old dining room.

John and Barbara McMullen, writer/consultants in New York's Jefferson Valley, combine the best of two eras. They write about today's computers, and they do it in a converted eighteenth century barn. They bought the building because its design let them isolate the upstairs living quarters from the downstairs working area where the livestock used to meditate. The two sections even have separate entrances.

Of course, when you ask yourself, "Hey buddy, got a spare room," the answer may be *no*. Do not despair.

Consider, for example, a walk-in closet. Just add a small desk, filing cabinet and lamp. Most closets come equipped with a door—a handy device that keeps the world out when you don't want to be distracted

238 The Writer's Digest *Handbook of Making Money Freelance Writing*

and keeps your office hidden when you don't want to think about work.

A closet may not be *your* salvation; but somewhere in your home a space yearns to be your office. It may be disguised as a living room corner or that spot in the bedroom where you park your dusty stationary bicycle. The location may well wear camouflage and blend stealthily into its background.

New York graphic designer Cassandra Malaxa wanted to anchor her office with her drawing board. The board's ideal site was a niche by the living room window, but a bookcase hogged that spot. Malaxa realized the books were important—not the furniture. She deep-sixed the bookcase, eased in the drawing board, and stacked the books neatly on the floor beneath the board, leaving herself some legroom.

THE PHILOSOPHY OF STUFF

Once you seize your space, it's time to fill it. Equipping a home office is not simply the feverish compilation of material goods. It's an opportunity for philosophy: What you need to be the best writer you can be, and where shall those needs be placed? Also, how much money can you spend to meet those needs? The answers to those musings will shape your home office. You're really selecting a playing field, and it must suit your game and style of play. You wouldn't try to develop your hockey skills on a golf course, would you?

Here are some hints:

• *Work surface.* Here's the place where you actually write, but other factors may affect its shape or size. Do you frequently consult books or files? Are you working with a computer and therefore with disks, references and maybe a mouse? What do you like to have at your fingertips while you work? This surface is usually a desktop, but people with computers sometimes prefer specially designed computer tables. (Longhand purists might move at a fast clip just by using a clipboard.)

Your work surface might be, as Groucho would say, "a common object, something found around the house." That was the experience of Joan Western Anderson, author of *Teen Is a Four-Letter Word: A Survival Kit for Parents.*

"There was a door left in the garage," explains the Arlington Heights, Illinois, author, "and I started lusting after it. I was the mother of five, and I couldn't find a surface that wasn't littered with pacifiers. Any kind of small desk I looked at just didn't have enough room."

That old closet door was the open sesame. Anderson painted it, and planted it atop a pair of two-drawer file cabinets.

• *Chair.* The more hours you spend in your office, the more important it is that you select a chair that keeps you comfortable and healthy. General criteria (each of us is shaped a little differently) suggest a chair with adjustable height, a back that tilts forward for typing, and a curved back to fit the spine's shape (Medical writer Mark Fuerst of Brooklyn keeps a throw pillow behind him to compensate for his chair's lack of curve.)

• *Something to write with.* I am a computer chauvinist. My computer's word processing program removes so many physical and mechanical obstacles to writing that I can concentrate purely on the act itself. Simple word processors are also fine as far as they go, but they won't help you engage in other computer delights, such as using your modem to research distant databases.

Electronic typewriters have a little bit of memory and do a couple of tricks. Self-correcting models, at least, are a big step ahead of manual typewriters.

• *Something to see with.* Rather than rely on overhead lighting, try for task-specific lighting—individual fixtures that pour light specifically on whatever it is you have to see. Light bulbs come in three flavors: incandescent (the old tungsten filament baby that echoes Tom Edison's original idea); halogen (an incandescent mutant that throws off much heat and light); and fluorescent (a bulb that gets much illumination from little wattage). Incandescent bulbs yield a warm light and cost the least. They also have the shortest life span and are the least energy efficient. Halogens emit so much light that they can produce uncomfortable glare. Also the abundant heat produced demands that you check the halogen fixture to make sure it is well ventilated. Fluorescents are the longest lasting and most energy-efficient of the three. Some find the light quality of most fluorescents to be harsh. A classic fixture is the so-called architect's lamp that fuses a fluorescent for brightness and an incandescent for warmth. When you set your lamp up, check for glare—light, direct or indirect, that shoots into your eyes. To identify sources of glare, look at the shiny surfaces you'll be working with (a computer screen, for instance) to see if any light bounces off those surfaces.

• *Someplace to store paper.* Basically, you almost need the equivalent of a set of Russian nesting dolls—a little doll within an identical but larger doll within an identical but larger doll within. . . . Instead of playing with dolls, we writers frolic with file folders, hanging folders and containers for the hanging folders.

The basic unit of all paper is the file folder. Keep related pieces of paper in a clearly identified folder. For example, I have a folder for ideas. A newspaper clipping or press release that sets off my article-generating enzymes gets tossed into the "ideas" folder. If I find or dig up more information about a particular idea at a later point, the idea gets a folder of its own. When I have enough information to write a proposal, a copy of the proposal goes into the folder. When the assignment comes, it is quickly trailed by pieces of paper—notes, interview transcripts, press releases, scribbled names of contacts, drafts, photocopied magazine and book pages from the library.

The article in process soon has not one but a group of file folders. Again, each folder contains related materials. I might keep transcriptions in one folder, photocopies in another and contacts in a third. The folders themselves are kept together in a stronger, roomier device called a hanging folder. Each of the hanging folder's four corners has a hook, thus enabling a folder to—well—hang within a cabinet.

We keep the folders stored in an organized arrangement. The kinds of things you group together in folders and the way you group the folders form the spirit of your filing system. Your system will be based on how you think. I keep the contacts for a particular article with the other material related to that article. That's because I think of the contact within the context of the article. Someone else might have a file called "contacts." Another someone might file contacts according to professions.

Now comes the fun part. What holds the hanging folders that in turn hold the file folders that hold the paper? Proud office tradition maintains that files belong in file cabinets.

My office includes both traditional frontfacing files (in which files are placed from front to back) and lateral files (in which the files are placed sideways from left to right in a long pull-out drawer). Remember Joan Anderson's door atop a pair of two-drawer file cabinets? The setup not only supports her work surface, it's also a compact approach to file storage, and keeps her files at her fingers while she works.

Those who have neither the money, space nor even the quantity of files to justify a New York skyline of cabinets need not fret. A wonderful variety of folder receptacles awaits you at the office supply store. These include 12-inch fiberboard cubes (with covers), plastic milk crate-like boxes, and laundry cart-type arrangements (complete with wheels). These all are compact, light and portable. They serve as efficiency-sized file cabinets or special project supplements to your fixed furniture.

- *Storage.* Obvious choices include shelves and desk drawers. In crafting your personal space, you'll have to make some personal decisions. Look for piggyback opportunities, creating storage areas above or below utilized spaces. Also pounce on unused territories. Debbi Kempton-Smith, author and columnist for *Glamour* magazine, stores books in her otherwise unused oven. Always remember that the more frequently you'll need something, the easier it should be to retrieve.

- *Telephone system.* If your writing activities include making phone calls, you'll need a telephone. A separate line placates the gods of accounting and privacy. (Readers, if you write in and say you have just one line and have been deducting it for years and have never been bothered by the IRS, please be sure to include your social security numbers. That helps our readers at the IRS find you and thus saves your government money.) Check out phones with such time-saving features as automatic redial and phone number storage. With the phone comes the responsibility of having an answering machine. Once you begin working with specific editors, the ability to retrieve your calls while you are somewhere else is a bare minimum.

- *Other machines.* You won't need a fax machine until people you do business with start asking, "Do you have a fax?" You won't need a personal copier until you discover that you're learning too many intimate details about the gang at the copy shop.

- *Extra toppings.* Your home office will evolve as you learn more about how you work and the materials you work with. For example, Joyce Baldwin loves bulletin boards. She has several in her basement office.

"I have a big calendar up there," said Baldwin, "and I use it to keep track of what's going on. I tend to post letters on one bulletin board, outlines on another, names and addresses on a third and notes on a fourth.

Gail Greco, a Rockville, Maryland, author who writes about business and entertaining, strays far from office supply stores to furnish her office. The Greco headquarters is replete with old advertising tins and baskets and ceramic crocks in place of shelves, drawers and file cabinets.

Despite the diversity of approaches, a certain harmony prevails in home office land. People add items that make work easier. Generally, there's no perfect time to get something. I didn't buy a call waiting service until I started doing a column that required lots of phone contact. I'm not sorry that I didn't shell out for call waiting during the years when I didn't really need it. Of course, a little prescience can help. A telephone with automatic redial and memory will save you time by sparing you from the repetition enforced by a plain phone. When you buy your computer, get your modem. It will be right there with you when you're ready to streamline your researching via faraway databases or to offer editors the service of electronic submissions. The main consideration is not the object or service being purchased. Instead, you need to know what problem it will solve, and how.

Many of us enter the writing life by living on scraps—scraps of encouragement, scraps of paper for our notes, scraps of time in which to think and scraps of space in which to do the actual work. It's exciting to create a home office and transform these various scraps into a beautiful quilt that protects and identifies you.

Welcome home.

How to Handle Distractions and Interruptions

BY LEONARD FELDER

S ound familiar? Julie is a novelist whose New Year's resolution was to stop procrastinating and finally complete her book. On a recent morning in which the creative juices were flowing wonderfully, she was interrupted by a phone call from her mother who "absolutely needed her advice on something that couldn't wait."

Hours later, Julie was still fuming at her mom for calling, and angry at herself for picking up the phone. As she says, "There's nothing worse than being in the middle of writing with an image in my mind finally beginning to take shape. Then along comes an interruption. The image falls apart. The blood boils. Worst of all, I spend the rest of the day frustrated because I can't get it back."

Whether the interruptions in *your* writing life come from other people (a phone call, a visitor), mechanical objects (a broken typewriter, a leaky faucet that drives you crazy) or you own inner concerns (a growling stomach, some unfinished business with a family member), there are creative ways to overcome these distractions:

PREVENTING INTERRUPTIONS AND DISTRACTIONS AHEAD OF TIME

Rather than waiting for the next derailment of your writing train of thought and then moaning "Woe is me," take preventive measures now:

1. **Get up early and write when there's no one to interrupt you.** According to poet and novelist May Sarton, author of more than 40 books: "It has to be the morning, before one's mind is all cluttered up, when the door to the subconscious is still open, when you first wake up. That's the creative time for me."

Larry McMurtry, author of *The Last Picture Show, Terms of*

Endearment, Lonesome Dove and *Texasville*, agrees: "I think the last time I was interrupted was in 1964 when my sons were two. Now I live alone and I write early and briefly when no one is awake enough to interrupt me."

Says novelist Gail Godwin, who wrote *A Mother and Two Daughters* and *A Southern Family*: "I start the day early, sometimes at 6:30 A.M. Most people don't phone before 9 A.M."

2. **Ask people ahead of time not to interrupt you, rather than waiting for them to make you angry.** Often the people we live and work with don't fully understand how important it is for a writer not to be interrupted. You may need to have a heart-to-heart discussion with each of these people so they will be more sensitive to your writing habits. Explain to them how fragile your writing time is and what they can do to help prevent distractions.

Barbara Ehrenreich, an essayist and social historian who wrote *The Hearts of Men, Remaking Love* and *For Her Own Good: 150 Years of the Experts' Advice to Women*, told me that when she was disrupted by someone she lived with, she "simply told him not to interrupt me, and he listened."

Sometimes the people you live with might need a more detailed definition of *interruption*. For example, I write at home and my wife, Linda, works at home, so there are times when I'm walking through the living room to get a book or a drink of water. Linda naturally assumed that my walking through the apartment meant I was open to conversation. But I explained to her that I'm still percolating ideas in my head even though I'm walking, pouring a glass of water or looking at a bookshelf.

My wife and I soon agreed that I shouldn't interrupt her and she shouldn't interrupt me when either of us is in our own thoughts. We reasoned it's better to assume that we're still uninterruptible unless we specifically let the other person know: "I'm not working right now. We can talk."

Clear agreements like these can prevent arguments and misunderstandings. Unless you tell your loved ones or roommates they shouldn't approach you at certain times, you are expecting them to read your mind—and that's not fair.

3. **Put up physical barriers to prevent distractions and interruptions.** There are numerous inexpensive devices that can make your writing life easier. For example, Gail Godwin ways, "I saved myself a lot of frustration by installing an answering machine." Answering

machines allow you to screen calls, save messages until you are ready to answer them and avoid nuisance calls.

In addition to answering machines there are other high-tech ways of ensuring your private time for writing. If you have a roommate who loves to listen to music while you work in silence, give him or her a pair of headphones. There are now excellent earphones for television sets, as well. Ask for an inexpensive set at your local electronics parts dealer.

For only a few dollars, you can buy the most valuable soundproofing device known to human beings—ear plugs. They come in plastic, wax, foam and other varieties, depending on the selection at your local pharmacy.

Another simple but effective privacy device is suggested by Shirley Conran, author of *Lace* and other novels. She says, "I lock the doors and switch off the telephone." Other writers have posted creative signs on the doors of their writing rooms, ranging from the polite "Please Do Not Disturb" to the outrageous "Genius at Work—Noisemakers Will Be Tortured."

4. **Take care of potential distractions before you sit down to write.** You can anticipate many of the things that might cause you to break your train of thought. For example, stock supplies before you sit down to write. If you write longhand, make sure you have the right kinds of paper, pens, pencils and erasers so you won't have to stop in the middle of an idea. Some writers sharpen their pencils and restock supplies at the end of each writing session to be ready the next day. Buying extra typewriter ribbons and correction tapes is also a good idea.

Many writers admit to getting hungry when they write. For instance, Barbara Ehrenreich says: "For me, hunger is still a distraction. I haven't figured out how to eat while writing."

Eat a light snack or meal prior to sitting down to write. While too much food can make you sleepy, a light amount of healthy food and a cup of tea, vegetable broth or water can keep your stomach from becoming disruptively noisy. Some writers install a coffee pot or a small refrigerator in their writing office, or keep healthy snacks or fruit on hand.

WHEN YOUR BEST EFFORTS FAIL

Despite precautionary measures, your writing is bound to be interrupted at some point. Here's how to respond to future distractions without getting overly stressed:

1. **Delay the interruption until a better time.** If you make the mistake of answering the phone or letting a visitor enter while you're writing, see if you can postpone dealing with the interruption until after you're done writing. You might say, "Can I handle this after five, when I'm done working?" Or you might delegate the task to someone else until you are available, by saying: "Maybe you should call so-and-so about that. I'll be available in about three hours if you still need me."

Many writers set aside certain times for writing and other times for handling errands and details of daily life. If mornings, for instance, are your sacred times for writing, postpone all other tasks until the afternoon. Or if your writing time is after the kids are asleep at 9 or 10 P.M., take care of everything else before they go to sleep.

2. **Have a sense of humor about interruptions.** You will be amazed at some of the subtle and manipulative ways people will try to distract you from your writing. Unless you learn to have a sense of humor about interruptions, they can take on too much importance.

For example, when your romantic partner or your children interrupt you by saying, "Oh, I'm sorry—I didn't realize that would interrupt you," you might as well laugh. Don't punish the innocent or those who love you too much to let you spend time away from them. Appreciate the strange ways people have of saying "I love you" or "I need you." But do make sure these people know what they have done and that it must not happen again. Having a sense of humor doesn't mean letting people walk all over you.

Many writers have learned to live with interruptions. Clive Cussler, who wrote *Cyclops*, *Deep Six* and *Raise the Titanic*, claims that in his home the interruptions are so unstoppable that "The little Dutch boy with his finger in the dike faces better odds than I do. Being one who writes at home and lives with his wife twenty-four hours a day, the interruptions are constant. However, since I am such a marvel of consideration, I muddle through. I'm also deluged by phone calls, phone calls, phone calls—from my agent, editor, accountant, etc. I simply have to cope."

Stephen Birmingham, who wrote *Our Crowd, Certain People* and *The Rest of Us*, agrees. "Having begun my writing career in a busy New York advertising agency, where interruptions from telephone calls, fellow workers, sudden summonses to meetings, etc., were a routine part of the day, I can cope with interruptions and they do not bother me at all."

Recently I taught a writing class for adults at UCLA Extension in Los Angeles. One of the participants told me: "I actually need a little chaos and disruption in order to write my best. If I'm alone in silence, I get anxious and blocked. But if there are kids playing in a nearby room or workmen pounding on the new addition to our home, I feel more like writing."

I myself have gotten into the habit of laughing silently to myself whenever the phone rings, someone knocks on the front door or an earthquake rumbles the furniture around me. The more I laugh at how these interruptions always seem to come at the moments when I'm most intent in my work, the easier it is to not panic and to get back to my writing.

3. **When interruptions occur, keep their impact to a minimum and ease back quickly to your writing.** Sometimes the key to dealing with distractions is to know how to get back into the rhythm of your writing without wasting too much time lamenting the interruption. For example, if your dog starts barking, you may want to see quickly if there's something important you need to deal with. If there isn't, simply go back to your train of thought without spending a lot of time getting angry at the dog for being noisy.

How do you submerge yourself in your writing again once you've been brought to the surface by a distraction or interruption?

Different writers have different techniques. Some take a short walk or stare into space until they begin to daydream creatively and lose touch with mundane concerns. Others look at a photograph or a drawing of the image or setting they are writing about, and thus enter the feelings and memories of that imagined situation. Still others become submerged again by meditating, relaxing or taking a quick nap.

A technique that always works for me is to wash dishes. That may sound silly, but the warm water has a soothing effect and the accomplishment of completing a dish or two gives me momentum to start writing again. Even if it doesn't help your writing, it certainly will give you a clean kitchen!

Some writers find that taking themselves out of a stressful environment and writing in a peaceful location is the key to becoming submerged. Novelist Shirley Conran tells how she finished a book despite the best efforts of her loved ones to distract her: "People you love tend to resent your attention not being focused on them, so I go away to a hotel or a friend's house the last two weeks of work on a book." Even then, Conran gets tested by her loved ones. "My husband telephoned me at my friend's house to report that my two sons were killing each other (there were even loud background yells). I rushed home to find peace reigned, white wine waited, Vivaldi played. *I went back to the friend's house and finished the book.*"

4. **Use each interruption as an opportunity to preclude the** *next* **interruption from this source.** Instead of becoming irritated each time someone distracts you, see each interruption as a chance to become more creative at ways of overcoming these distractions. Each time the phone rings, your word processor breaks down, or the smell of good food distracts your from your writing, jot down the source of the interruption and brainstorm later on how you can preclude the next one.

If a family member or roommate disrupts your writing with an urgent request (such as the cat getting caught up a tree), you might say, "I'll take care of it this time, but let's make arrangements to make sure next time I won't need to be interrupted." Or if your loved ones start thinking of you as someone who must cater to their every whim, you might say, "I realize you'll be home early for supper, but I can't break away. I've left some lasagna in the freezer for you. Call Aunt Susie if you have any questions."

Think back over the past few weeks, months and years. What has interrupted or distracted you while writing? What could you have done to prevent these disruptions? What can you do right away to make sure these same types of distractions don't occur again? Brainstorm ways to prevent interruptions with other writers or other disciplined individuals.

Rather than feeling victimized or blaming others for the stops and starts in your work, take charge of this crucial aspect of being a creative person. The sooner you become more adept at preventing, coping with and dealing more effectively with these disruptions, the more you will succeed as a productive writer.

GETTING AN OUT-OF-HOME OFFICE

BY ROBERT W. BLY

E conomics dictate that most freelance writers should stick to a home office. Rented offices cost money, and most beginning freelancers just don't make enough to justify the expense.

And for many people, working at home is the ultimate lifestyle—no commuting, no office politics, no dressing up in a suit and tie. But despite these benefits, a lot of at-home professionals (including writers) eventually consider getting an outside office. Here are some of the most common reasons why:

• *A change of scene.* After seven years of staring out the same bedroom window at the same tree five days a week, fifty weeks a year, I wanted a change. But there was no other room in my house I could use.

• *Separate your work from your personal life.* A home office makes that difficult. Clients call during dinner; you get faxes at 9 at night. An outside office affords you more privacy and a place to leave your worries when you come home.

• *No kids.* When my son Alex was born, his crying made it difficult to conduct business over the telephone—his bedroom was next to *my* office/bedroom. When he became a toddler, he wanted to play with me constantly during the day.

• *There are too many distractions at home.* Children aren't the only distraction. If shopping, housework, lawn care, TV and the refrigerator beckon too frequently, an outside office will eliminate these distractions. My productivity doubled when I moved to an outside office.

• *Outgrowing your space.* After my tenth year as a freelancer, I had almost ten times as many papers in my files as I had in my first year in business. I had a lot more equipment, too.

• *Clients visit.* Meeting clients in a rented office doesn't disrupt your home life and keeps the presence of pets, children and friends from creating an unprofessional setting.

• *Hire a staff.* Hiring a full- or part-time secretary or

researcher requires another workspace. Your home office may be too cramped. And your spouse and children may object to the invasion of privacy.

• *Neighbors complain.* This rarely happens, but the fact is that most home-based businesses are run in offices not zoned for business. An outside office in a business district eliminates this concern and protects you from neighbors who want to keep the neighborhood free of commercial enterprises.

Five key factors to consider when evaluating office space are size, location, luxury, type of office setup and cost.

Take the minimum size space that will meet your needs. Don't overpay a larger-than-necessary office to accommodate future growth. If you end up needing a bigger office later, you can always move.

As for location, you want a nice, safe neighborhood, but it probably isn't necessary to be in the heart of the local business center. Offices in suburbs and rural areas are *much* less expensive than office space in major cities. An office close to your home will minimize commuting.

You also don't need a fancy office. One with good lighting, adequate heat and electric outlets should suffice. For me, an office with a window and a good view is also important.

Some of the best deals can be found with converted houses and other small office buildings owned by local landlord/entrepreneurs. Oftentimes these owners are least able to afford prolonged vacancies and will negotiate terms with you to get you as a tenant. If you support services such as typing, faxing and photocopying, consider renting space in a small office suite shared by self-employed professionals. Large office buildings are often too costly, but recent high vacancy rates in some areas of the country have made owners of such buildings more flexible.

Rent the office only if you can comfortably afford the monthly payments. Aim for rent payments of less than 5 percent (and certainly no more than 10 percent) of your annual income.

Don't hesitate to be a fussy buyer and negotiate a lower rental than is advertised or initially proposed for the office you want. Most landlords require a security deposit equal to the first month's rent plus the first month's rent in advance. If they ask you to sign a lease, show it to your lawyer first.

Writing by the Light of the Moon

BY ROBERT W. BLY

I f you're not ready to take the plunge into full-time freelancing, moonlighting is an attractive alternative. Moonlighting enables you to write and earn extra income without the financial insecurity of full-time self-employment. But be warned: In addition to its many rewards, moonlighting has its own share of problems and pitfalls.

Moonlighting allows you to "practice" being a freelance writer before you make the decision to leave your day job and pursue freelancing full-time. It's a risk-free way to decide whether freelance writing is the right career for you. Your moonlighting activities bring in extra income, bylines and clips of published articles. Because you're not dependent on freelance writing for economic survival, you can pick and choose your assignments, fret less over rejections, and enjoy the luxury of writing without the unrelenting pressure to earn a living from it.

There are disadvantages, of course. If you already have a full-time job, you may not be free to attend client meetings, do research or interview subjects during normal business hours. When you come home exhausted from a hard day at the office, and it's a choice between putting in an hour or two at the word processor versus watching *Wheel of Fortune* and *Jeopardy!*, TV frequently wins out.

Okay. Let's say you'd *still* like to try moonlighting. Here are some of the key considerations.

CAN YOU MOONLIGHT?

One question that comes to mind as you think about moonlighting is, "Will I get in trouble with my employer if I work on the side?

The answer depends on your individual situation.

First, discreetly check your employment contract or company policy manual. Don't ask your manager whether it's okay to moonlight. Don't tell the personnel department you're interested in freelancing on the side.

If your contract or employee manual expressly prohibits moonlighting, you could risk being fired by doing so. If your company doesn't forbid moonlighting, but does discourage it, then you have a decision to make: Are you willing to risk moonlighting—and being discovered—if it could result in a reprimand or be harmful to your career?

Analyze the corporate culture of your firm. Perhaps you work at a company where management doesn't care what you do in your spare time. As long as you maintain good performance on the job. If that's the case—go for it.

If you feel your boss would be likely to approve of your moonlighting, then by all means mention it and ask for his or her permission. That way, if someone else in the company objects, you have already cleared it with your immediate superior.

If you feel your boss would disapprove of your moonlighting, but would not take action against you, then go ahead and do it. But don't tell him or her. Again, be discreet.

That brings us to another question: Can you conduct your moonlighting activities discreetly? For instance, you can probably moonlight as a ghostwriter with no one ever being wiser. But if you're writing cover stories for national magazines, sooner or later your moonlighting will be discovered by others in your firm.

There are several other factors that determine whether it's feasible for you to moonlight:

• Do you have enough personal freedom on the job and flexibility in your work schedule to occasionally conduct freelance activities, such as interviewing subjects or meeting with publishers, during normal business hours?

• Can you take an occasional personal day or vacation day and use it to conduct freelance activities? For example, my former boss at Westinghouse uses most of his five weeks of vacation to do freelance work for his outside corporate clients.

• Do you have the time and energy to handle moonlighting assignments during evenings and weekends . . . and are you willing to give up your free time to do so? (You may be saying "yes" now. But many quickly tire of moonlighting when they see others relaxing and having fun evenings and weekends while they work away.)

• Can you find clients, editors and publishers willing to work with you on a moonlighting basis? Generally, this isn't a problem. Some will, some won't. Fortunately, there is more than enough business out there to keep you busy.

- Are you ethically comfortable with the idea of moonlighting? Or do you feel that your are somehow "cheating" your day-time employer? Many companies frown on moonlighting because they believe it tires people and makes them less productive in their nine to five endeavors. Do you agree?
- Can you withstand the stress and pressure of having two jobs?

SPECIAL PROBLEMS—AND HOW TO BEAT THEM

That last question—can you hold down two jobs—addresses one of the biggest problems faced by moonlighters. I've heard several clients of mine complain, "I've hired moonlighters, but when they got busy in their regular jobs, they neglected my work and didn't return my phone calls."

When your full-time work interferes with your moonlighting, it's easy to fall behind on your moonlighting projects. But your writing clients will expect you to meet your deadlines the same as their full-time freelancers do.

The best way to make sure you meet your freelance writing deadlines is to not take on too much work.

I recommend that moonlighters handle only one assignment at a time. Also avoid projects with too-tight deadlines. Full-time freelancers may need to take on many rush jobs at once to keep the cash flowing and pay the rent. As a moonlighter, you probably don't have that pressure.

Another special problem, especially for freelancers handling corporate and advertising assignments, is whether to let clients know you are a moonlighter.

When you're seeking an assignment, there's no need to highlight the fact that you're moonlighting. If the client wants you to perform services at times that would be inconvenient because of your regular job, suggest that meeting or conferences take place after 5 P.M. or during the lunch hour. If a client asks whether you're a moonlighter, explain your situation this way: "Yes, in addition to handling writing assignments for numerous clients and publications, I also have a staff job as a senior writer for XYZ Company." Don't use the term *moonlighter*—which has, for some, a negative connotation. And don't apologize. Treat your full-time job (especially if it's a writing job) as a credential that shows you're the best, rather than a drawback.

Another difficulty for moonlighters is the inability to accept phone calls from your freelance clients during normal business hours. If the calls are infrequent and your company has no objection, you can make a few phone calls from the office during business hours.

Otherwise, give clients your home telephone number and install a phone answering machine to take their calls while you are at work. A remote feature available on answering machines lets you collect your messages while you're at work. Then you get back to clients during a break or lunch.

A more difficult stumbling block is not being free during the day to make sales calls, attend editorial conferences, meet with agents and publishers, interview subjects, visit distant locations or do other writing-related activities that require travel or personal contact.

One solution is to take your vacation time by the day or half-day for these tasks. This is difficult for those with little vacation; easier for people who get three or more weeks per year.

If your employer is flexible about hours, perhaps you can arrange to have some time off during the day, which you make up on evenings or weekends.

OVERCOMING GUILT

You may feel guilty about pursuing freelance writing on a part-time basis. You may feel you're "cheating" your employer by not devoting your exclusive attention to your regular job, or by sneaking out now and then to attend to some freelance writing matters.

Similarly, if you're married or are in a relationship, you may feel you're being selfish when you sit alone to write rather than spend leisure time with your partner. Parents especially feel a strain when their writing and their children compete for attention.

This is an issue you must resolve in your own mind; I can't do it for you. It may help, however, if you set a schedule and clearly allocate time for writing versus other pursuits.

Bill Greene, a promotions writer for ABC-TV, moonlights as a suspense novelist. He lives close to the office, so commuting time is minimal. When he gets home, he writes in his study for two hours until dinner is ready, then spends the rest of the time with his family or just relaxing. Having a schedule and set amount of time for moonlighting, and not exceeding that limit, helps separate work from personal life and prevents guilt feelings.

Conflict with your day job may not be as easily resolved. When I moonlighted, I felt terribly guilty about using the company phone (though most other employees made far more personal calls than I did), rushing out of the office at 5 P.M. to get home and write, taking an occasional long lunch to do an interview, and not devoting myself 100 percent to the company and its business.

I was never able to resolve this guilt. That's why I quit my job and began freelancing full-time.

You have to do what works for you, and this is something that all employed people, not just moonlighters, must cope with. Moonlighters aren't the only employees who occasionally use the office copier for personal copying, for instance; many do. Is this acceptable? Your behavior must conform to the personal code of ethics that makes you comfortable.

MOONLIGHTER SPECIALS

Your personal interests, energy and ambition will dictate the types of writing projects you tackle as a moonlighter. But there are certain assignments that are better "second jobs" than others.

The rule of thumb: The less contact the assignment requires with other people, the better.

The rationale is simple: The responsibilities of a full-time job or raising a family make it difficult for moonlighters to attend to writing-related tasks during everyone else's regular business hours. I discussed ways to minimize this concern earlier, but the best approach is to avoid the situation as often as possible.

If you're a magazine article writer, look to how-to, service, informational, confession, humor, personal observation and other articles that can be written from firsthand knowledge or library research. These articles don't require interviewing subjects, most of whom are available only during daytime hours.

Interviews, profiles, celebrity bios, investigative journalism and other types of articles requiring extensive interviewing, travel and research are difficult to handle when you're a moonlighter tied to a desk job from nine to five.

The same goes with books. How-to, reference, humor, popular science, history, children's, business, computer and fiction are easier for the moonlighter to do than biography, current affairs, investigative journalism, exposé, social issues and similar research-intensive books that may require a full-time effort.

If you're freelancing for business and corporate clients, the best projects are ads, brochures, sales letters, direct mail packages, audio-visual scripts and other short copy assignments. These can be handled primarily by mail and phone, with perhaps only one or two meetings with the client.

On the other hand, annual reports, company newsletters, executive speeches, computer manuals and other lengthier assignments requiring a lot of interviewing, meetings and back-and-forth contact are more difficult.

THE BASICS OF MOONLIGHTING

The only *real* difference between a moonlighting writer and a full-time writer is the number of hours each must devote to other tasks. Once the moonlighter sits down to write, he or she operates in essentially the same manner as the full-time writer. The rules for dealing with publishers and agents, clients and sources, accountants and tax collectors don't change according to the number of hours you log at the word processor.

If there is a difference, it's that moonlighters need much less work than full-time writers to keep busy—or pay the bills. Moonlighting novelists may have the luxury of polishing a book longer before turning to its sequel. Article writers may push aside a few luke-warm ideas in favor of topics that truly excite them.

Many moonlighters do no marketing or selling at all and are busy just from the requests that come in "over the transom." Perhaps you get occasional requests to handle moonlighting projects from people who know you are a writer. If you accept such assignments, and inform these people that you are actively seeking more freelance projects, you may get all the work you can handle just from referrals and word of mouth.

If your company deals with printers, ad agencies, graphic arts studios, public relations agencies, trade publications and other such vendors, these vendors could be potential clients for your—or, if you feel there would be a conflict, you can at least ask them to recommend you for writing assignments to others they know who might need a freelance writer.

If your full-time job dictates you keep your moonlighting activities quiet, make sure a vendor will keep your request for work or referrals confidential. Other traditional methods to generate assignments—query letters to magazine editors, book proposals to agents and publishers, sales letters to potential corporate clients—are not subject to public scrutiny and thus are ideal for moonlighters.

Avoid marketing techniques such as print advertising, networking and telephone selling. These make your moonlighting activities extremely visible and may get you into trouble.

And *never* reply to a blind help-wanted ad in the hopes of getting freelance work from the advertiser. Once I replied to an ad that read "Ad Agency Needs Freelance Writer for Special Assignments." It turned out to be the ad agency that handled all the advertising for the company for whom I worked as advertising manager.

THE BEST QUESTION

How much extra money can you make as a moonlighter? It depends on how well you are paid and how much you can do.

If you want to write a book, be aware that the *average* advance for a first nonfiction book or novel ranges from $5,000 to about $7,500. And it can easily take a year of moonlighting to complete the book. So, your earnings for that year would be equal to the advance. Future sales may result in additional income from royalties, but don't count on it: The majority of books don't earn back their advance.

How about article writing? Say your get $600 per article and can moonlight two articles a month. That's an extra $1,200 per month in your pocket. (*But* article payments can begin as low as $5, depending on where you sell your writing.)

Freelancing for ad agencies, corporations, PR firms and other corporate clients will bring a somewhat higher rate of return. Let's say you write audiovisual scripts and get $3,000 per script. If you do one a month, that translates into earnings of $36,000 a year—enough to improve your lifestyle considerably.

For more information on pay rates, see the "How much should I charge?" section of *Writer's Market.*

TRADING NIGHT FOR DAY

If moonlighting allows you to "practice" being a freelancer before making the break to full-time writing, when do you make that transition?

There's no ideal time. I'd say do it when you have enough money in the bank to live for one year, have three or four steady clients (magazine editors, corporate clients or book publishers), and feel you could earn enough to live on if you devoted yourself to freelancing full time.

Of course, you might choose to *never* leave your day job. Just because Tom Clancy quit the insurance business after *The Hunt for Red*

October ensured his future does not mean the moonlighter must eventually become the full-timer. Poet William Carlos Williams never quit being a New Jersey physician, for instance.

People moonlight as writers for all sorts of reasons. Maybe you are looking to sock away some extra income for a child's college education, or find the cash to add a room to your house, or satisfy the itch to see your name in print, or publicize a cause that's important to you, or . . . well, *any* reason is a good enough one.

Once you couple that ambition with the energy it takes to go back to work at your keyboard after you come home from the office, you'll have all that is necessary to be a successful moonlighter.

Which Is Better, Getting Paid by the Week or by the Word?

BY ART SPIKOL

I f you've ever thought about getting a job as a writer—I'm talking about a full-time position where you get paid to write and actually take home a regular salary—you're not alone. Practically every writer has, although freelancers are far less likely to want jobs than spare-timers. (By way of definition, most of those who consider themselves freelance writers are really spare-timers who write in their spare time doing something else full-time.) Having a full-time writing job is, for the most, The American Dream, writer's style.

Well, I've had several writing jobs, and I've learned that there are several ways to break in:

1. Don't want the job.
2. Be in the right place at the right time.
3. Go after somebody else's job.
4. Work for free.

(This list is incomplete but not by much.)

I am not talking only about jobs in publishing, but the broad spectrum of jobs that involve writing—including some you may not respect. It's easy to be a snob and say you would never take a job working for anything less than *The Atlantic*—but we all know that's a lie, and therefore, as a service to our less fussy readers, I'm writing this column with the idea in mind that at least some of you may be willing to work at just about any kind of writing job, if only someone would offer it.

I remember my first writing job (I must admit that my employers didn't consider it such), which was writing the weather forecast for the now-defunct *Philadelphia Evening Bulletin*. I was seventeen, fresh out of high school, and the *Bulletin's* management thought I was just another copy boy. But I knew better. When I would ride home on the Frankfort elevated after a hard day's work and watch my fellow passengers reading page one of the *Bulletin*, I knew they were reading the weather. And I had tough competition: Those were the days of the McCarthy Army hearings.

Now, it may seem that there could not have been much creativity in such a job, but again I knew better. A job is what you make of it, and it was amazing how many ways you could take the weather bureau's mundane description of upcoming events—for instance, "partly sunny today"—and really make it sing.

There was, for instance, *partly cloudy today* (after all, if it was partly sunny, what was it during the time when it wasn't sunny? Right!), *somewhat overcast today, mostly clear today, some sunshine today, chance of cloudiness today, partially cloudy today,* and more. I felt like I had all the adjectives and adverbs in the English language to play with. And it paid $32 a week.

I learned a lot on that job, as I have on most jobs I've had, so I recommend a job highly. Whether you need one or not. Today I prefer not to have one, but that's because I am finished learning what a job can teach. Besides, I like working out of my home and other habits few bosses will tolerate. I can roll out of bed and into a pair of jeans and into my office. On goes the stereo. Up goes the coffee. On goes the computer, glowing warmly at me . I do not pretend that a job can compete with such advantages. But it took the jobs to give me the track record, the self-discipline and the ability to do a lot of writing in a short time. No matter how you cut it, a freelancer's deadline is not the same as the deadline you have to meet on the job. Freelancers have more time, more space. They get paid by the job, so nobody cares if it takes them a hundred hours. When you're pulling down a salary, however, you get paid even when you goof off—and somebody's going to make sure that every minute is accountable.

As I said, a good training ground.

What can you earn? First of all, there's no point in talking about starting salaries, because they're whatever the traffic will bear, so we'll limit our figures to what you can expect after a couple of years of proven performance. Second, it depends not so much on what you do as where you do it. For instance, a decent advertising copywriter in a major metropolitan area these days can command a salary of $25,000 and higher; a heavy-weight with lots of TV experience can get $55,000 or so. In a small community, most often much less. And in New York, the numbers are off the wall—two or three years experience will get you $40,000, a few more years up to $75,000 to $80,000. And group heads or creative directors earn between $125,000 and $200,000. Says a friend of mine who works there, "Win a Clio and you can write your own ticket—you can zoom from $30,000 to $90,000 in one day."

It's easy to put advertising down, but I've never found a better arena in which to learn how to say exactly what needs to be said in as many words as it should take to say it. And once you're used to slanting for specific markets, other kinds of writing come easy.

Naturally, it's tougher to break into advertising than other writing positions, because while creativity is important, experience and track record are paramount. It's understandable, what with ad space in some publications selling for tens of thousands of dollars a page and TV time going for six figures per minute: Those ads had better work. So there's a premium not only on the jobs, which are highly competitive, but also on who can come up with the persuasive, the memorable. You may think you can do it, and maybe you can, but before you'll get a chance to sell somebody else's product, you'll have to sell your own. And that's *you*.

That kind of money for writing is rare outside of advertising unless you can break into TV or movie scriptwriting. So if you go to work for a national magazine, you're going to make some decent money (all of this is relative, of course, but bear with me), but when people say the money's better in advertising they mean that there are far more ad agencies than publications. Try to leave a $45,000 job in publishing and you'll quickly find your options limited; try it in advertising and you'll probably find another job in a few weeks. (Also, quantum leaps in salary are always more likely to occur when you leave one job for another.) If you work at a city magazine, and the city happens to be a major one, you can figure on a salary from the thirties to the mid five-figure range. In a somewhat smaller city, you can figure on about two-thirds of that. And if you're in a small city, you're a captive audience, totally exploitable. It figures: Small-city magazines have fewer readers, which translates into lower ad page rates, which means less income.

NETWORKING PROGRAMMING

To get a job in anything, networking works best. It goes like this: You have a friend who works for the kind of company you'd like to work for, or a friend who has a friend. You try to pull every available string, call in every marker, so that the next time a position opens, you get an interview. Not only that: You're also highly recommended. It's the best way to walk through a door, and it's why some people join organizations—to get to know some people who can open those doors.

(Sounds a lot like joining a country club in order to sell insurance? It is. *C'est la vie.*)

But not everybody can have well-placed friends, and maybe you'll have to try for a job the old-fashion way—by answering an ad. The problem then becomes, how do I separate myself from the masses?

Well, sometimes you don't. If you don't have what it takes to land the job, if your reach exceeds your grasp, as the cliché goes, don't waste your time. But if you think you have something unique or particularly suited for the job, even if you're not qualified in every area, you're only out a stamp. Go for it.

Of course, you'll have to offer proof that you can do the job. In any writing job, that proof is usually offered in terms of prior work. And even if you don't have the specific experience they're looking for, don't forget that writing is a particularly transferable skill.

Somebody looking for a PR writer for the health-care field, for instance, would be crazy not to be interested in a writer who's written for the scientific or medical press. Conversely, an editor looking for a writer or associate editor for a health-care publication probably wouldn't mind speaking with a good PR writer with a strong interest in and sensitivity to those fields. There's a lot of crossover writing.

But there's also a lot of prejudice. A magazine editor might frown upon somebody with a background in PR writing. So if you get that far, you can frown on it too—just say you've been dying to get out.

Naturally, you'll custom-tailor your resume so that you sound ideal for the job. But how about the cover letter—the first thing the recipient will see?

I've been on the hiring end a great deal, and I will tell you that there's no formula. It's not uncommon for a good help wanted ad to pull eighty to one hundred responses, and, because nobody wants to conduct eighty to one hundred interviews, there's a weeding-out process involved. If your resume doesn't cut it, if you know you're much better in person or in your samples, now's the time to be a writer. Write a knockout of a letter, one that will make the case your resume fails to make.

There are no rules regarding this, but you can't go wrong assuming that you have about three seconds to capture someone's interest—and the longer the letter is, the more formidable the task of reading it. So say it good and say it fast. If you can write a letter so short—and so powerful—that it can't help but be read, that won't go unnoticed. At least, not by someone who's looking to hire a writer.

A guy once wrote me that kind of letter. It was four words long. It said, "I can flat write." That was all it said, but in those four words it told me that this was a guy with courage, who knew the effectiveness of brevity, and who knew his way around words. It reminded me, in a sense, of what a jazz musician might say: "Sure, I can play Bach. But when I want to communicate, this is what I do." That four-word letter was far better than his resume, but he got the interview—and the job.

It's like ad copy. Only the product is you.

BACK TO SQUARE ONE

At the beginning of this column, I referred to four somewhat unorthodox ways of getting a job in writing.

You may have thought I was trying to be funny. Well, I was. But serious, too.

Let's go back. I said, *Don't want the job*. It is, in fact, just about the most effective way to get someone to hire you. People who don't want jobs almost always have the upper hand: Suddenly, the interviewer becomes the interviewee. "You don't want the job? Why? What's the matter with us?" It's true; ask any freelancer—because they're usually the people who are offered the jobs and don't want them.

You see, anybody who can sustain a career as a freelancer is not only good, but also dependable. Now, that's what every employer wants—quality and dependability. So it's not unusual for freelancers to be offered jobs. They almost always turn them down, but some allow themselves to be seduced. And some of them even last for a while.

This is a roundabout way of saying, If you want a job, prove yourself as a freelancer, and then make 'em beg.

Next, *Be in the right place at the right time*. Easy to say, you figure, but how do you know what the right place is? Well, the right place is any place where they have a need for writers. You may have to take the wrong job to be there—for instance, you may go to work for a magazine and find yourself working as a receptionist or the person in charge of the classified ads—but the idea is to be there, make friends, and gradually let people see what you can do. If you have talent and you're willing to push a little, it'll be recognized.

Next, *Go after somebody else's job*. This, too, is easier said than done, but you may see articles or columns being written that you know you can write better. Prove it. (And remember, if you think a piece of writing isn't up to par, it's probably annoying the hell out of an editor, too.)

Finally, *Work for free*. This is for the very young because it appeals primarily to those who have no fiscal responsibilities. Try to get an internship or an apprenticeship. Run an ad: "I'll do free research, typing, etc., for writer or editor in return for hands-on experience and training." Call an ad agency, a cable TV network, a newspaper, and offer your time. I've seen careers grow out of internships.

Do these really work? Sometimes. Whaddya want—a guarantee?

When to Quit Your Day Job

BY DANA K. CASSELL

J ust about every writer who's sold an article or a story has day-dreamed about writing full-time. A lot of us have even chucked our day jobs and tried to make a go of it. Unfortunately, many part-timers find themselves unable to make the transition to self-supporting, full-time writing.

Sometimes they fail because of lack of preparation; more frequently they simply fail to follow their plans.

My own personal experiences—which reflect those of a couple thousand other writers I've met while serving as executive director of a freelance writers' network—convinced me that a successful full-time freelance writing career demands both ability *and* attention to a variety of critical technical concerns.

ABILITY

You wouldn't undertake a cross-country auto trip without first knowing how to drive and having an able vehicle. Likewise, before going full-time it makes sense to have some assurances that you're a sufficiently capable freelance writer.

Note that I used the adjectives *capable freelance* writer and not *great* writer. Successful, money-making, full-time freelancers are not neces-sarily the best writers around. They *do* have the ability to target read-ers with appropriate material, and to communicate effectively with those readers.

Unfortunately, there's no "writer's license" test to tell you when your skills are equal to the challenge of the full-time route. But there are criteria you can use to test yourself.

Some hopeful full-timers hone and evaluate their writing skills through staff jobs with newspapers, magazines or corporations before freelancing seriously. If you can satisfy your readers and superiors in a writing-related job for a few years, you should feel secure in your ability to communicate well on paper.

Many of us simply learn by doing. I remember my own early freelance days, when I was "becoming a writer." Whatever *Writer's Digest* said to do that month is what I wrote—until the next issue came out and I tried *its* suggestions. The sales were sporadic at first, as I learned, tested my skills in the marketplace and refined my material. Then, after five years with a total of twenty-one freelance sales, I suddenly sold twenty-eight manuscripts during a single year. The following year I maintained the pace, with thirty-two additional sales. It was during that year I felt secure enough about my ability to consider writing full-time.

Writer Christine Adamec (*The Encyclopedia of Adoption*) decided to make her move after she started selling magazine features on a regular basis. "When I always had an assignment to work on, so there wasn't any down time, I realized I could actually use the word *writer* to describe myself. Once I'd overcome that hesitation to think of myself as a writer, I was able to go full-time. At that time I was selling at least two or three magazine features a month."

As critical as it is to communicate effectively with readers, you also must be able to target those readers with appropriate material. Rare is the writer who is kept busy solely from assignments initiated by editors. Sure, once editors learn you are available full-time and thus more likely to be able to meet short or emergency deadlines, you can expect a few more phone calls. Consider those assignments the gravy—they're a bonus for your writing business, not the basis for it.

Your day-to-day, routine meat-and-potatoes work will result from the query letters and proposals you send to editors. Therefore, you must feel secure in your ability to submit the right ideas to the right publications at the right time—most of the time. No writer scores with *every* idea the first time. But you at least need to be able to make a hit often enough to produce adequate income to stay in business.

And that rule is absolute regardless of the field you write in.

Measuring your ability according to these factors only tells you if you're equipped to meet the challenge of full-time freelancing. Whether or not you can make the transition successfully will depend on how well you follow your plan—allowing sufficient time for such technical concerns as marketing, administration, production and study. These "part-time" tasks will make or break you as a full-time writer, so let's discuss each one in detail.

MARKETING

Marketing can be defined as selecting, selling, advertising, packaging and delivering goods or services. It is critical to your success. Without it, even the most eloquent writing will sit in a desk drawer unread.

When I discovered this basic truth, I went from a writing hobbyist to a full-time writer. As I've already described, my part-time efforts were varied, with sales ranging from children's short stories to greeting card verse to women's nonfiction to business articles.

When I decided to get serious about my writing, I started with the "selection" phase of marketing and analyzed my sales up to that point. I listed each sale according to type of material (puzzle, juvenile fiction, trade journal article, women's article, etc.). Then I compared the number of ideas queried in each field, and the number of go-aheads or assignments in each field. Next I compared the number of manuscripts submitted in each field, and the number of sales in each field. By comparing ratios, it was apparent that my natural "market" was the trade journal field; it was there that I needed the fewest number of queries mailed to generate the most go-aheads received, and where I earned the highest manuscript submission to manuscript sale ratio. Therefore, I concentrated on the trade journal field when I went full-time.

You may not *want* to specialize in a single subject or market area, but at least give the idea serious thought. Virtually every full-time writer I've known concentrates in one or two areas. Jackie Lynn, a full-time business magazine freelancer, told me if she were to begin her writing career over again, "I would be more focused. For a while I couldn't decide what I wanted to do and I'd flitter from one thing to another. Once I made up my mind that I couldn't write absolutely fabulous short fiction, and really good business articles, and the Great American Novel, *and* a how-to book all at the same time, I became more productive and my income went up."

When you focus (or concentrate or specialize) your writing in one, two or even three areas, several benefits result:

• You have a better chance of reusing your costly (in terms of time and money) research. A hobbyist can afford to spend sixteen hours and several dollars researching a piece just because it's interesting, but the successful full-time professional uses that research to write and sell additional related articles—raising her overall dollar-per-hour-invested rate. I like to call this "making your research earn its keep."

- Editors soon perceive you as an "expert," and give you more assignments. One editor assigns me at least an article every year on a security topic. While I sent her several queries over a period of many months on that subject years ago, I never did score with one of my ideas. But—and this is why specialization can pay off—she called *me* when she later wanted one of her ideas on a related subject written. My concentration in several business subjects (security, marketing, retailing) has also led to assigned article series—even one seven-article supplement.

- Because you soon build comprehensive reference/source files in a specialty field, future writing in that field will be easier and faster—and, therefore, more profitable. For example, I'd already written and sold more than a hundred articles on retail advertising/promotion when I proposed my book, *How to Advertise and Promote Your Retail Store.* Not only did this experience help me get the book contract, it made writing the book a breeze.

You don't need to resign yourself to *only* writing about one subject for the rest of your career. That's boring. Writing about something different, or trying a new writing field once in a while, keeps life interesting, forestalls writer's block, and can even lead to unexpected profit centers.

The success secret is to concentrate at least 80 percent of your efforts in your proven field(s), then experiment with, or test new fields with, up to 20 percent. Periodically reexamine your ratios, and you'll note declining subjects and markets *before* they become cold, as well as spot new ones to pursue while they're still hot.

I've already mentioned the importance of making the most of one's research and material by slanting, reslanting, reworking and reprinting.

When you get into reslanting and reselling, you soon realize that your income-per-hour is more important that your income-per-sale. This is another concept that separates most part-timers from full-timers. It's easy, when writing is an avocation, to look solely at how much money an article will bring from a particular magazine before submitting it.

But the successful full-timer looks further than the numbers on the check. When you only have a limited number of hours in a week to meet your income needs, the number of work hours it will take to earn a particular fee becomes as important as the amount. A $100 payment for a reprint that takes fifteen minutes to submit pays a better hourly wage than does a new $800 article that takes twenty hours to research and write (with attending research costs). For this reason, the full-timer considers *total* income potential before tackling any project.

I've spent a chunk of space here on marketing because it's so important. I used to tell workshop audiences that effective marketing was 90 percent of writing success, but no one wanted to believe it so I dropped back to 80 percent. (But it's really closer to 90 percent for most full-time writers.)

ADMINISTRATION

Attention to the administration side of business also takes on added importance when you become a full-time freelancer—a fact that dismays many "creative" types. It's unusual, in fact, to find a writer who welcomes recordkeeping and other administrative chores. Full-time magazine writer David Kohn says, "A business really consists of two parts: One is doing well what you do; the other is running a business that does well doing what you do. I think I write well, but I'm still learning a lot about running a business, and I don't know that I'm a natural entrepreneurial type. It's always difficult to be a business person if you're not naturally inclined that way. Unfortunately, it's also a necessity."

Certainly, maintaining records to keep the IRS happy is necessary and important for all income-producing writers. But the full-time writer is a small-business owner and must "manage" the business in addition to selling and writing.

Among the administrative or management areas of concern are planning, time management, purchasing, maintenance and financial management.

Each management area could fill an article of its own; in fact, several general small-business management books are available on each of these topics. It's a good idea to keep a few current ones near your desk for study and reference, but we can touch on some of these topics now.

Planning covers everything from tomorrow's schedule to annual marketing plans. Once you've worked out goals and a sales strategy, you know how many queries, proposals, brochures or whatever to send each week or each day. you also will need a production plan: How many articles, stories, outlines, scripts, etc., are you going to work on or complete each week or each month?

Writers who have been squeezing in writing hours among regular jobs, household chores and family obligations often enter full-time life figuring they'll now have all the time in the world. *Beware this trap!*

Too much time often leads to procrastination and *less* productivity than a busy part-timer might achieve. So time use is an important management area. The full-time writer usually has more control over working hours, and can consider the "inner body clock rhythms" when scheduling different kinds of work.

Management of those work hours becomes especially critical when assignments pile up and that scheduled forty-hour week stretches into fifty—even sixty or more—hours. Thus, you need to employ the basic time management principles:

- Consolidate similar tasks (correspondence, phone calls, filing, errands).
- Tackle tough, important jobs first.
- Delegate to family members, job-hungry high school students and independent contractors certain tasks (such as stuffing/labeling, breaking down long-distance phone records, typing/word processing, interview tape transcriptions, household chores).
- Decide which paperwork can be streamlined or eliminated.
- Log and analyze time use.
- Establish priorities.
- Maintain energy with exercise breaks, appropriate foods, proper lighting.
- Streamline mail handling and telephone techniques.

When writing income is used to pay for life's necessities, and not primarily the extras (as part-time writing income frequently is), the administration of that income achieves new prominence. Purchases of equipment, supplies and maintenance contracts take additional planning and study. The chore of managing an unpredictable income can make or break the full-timer fast.

PRODUCTION

This is our actual business: producing articles, stories, books, ad copy, video scripts and so on. Therefore, a significant portion of our time must necessarily be spent on production. (I'll pass on my recommendations shortly.)

If you frequently run up against writer's block, or consistently miss deadlines as a part-time writer, those syndromes will not disappear when you go full-time. If anything, they will get worse when the stress of unpaid bills or the crunch of several assignments mounts.

To be successful, the full-time writer must juggle the research of six or eight different projects, the writing of five or six drafts in varying stages of completion, possibly two or three photographic sessions, plus the polishing and submission of three or four additional projects—all in the same week. It helps to be organized; the disorganized "creative" type sometimes runs into problems.

While I stressed earlier the importance of becoming "known" in a few subject or skill areas, most writers I've watched succeed as full-timers have kept their options open. Wise use of that 20 percent experimental writing I suggested can make a big difference.

Because I talked to so many business owners and managers while researching business articles, plus specialized in articles on advertising/promotion, it wasn't long before I was approached to write ad copy, brochure copy and public relations material.

While I've never pushed to make this a major portion of my writing business (I prefer to write articles and books), it has provided quick money when needed, has led me to new business sources, and has stimulated new article or book chapter ideas. Plus, I appreciate some variety.

Joseph Straub knows firsthand the value of reserving some production time for "different" kinds of work or clients. "For over a year I edited a management newsletter, which was wonderful work. The pay was great, but with one phone call management canceled the newsletter through no fault of mine, and bam, I was out of a job. That one experience taught me to never, ever rely on one client or one field. I like to keep my options open."

From these examples, you can see how, to the successful full-time writer, production means more than meeting a few deadlines. It includes scheduling the different components of production to maximize time use, plus deciding *what* to produce so as to keep current clients and editors happy, as well as preparing for future business needs. Most of all, it requires assuming the posture of a "communicator with words" rather than that of solely an article writer (or whatever).

STUDY

The most successful full-time freelancers I know are the first to attend seminars and conferences, read books on writing, and generally keep learning. Study *is* a very important tool.

There are always bad writing habits to spot and break, and good

272 *The* Writer's Digest *Handbook of Making Money Freelance Writing*

ones to pick up; new fields to explore and consider; and other writers to share experiences with and learn from. The more established a writer becomes, the less he or she usually learns from seminar speakers, but the more benefits spending a day with other writers can offer: from "brain-picking" about methods, markets and contacts to simply finding rejuvenation outside our solitary offices.

Over the years, I've accumulated an extensive library of books and tapes targeted to writers. Their main value to me has been as motivating tools: reading a couple of chapters a day, or one book a week, or listening to a tape while exercising or washing dishes does more to energize my creativity than educate my brain. And for the full-time writer, *that* can be more important. Some writers judiciously schedule writing seminars for this very reason; whenever their spirits begin to sag or the office walls begin to close in, they will use a seminar as a B-12 shot.

Likewise, virtually all full-time writers I know read several writers' magazines and newsletters—always keeping on top of the latest market information, publishing trends, new areas to possibly pursue and so on.

SCHEDULING

How in the world does a person cover all these areas? With scheduling.

While every situation is different, a basic starting place for planning is to allocate your time and energy in these proportions:

Marketing—25 percent
Administration—12½ percent
Production—50 percent
Study—12½ percent

This is only a starting point, a rule of thumb. If your full-time business will consist of two or three novels a year, you may decide to reduce the marketing and administration percentages, while increasing the production—and maybe emphasizing the study a bit more. Or, if your business is largely high-fee direct mail copy, you may need to allocate more time to marketing and less to production.

Okay, so now you've completed your preparation and you know you're ready to make the jump to a full-time career. Will you succeed?

I've watched enough people go from beginners or part-timers to successful full-timers over the past nine years to offer an enthusiastic "Yes, you can . . ."

But, during the same time I've also watched a good number try it and not make it. So I temper my enthusiasm with ". . . but it isn't always easy."

You need to take a long, hard, honest look at yourself and your situation. Will you carefully lay out and closely follow your plan? Do you have the ability to communicate effectively with readers and to target those readers with appropriate material? And do you have the financial cushion to carry you through the dry spells?

Yes?

Congratulations.

Is It Time to
Quit Your Day Job?

BY LAWRENCE BLOCK

Dear Geoffrey,

I enjoyed our lunch the other day, and, as always, I enjoyed the conversation. Since then I've found myself thinking about some of the things we discussed. I find myself moved to write to you. I also find myself facing a deadline—it's time to write this month's column. A single stone ought to do for both birds; with your indulgence, and my readers', I'll write my column in the form of a letter to your estimable self.

As you'll recall (though it will be new information to the eager multitude of readers), at lunch you recounted some of your recent successes. An article placed here, a short story sold here and anthologized there, another story nominated for a major award in its genre, and a book just published and well received.

Then you went on to mention a letter you had lately received from a novelist friend. He too had been apprised of your recent successes as a writer, and he had some advice. "Geoffrey," he wrote, "it's time for you to quit your day job."

Don't quit your day job, of course, is what a musician says to let another musician know he thinks he's of less than professional caliber. Your friend was telling you that you are indeed ready to join the pro ranks; beyond that, he was saying that the crutch of steady employment was one you no longer needed. Once it had helped keep you steady on your feet, but now it was only slowing you down and holding you back.

But, you went on to say, you had thought it all over and decided you were not about to quit your day job. Full-time freelancing was definitely something you wanted sooner or later, but you were not ready to take the plunge, not just yet.

You spoke of rent increases, of the cost of putting children through school, of all the thousand financial ills that flesh is heir to.

And I've been thinking about our conversation ever since.

There are moments when the answer seems very clear to me. "He's absolutely right," I'll say to myself. "He should keep the job. Among other things, it enables the man to *enjoy* writing. He gets home from the office, he plugs in his word processor, and he's as happy as a buffalo in chips. If he didn't have an office to go to, if he had to start each morning by facing the high-tech equivalent of a blank sheet of paper, he wouldn't be so sanguine about it. Anyway, security's not the worst deal around. Assuming that discontent is inevitable, part of the human condition, isn't it better to be discontented with a steady income than discontented without it? Better to be gainfully employed in an engaging profession and wishing you were writing full-time than hacking away day and night and wishing you had a steady paycheck coming in?"

Another day the opposite answer will seem every bit as self-evident. "He's sick of the damned job," I'll tell myself, "and he's learned as much as he can learn from it and gone as far as he can go with it, and now it's only hobbling him. He's waiting for a perfect time to quit, a safe time, and there is no such thing. You can't step safely into freelance writing. The place is an economic lion's den. Insecurity comes with the territory. But he wants to be sensible and responsible, and he wants to look like (and even to be) a good father and family man, and in the process he's letting his life slip by and missing out on what he really wants to do."

Most of the time, however, I'm not so sure. After all, I rarely know for certain what *I* should do, so where do I get off making major decisions for other people?

Still, the question demands consideration. Most of us at least start off doing something else for a living, launching our writing careers early in the morning or late at night or on the weekends. Most of us dream of quitting our day jobs, and very likely wonder whether we've held onto the thing too long or let go of it too soon.

In my own case, it took no particular courage for me to begin writing full-time. I started publishing fiction while still in college, and by the time I left I had a publisher who was eager to take a book a month from me. This may sound like guaranteed wealth, but in fact it was hardly that; the fellow paid me $600 a book, or $540 after my agent's commission, and this is not a great deal of money now and wasn't great wealth even back then.

Still, it was a living. More to the point, it was at least as much as I could have been confident of earning by any other lawful means. I had left college without a degree, and had never held anything but a menial position, and there was really not a great deal that I was qualified to do.

As you can see, there was an obvious dollars-and-cents argument for my writing full-time. But dollars-and-cents considerations are rarely the primary determinant. The writer's temperament, it seems to me, plays a greater role.

Two contrasting examples spring to mind, both of them writers of thrillers. First let me tell you about a fellow I've known for years. When I first met him he was a couple of years out of college with a graduate degree in history. He was newly married, living in Manhattan and employed as the slightly underpaid editor of a trade journal. He had recently become friendly with several novelists, myself among them, and decided that he liked the life the rest of us appeared to be living. (He only saw us at parties, at which time we tended to be carefree and drunk, so he very likely thought we were like that all the time. Which, come to think of it, we pretty much were.)

He had never tried writing anything before, but he put his mind to it and came up with what struck him as a good idea for a book. Then one Monday morning he called in sick and started writing, and he kept at it all day. He did the same thing Tuesday, and Wednesday, and on Thursday he called the office again and told them he was quitting. He stayed at his desk five or six days a week for the next six or eight weeks, and at the end of that time he had finished a book.

Well, it was terrible, but that's beside the point. He went on to write a second book, which was still unpublishable but was light years ahead of the first effort. And he wrote a third book, and that one sold.

And he has been writing and publishing ever since. Not

without misadventure—there was a stretch when nothing went right and several books in succession went begging, and he had to take a bartending job. But that was just a bad patch, of the sort to be found in most writing careers. The fact remains that he had managed to go from a standing start and make of himself a published full-time writer in a matter of months.

My contrasting example is an even more successful thriller writer who began publishing while teaching at a large university. While his first few books did not make him rich, his sales increased sharply, and a couple of movie sales boosted his income dramatically. His agent was soon urging him to quit his day job, as it were, especially in view of the fact that he had no deep and abiding love for teaching but had been staying with it because it was steady and secure.

And he had a great deal of difficulty letting go of it. Writing part-time, he was making a healthy six-figure income, yet he found reasons to hang onto his professorship. "I'm not sure I should let go of this," he told a mutual friend. "You know, they've got a really good medical insurance set-up here."

I suppose a big factor in this equation is just how comfortable you are with risk. I don't think there's any way to make freelancing altogether risk-free. Even the writer just mentioned, with his high income and his receptive market, could not ensure against the possibility that his creative well might run suddenly dry. As a tenured professor, he could count on a lifelong good income so long as he showed up each day, whether or not he came up with anything inspiring to say to his classes. But writers don't get paid just to show up. They have to produce.

There is no particular virtue in being comfortable with risk; indeed, the world is awash in degenerate gamblers who are distinctly uncomfortable without it. It's true, though, that we're always much quicker to applaud the person who takes a chance than the one who plays it safe. The studio audiences at television game shows always cheer for the lady who gives up the washer-dryer to go for what's behind Curtain Number Three.

It must have been more than thirty years ago that I read an article in *Writer's Digest* by Richard S. Prather, creator of Shell Scott, surely the greatest of the soft-boiled private eyes.

Mr. Prather wrote of his decision to quit his job and give writing his best shot. He had realized, he wrote, that nobody starves to death in America, and so he'd set up housekeeping in a trailer and kept at it until, miracle of miracles, he'd written and sold a couple of books.

Nobody starves in this country. That impressed me enormously at the time, and I rather suspect that I've been a little more of a risk-taker for having internalized this bit of wisdom. I don't know that it's as true as it was thirty years ago; the throngs of homeless people on the city streets suggest that, if people don't literally starve to death, some come rather closer to it than I would care to. Still, I know dozens of people who have supported themselves solely and exclusively by writing for a substantial number of years, and none of us have missed meals or been forced to sleep on the subway. Almost all of us have done without things we would have enjoyed having, and almost all of us have gone through times when the wolf was encamped on our doorsteps. And, while I have no hard data on this, it seems to me that almost all of us would do it all again.

Ah, Geoffrey. My conclusion—and it was probably a foregone one—is that I don't know whether or not you should quit your day job. How could I know? How could anyone know but you yourself?

There are, God knows, reasons beyond security for holding onto a job. Some writers go nuts without the human contact that regular employment provides. Some of us draw input from our daily work that enriches our writing. Some of us are freer to take risks in our writing because we've elected to play it safe vocationally. (When I'm tempted to congratulate myself for my daring in setting out as a freelancer, I have to remind myself how long I went on doing sure-thing formula paperback fiction for $600 a book. That was the day job that I had trouble walking away from.)

When all is said and done (and it certainly seems to be), the only advice I'm comfortable giving you is that you do what you want. Not what you *feel* like doing. Not what you think you *should* do.

Good luck with that—whatever it turns out to be.

Proving You Can Pay the Freight

BY SUE FAGALDE LICK

One of the challenges of being a writer is proving that you work for a living. Bankers, landlords and government agencies often look at writers as free spirits without jobs—they're creative, but you can't trust them to pay the rent. Since many people don't understand writing is a business, we have to be prepared to prove it. Documenting our employment status may be among the most important writing we ever do.

You'll likely encounter the most questions when applying for a home loan. Bankers look for consistency and dependability. They want to see a spotless credit record that shows you always pay your bills and aren't overloaded with debts. They also want to see that you make enough to consistently stash some money in the bank. Suddenly pouring a large amount into your account to impress the loan people won't work.

Tax returns can be the trickiest part. As a self-employed person with no tax withheld from your checks, you and your accountant will usually try to decrease your net income by pumping up your expenses. But that's the wrong face to show if you want to buy a house. You may have to take fewer deductions and pay more taxes for a couple of years so that your returns will show a profit.

Mortgage broker Debbie Moore suggests using a blank Schedule C, the federal income tax form on which business income and expenses are reported, to estimate for a loan officer what this year's figures will be. If possible, include letters from editors with whom you have contracts to prove that money will be coming in. Consistency is important. If you show yourself suddenly making $50,000 more this year than you averaged the past two years, the loan company will suspect you're making it up. Growth is good, but be realistic.

In the home loan business, says Chuck Castagnolo, a loan

underwriter for Home Federal Savings, applicants are pieces of paper, not people. Everything needs to be fully documented and provable, so that any one of the many people who see those papers can read the story they tell. "It has to be a complete story," he says.

Your credibility as a professional can be scrutinized in other financial situations, too. Gregg Levoy, author of *This Business of Writing* (Writer's Digest Books), has found some landlords reluctant to rent to freelancers because writers' incomes fluctuate.

Levoy admits he sometimes slightly inflates his monthly income on his rental applications. "It's a small ethical slip that I'm willing to endure in order to have a home," he says. He puts down a figure that reflects one of his more profitable months, knowing that he can't make any promises about his future income. However, he can show that he has paid off every past financial commitment. "I know that I'm always going to pay the rent," he says. He also lists his occupation as *journalist* on rental applications, instead of *writer*. "It strikes me that journalist sounds more stable. Too many people envision a writer as an artist starving in a garret."

Credit cards, car loans and personal loans may also require writers to prove their financial status. Credit history and two years of tax forms will be called up as proof.

Tony Sing, a credit card officer for Wells Fargo Bank, says self-employed applicants generally need to have been in business for at least three years. (Businesses less than two years old are expected to lose money.)

When applying for personal loans, your debt-to-income ratio is considered. An individual should not be paying more than 40 percent of his or her income to outstanding debts.

If you haven't been freelancing for at least two years or don't make enough money to support yourself, you probably have some other source of income, whether it's a working spouse, a full- or part-time job, or a contract to produce newsletters, reports or articles. Use whatever you've got to prove your credibility.

If you're planning to make the leap from a job to full-time freelancing, prepare in advance by getting credit cards, loans and insurance established while you still have a regular paycheck to back you up.

Once you're out on your own, giving yourself a company name can help, says Louisa Rogers, a freelancer who frequently gives seminars on magazine article writing. Even if "Jane Smith Associates" consists of Jane and the kid who types envelopes once a month, it *sounds* impressive.

Attitude counts for a lot. "What you say doesn't matter so much as does the fact that you act confident," Rogers says. If your career is in the early stages, you can still act as if you're a pro. "The more you convince yourself, the more you convince the world."

Bring Your Writing Up to Speed

BY HANK NUWER

I t's a sad fact of the writing life. Many magazines pay the same fees they did in the good old days—even though the cost of rent, food and living has long since shinnied upward. The ever-shrinking dollar has created two categories of writers: the quick and the dead-broke.

In tough economic times, it's the prolific who survive. If you're free-lancing full-time, you must take on lots of assignments to make a living.

I'm no exception—especially now that I have a kid at college. I wrote two books and more than twenty articles last year. I'll match that total this year. And in past years, when I haven't had a book to write, I've completed as many as forty magazine assignments.

I'm hardly alone in my productivity. Magazine journalist Louis Bignami has cranked out more than twelve books and ten thousand articles since turning to full-time freelancing in 1969.

"I try to do six 2,000-word articles a week," says Bignami, who sees the key to financial success in calculating dollars *per hour*, not *per word*. "I have discovered that a couple of $150 articles a day are easier to produce than a 2,500-word piece for a major market that might pay $1,000 but takes a week plus field time to write."

My vanity, however, demands that I frequently see my byline in national magazines—even if writing fewer pieces reduces my annual income. But I share one quality with Bignami: I've become a speed writer. After all, I can't afford to spend a month on a piece that pays $250. And I'd make my accountant unhappy if I spent a month on any single piece, even if it paid $2,500.

It's not easy writing several articles per month, but it *is* possible to make a living writing if you think and act fast. If you've been snoozing, you've been losing. Follow these hard (and fast) guidelines, and get your writing up to speed.

LOG IN THE HOURS

You must acquire what Atlanta writer Gloria G. Brame, co-author of *Different Loving*, calls a "slave drive mentality."

I personally work ten to twelve hours daily (I'm up at 4 A.M.), five days a week, and put in between two and eight hours on weekends. Twice a month I take a weekend off like "normal" people do. Still, I'm a backsliding hedonist compared to Brame. She works seven days a week, for at least a few hours, and her workday begins in the late evening and ends at dawn.

Are *you* working as hard as you must? Keep an hourly log and ruthlessly assess how you spend your time. You must keep regular and consistent hours, absolutely refusing to succumb to distractions. "Keep in mind that however minute is today's contribution, in the long run it will pay off," says Brame.

CRANKING COPY

There are many reasons writers self-detonate when they need to write fast. Some struggle with the framework of every piece, thus turning their hourly rate to about what they'd make by tending bar. Some disappear in the quicksand of research. Others are unwilling or unable to juggle more than one project at a time.

If you often have trouble getting started, take comfort in knowing that every writer has frozen occasionally when it came time to sit and deliver. Fortunately for most of us, an encroaching deadline is enough to set our creative juices flowing. "Frankly, I think terror is what helps one write nonfiction quickly," confesses Brame. Or, as Arizona-based writer Diana Gabaldon puts it, "You don't overcome the fear of writing—you just write anyway."

Thus, the only secret to turning out copy is . . . to turn out copy. "Crack that blank screen with something," advises Christopher J. Galvin, former associate editor of *CompuServe Magazine*. "If it doesn't fit once the article's done, try something else."

For Jennie Howard, my former editor at *The Saturday Evening Post*, that *something* on the screen is a quotable quote. Her personal method of giving her freelance articles an instant structure is to scan her interview transcripts and pull out the best quotes she can find. Then she'll string these quotes throughout the pages she's allotted to the assignment.

"Oh, that one sounds good near the beginning," she'll say. Or, "I definitely want to close with that one."

Voilá, the screen is no longer virgin territory, and therefore no longer terrifying. And great quotes are sparkling to read, informative and loaded with personality.

As Howard proceeds, she'll rearrange, paraphrase and even delete many of these direct quotes. But by then she's in high gear, and the quotes long since have served their purpose.

For me, an outline accomplishes the same purpose. I not only print a copy of a detailed outline to tape above my computer, but I also use one as an icebreaker. When it's on the screen, it provides a framework for the article I need to write. In effect, once it's done, I simply fill in the blanks on the outline.

To fill those gaps, I organize my thoughts with the aid of file folders I study the outline and consciously divide the piece into sections. I assign a key word to each section and type that key word on a label which, in turn, I slap onto a file folder. My research and the transcripts from interviews then go into these folders.

ONE-MINUTE MANAGING

My method here is similar to the system Gloria Brame uses to organize her material. We both first gather our pages of transcripts. Ordinarily, wading through all that verbiage can be time-consuming and may even produce panic attacks in the uninitiated. To make all that material manageable, it's essential to excise what you don't need.

Take a highlighting marker and strike through the interview questions, redundancies and digressions. (Keep an extra file on disk, and you can accomplish the same task on your computer and print a clean copy to work from.) This done, your vast amounts of transcript material become far more usable and bite-sized, says Brame.

Now take your scissors, cut apart the interview, and place sections pertaining to one another in the appropriate file folders. It doesn't matter if you have material from a half-dozen interviewees in the same file as long as you always know who's speaking. While transcribing, I mark every quotation with the initials of the person speaking (*GB* for *Gloria Brame*, for example).

Arrange the files in roughly the order you expect to insert them in your outlined piece. Keep them at hand as you write.

I use the same system to organize the pages of my photocopied research. I break them down and add them to the file folders, too. Once all that material is neatly packaged, it's no longer quite so daunting.

Don't be alarmed if you use only a fraction of your interviews and research. And don't try stuffing this unused material into your piece until the article resembles an exploding suitcase. If you've done your job, you'll always have stuff left over. "I estimate that I ended up using only one-third of my interview materials and roughly half of my research," says Brame of her book *Different Loving*, a serious study of out-of-the-mainstream sexual practices.

LEAD ME NOT INTO PROCRASTINATION

One of the most daunting hurdles a writer faces when trying to jump start a piece is the lead. It's too easy to become bogged down in the search for the perfect opening. Galvin admits that lead writing is, for him the hardest part of writing an article. His solution: "Pick the anecdote, quote or example that caught your attention most during the research, write it and *move on.*"

No one can write an engaging lead (or article for that matter) without knowing the target magazine's concept and audience, adds Galvin. In addition, you must communicate with the person assigning you the piece to make sure you don't begin researching and writing without a clear and genuine article focus. "Your editor should give you one, so ask for it by name," he says.

Dominick Bosco, a former *Prevention* senior editor and author of *Alone With the Devil*, says leads frustrate him, as well. When not on deadline, he's been known to spend two hours writing the first half page of a short piece, even when the rest of the article requires only another three hours. Not something a "fast writer" can afford to do.

"Skip the lead and come back to it later," says Bosco. Once the bulk of your article is safely on disk, you'll be able to fiddle with your lead without the added burden of wondering whether the rest of the piece will be equally slow to materialize. Having 80 percent of the article already done is a great confidence booster, he adds.

And first writing the bulk of an article sometimes leads to a *better* opening than the writer might otherwise have concocted, Bosco says. A lead gives a ready promise that certain expectations will be fulfilled in an article. Once the writer knows *precisely* what's coming in the rest of the piece, it can become easier to phrase that promise properly.

No matter what order you arrive at them, once your piece has a decent lead and the skeleton of a body, it's time to flesh things out. But there are some pieces that never seem to sing—they always sound like a rough draft, even after several time-eating revisions. Gloria Brame suggests paying attention to the style and tone of an article at these times: Are they consistent from start to finish? Go over the piece with a fine-tooth comb, searching out (and correcting) any glaring errors and flaws in thinking.

At this final stage, it's also important to purge repetition and tighten all transitions. See if your piece has any questions that still need answering. At this time you should phone your sources if you need additions or clarifications. Don't pray that your editors won't notice. They will—to your detriment.

And since accuracy is a characteristic of all professional writers, you must eliminate typographical errors and double-check all spellings— especially the names of sources. (Hint: Even though I create on a computer, I print a hard copy to proofread before sending a manuscript to an editor. Things slip past me on the screen.)

DEALING WITH DEADLINES

If you're going to be turning out a great deal of material, you must successfully contend with deadlines. Yet some writers, particularly those without newspaper backgrounds, find that they write well *until* a deadline stares them in the eye; then they freeze.

Russell Wild, an oft-published health writer and co-author of *Boost Your Brain Power*, says he's taught himself to calmly accept the frequent deadlines he faces as a Rodale Press senior editor. He insists that playing "mental tricks" on himself helps him defeat the tyranny of deadlines. "I convince myself the deadline is sooner than it actually is," says Wild, who boasts that he's rarely handed an editor a late piece. "I give myself false (early) deadlines . . . and it works."

Some writers sit on assignments too long, and then find themselves paralyzed as their due dates stalk them. Not Wild. "I can't stand to work furiously right before a deadline," he says. "I work furiously my first day on an assignment. When my deadline comes, I can go into my home run trot as I approach the plate."

Dominick Bosco tries to mitigate the pressure attached to a single article deadline by giving himself multiple deadlines *within* that deadline. "A trick I use is to break a piece into bite-sized chunks," he says.

Thus, if he's procrastinated until a deadline arrives and must write ten pages by the end of the day, thinking about the unstarted piece as a whole tends to intimidate, he says.

"Instead, I say to myself, 'Okay, I will write three pages before lunch,'" says Bosco. That task done, he can eat without stress and give himself another three-page deadline before he allows himself to collect his mail. Then he'll set another three-page deadline before he can leave his computer to eat supper. When he comes back, he will finish the remaining page and then go back over his article to polish it.

I do virtually the same thing, but I'm a little more positive about it. I don't play tricks on myself—I take more bribes than a Chicago alderman.

"Just finish one page by lunch, and you can have a cup of coffee," I tell myself. "Finish four pages by lunch, and you can eat that bean burrito you're craving. Make your deadline by 5 P.M., and you can go to the gym to work out and relax in the hot tub." If that's simplistic, so be it. Whatever works, says I.

Bosco, Brame and I all agree that the secret of a book author's productivity is to break every chapter of a long manuscript into similar chunks. "What really helped us was establishing lots of realistic interim deadlines," says Brame about her co-writing of *Different Loving*. Without such deadlines, she and her two co-authors tended to relax too much, and the project floundered.

BRINGING EQUIPMENT UP TO SPEED

Some writers never become speedy because they fail to take advantage of new technology. Maybe it was true years ago that all a writer needed to succeed was a typewriter, but technologically advanced editors like Galvin don't take computerless writers seriously. In short, if you're not computer literate yet, you're a functionally illiterate writer. And if you *do* compose on a computer, you should teach yourself at least one new computer function a week, just to stay even with cyberspace-cadet competitors who've teethed on Nintendo.

Even the mechanically impaired (like me) have no excuse. Visit the placement office of your local technical college or put ads in Help Wanted sections until you find a qualified computer whiz willing to come to your home on an "as-needed" basis.

If I can do it, you can do it. It took me a long time to master my word processing program. But through sheer doggedness and force of will, I've become conversant with software functions that help me instantaneously cut, splice, store, edit and so on.

Handing in a typewritten manuscript is, in some markets, as unacceptable today as a handwritten manuscript would have been in 1963 (the year I sold my first article to a Buffalo newspaper, at age sixteen). Since 1990, I've received book contracts that *require* me to submit the completed text on a disk, along with the manuscript copy.

Magazines, too, have joined the age of technology. All my submissions to *CompuServe* are sent electronically by modem. *Pennsylvania Angler* won't even read queries or manuscripts sent on paper.

But I'm glad the markets compelled me to take my Underwood to the dump. My IBM-compatible machine has easily quadrupled my previous output. A computer makes multiple submission of query letters (with necessary adjustments mandated by each market) a breeze. It allows me to restructure an entire book with just a few keystrokes, moving thousand-word blocks of text in a fraction of the time it used to take me to scissor apart a manuscript and reformat it with transparent tape.

"Word processing means saying good-bye to that less-than-perfect liquid correction goop which, in some cases, can ensure your manuscript's final resting place in the deep-six file," says Galvin.

In addition, computer-mediated communications on big networks like CompuServe give writers fast access to a wide pool of contacts that could otherwise only be obtained by cold-calling experts whose names you've gathered in time-consuming, traditional ways, says Galvin. By way of example, for this piece I electronically contacted Gloria Brame on CompuServe's Literary Forum, an on-line clubhouse inhabited by hundreds of poets, authors and other reputable scribblers.

For past articles I've contacted experts in forums devoted to such diverse interests as health and fitness, sex, tropical fish collecting, genealogy, gardening and journalism. On-line networks allow me to send questions to as many interviewees as needed via electronic mail. The respondents type their answers and zip them back, "essentially providing a transcript without your having to put it together," says Galvin. For practical and ethical considerations, if you've contacted someone on-line whom you don't know personally, it's standard procedure to confirm your electronic interviewee's identity and reliability with a follow-up phone call, cautions the editor.

IS YOUR HOME OFFICE BUILT FOR SPEED?

To make money you need to spend money—on equipment that will free extra hours to write. My home office, for example, is outfitted with every time-saving device that I can justifiably write off on my taxes. Seven metal shelves are filled with office supplies. They flank my five filing cabinets, my bookcase filled with reference books and my bookkeeping station. The copy machine keeps me from driving eight miles to the nearest print shop every time I submit receipts. My computer and modem allow me to do research from my chair and even submit pieces electronically—as some magazines now require, not simply recommend. The fax machine has bailed me out innumerable times. (In fact, I faxed this very article to *Writer's Digest* during the Blizzard of 1993, when my local post office shut down.)

I also make sure my office has minimal distractions. There are no windows for me to gaze out longingly. I keep a pitcher of ice water or pot of coffee at arm's length and drink from a no-spill, lidded cup. The answering machine screens all calls (sorry, Mom), and a sign on my door warns trespassers that "survivors will be prosecuted." I enter my business related receipts daily so that they don't accumulate and overwhelm me.

If you're not as well organized, look no further when placing the blame for your lack of output. Says Brame: "The keys to completing a project are goal-setting, discipline and exacting organization."

Remember, though, that one of the main reasons you became a writer was that you thought the job would be fun. While it's necessary to take on lots of work, never bite off so much that you begin to regard what you do as drudgery.

"Treat every project like an adventure," says Brame. But make sure it's an adventure in success.

How to Chart Your Path to the Best-seller List

BY RUSSELL GALEN

When Lou Aronica headed up Spectra, Bantam's science fiction and fantasy imprint, I sent him a manuscript. I knew Lou at the beginning of his career when he was the assistant to another editor to whom I'd sold some westerns. The manuscript was a first novel by someone who'd gotten a bit of attention in the magazines.

Lou called me up quickly and started firing questions about the author. How old was he? Did he have a job? If so, was it a lifelong career or merely something to keep bread on the table over the short run? What were his next four or five books going to be about? How long did it take for this man to write a completed manuscript? Where did he want to be ten years from now as an author?

I answered all the questions and then said: "Excuse me, Lou. Did you like the manuscript or not?"

"Of course I liked it," he said. "The guy is brilliant—you know that."

"So, are you making an offer for it, or what?"

"I'll make an offer when and if I'm convinced that this is an author for whom we can build a master plan for the future."

And I said to myself, this guy is going to go far. (He has. Lou's now vice president and publisher at Berkeley Publishing Group.) Most editors think only of the book that's being offered: Will it or won't it sell? But the smartest of them are interested in finding authors, not just books. They know that the biggest successes come from long-term master publishing plans that stretch over many books. (Incidentally, Lou liked the author's ideas for future books and was impressed by his plan to quit his job one day and write full-time. I wound up selling him the novel plus the author's next three books.)

If you're an author who is not already highly successful, whether you're on your first or your twentieth book, understand something right now: You're a risk—probably a big risk. These days a book must sell a *lot* of copies to make even a small profit, and the odds are that unless you have a guaranteed blockbuster, your book is going to lose money.

So why should a publisher even give you the time of day? Because, unless your cover letter begins by saying, "By the time you read this I will have thrown myself off the Brooklyn Bridge," *you have potential.* Who's to say, no matter how modest your achievements are, that your next book, or your ninth, won't be the book that is so successful that it will put all three of that publisher's kids through college? Just as the bomb squad must view every paper bag as a potential bomb, the publisher must view every author—and I mean *every*—as a potential star.

This point of view has been rising dramatically in the past couple of years, as midlist, modest-selling books drop in sales and the industry becomes more blockbuster obsessed. This is because blockbusters are hard to find. An editor might get lucky and have Stephen King decide he wants to leave his publisher and come with him; more often, he must grow his own stars, find beginning authors with potential and then groom and develop them. More and more editors now understand that if they want to be successful ten years from now they'd better start looking for the authors who'll be successful ten years from now, not just the ones who are successful now.

Which brings us to you. Where will you be ten years from now? If you don't know the answer to that question, you need a master plan— a sense of where you want your writing career to go so you can make decisions based on whether your actions bring you closer to or further from that goal. A complete guide to forming a master plan for your own career follows, but it should be easy to understand the basic idea: You should start thinking not just in terms of "How do I get this current project sold?" but "What steps should I be taking now that eventually will get my work on the best-seller list?"

You don't really need to know about all this if you *just* want to get a sale. But you do if you want to be very successful one day, partly because having a master plan is your best bet at being successful, and partly because the editors with long-term visions are the ones who can take you to the top and thus the ones to whom you most want to sell. You won't get them interested unless you learn to speak their language, and learn what they're looking for and how to convince them that you're it.

Before you start building your plan, let's go over the ground rules these editors follow in what I like to call Long-Term Land.

GALEN'S GUIDE TO LONG-TERM LAND

The word "inexperienced" isn't the pejorative in this language that it usually is. Remember that in Long-Term Land, there are only three states of being: on the rise, successful and washed-up. If you're not already successful, it's far better to paint yourself as on the way up rather than as having had your shot and blown it. Thus, while you might ordinarily be tempted to bloat a resume and make yourself out to have been around a while, that will backfire here. The writer with twenty unspectacular book credits looks not like a solid pro, but like someone who has already peaked.

Of course, if you *have* been around a while, all is far from lost: There are other ways around this problem. Even the most cynical editor realizes that it can take some writers a long time to hit their stride. Authors like Martin Cruz Smith and Marion Zimmer Bradley published scores of paperbacks and were around for decades before finally producing the hardcover best-sellers (*Gorky Park* and *The Mists of Avalon* respectively) that made them famous. Great manuscripts, aggressive agents and imaginative, open-minded publishers made it possible. The point is that Cruz's and Bradley's track records were obstacles to be overcome; you must understands this and be careful of the way you describe your track record.

Similarly it's better to be young. I'll be blunt and tell you, at the risk of offending or disappointing some readers, that I'm nervous about taking on a new client "of a certain age," unless, of course, he or she is already highly successful. It's hard to tell an editor with a straight face that a 60-year-old is poised to take off on a brilliant career; again, it does happen, but it's hard to get an editor to believe it. Even if the older writer does become successful, how many years does he have left during which he, I and his publisher can reap the rewards?

Of course, I'll take on and sell a truly good book by an author of any age even if I don't believe a big breakthrough is coming. And there are many editors who are blind to this issue (and most of the others I'll be discussing). But for the best editors, being fifty or older is a negative, though not an insurmountable one. If your book is just so-so, I might take it on if you're a promising newcomer, but not if you're a old-timer. Long-Term Land is like the beach: Being young helps.

Understand that these editors are buying you, not just your

manuscript. They want to be convinced that you are dedicated to becoming successful; that you have more than one book in you; that your present work is better than your past work, and that your future work will be even better; that you're looking for a publishing relationship, a long-term home for your work, and not just a deal. Learn which of your qualities are assets in Long-Term Land and emphasize them; learn which are negatives and de-emphasize them.

Don't boast that you can write a novel in eleven days, as one writer did to me recently, when an editor is looking for evidence that you take pains to make each book as good as it can possibly be. Don't boast that you always meet your deadlines, when that is far less important to editors than evidence that you strive to make each book better than the one before. Don't mention that you're sure the book you're working on now is going to be a hit, when we really want to hear that you're aiming so high and thinking so grandly that, far from being cocky about your success, you're scared to death you might fail. Don't tell the editor that you're not devoted to, but are merely dabbling in, the genre of your present submission. (What romance editor, for example, looking for writers who can be built into stars, is going to respond to a letter from a mystery writer saying, "I thought I'd give this genre a whirl, just to get a break from my regular stuff"?)

Don't be afraid to reveal that inside you is a seething, fiery core of ambition and lust for success that would appall Napoleon.

DRAWING UP YOUR BATTLE PLAN

Michael McQuay isn't out to rule France, but he is an ambitious writer. After writing and selling—without an agent—his first five science fiction novels, Mike sensed that something was wrong with his career. He knew he was good, but his sales didn't really show it. There was no growth, no sense that things would improve if he'd just hang in and keep writing.

So he came to me and we hammered out a master plan. While his story is still far from its ending, it is far enough along to illustrate some basic points about your own master plan.

It isn't any easier or quicker to become a successful writer than it is to become a brain surgeon. Kids in their first year of medical school don't whine to their professors, "When do we start making some real money, sir?" They know they have ten years of schooling ahead of them first. Writing a successful book isn't any easier than slicing away at people's cerebrums, and it takes just as long to learn how to do it right.

I'll give you the same warning I gave Mike: It will be five years before you see any results from the plan at all, and ten years before you achieve our goal.

Andrew Carnegie's advice for becoming wealthy is important: "Put all your eggs into one basket and then watch that basket." I studied McQuay's writing and determined that his strength was in his savagely powerful characters and strong story lines. Therefore, mainstream suspense fiction, which showcases these same elements, was going to be the field in which he would one day make his stand. From that moment on, every choice we made, every new story he created, was designed to further his reputation in this one field. He still wrote science fiction at that point because that's where the easy sales came for him, but his science fiction became increasingly contemporary, increasingly realistic, less farfetched and exotic. He gradually would move over to writing exclusively mainstream suspense fiction.

There's not much overlap between groups of readers. Romance readers don't read westerns; thriller readers don't buy biographies and so on. So if you're bouncing around doing many different kinds of books, you're reaching different audiences with each book. Individual readers aren't staying with you from book to book, forming a loyalty to you; they're reading only the one book you've written for them, and then abandoning you. By contrast, if you stay in the same field, readers in that field will be reading two, three, four books by you in a row, and becoming loyal fans.

By building on this core audience, you can create momentum. With each new book, you only have to find a small group of new readers in order to have sales figures that are going steadily up. Let's say that a new book can, with luck, find 100,000 readers who had never before heard of the author. If each new book is in a new field, it must find 100,000 brand new readers every time—and if you slip up even once and sell only 55,000 (which will happen sooner or later), you're seen as someone whose sales are going down, a loser, a has-been. But if you stay in the same field, your second book is going to be picked up pretty much automatically by the 100,000 readers of your first, if it's any good. Thus, you must find only, say, 50,000 brand-new converts in order to have a dramatic increase in your sales. If your new audience base of 150,000 gets you 80,000 new converts for the third book, your new audience base of 230,000 gets you 120,000 converts for the novel after that, and so on, it's not going to be long before you're selling in the millions.

Decide in advance what kind of writer you want to be, and then bend every effort toward making it in that one field. It's no disaster if you need a little variety now and then and want to do a different kind of book, but you should have a home base.

You can't execute a master plan alone. It's essential that your agent and publisher think in terms of your long-term future and share your hopes and dreams. If your editor feels he has no future with the company, or if your agent is planning to quit as soon as she finds a husband, or if your agent or editor simply can't think beyond tomorrow, you're with the wrong person. Such people—and they are *the most common type,* so keep an eye out for them—will discourage you from doing what's best for you if it makes this week easier for them.

Now is not the time to take it easy. I want to stress here that a master plan involves far more than cranking out books that hew to some secret formula. More important than all my little points is that you do the work of your life. Mike did. Each book was better than the one before. If the plan had an editorial effect on Mike's work, it was in the tremendous level of inspiration that it supplied him. He felt as if he were working not just to fulfill a contract and get the latest advance, but to achieve something of vast scope, to make a ten-year plan a reality.

It's like the difference between having sex just to have sex, and having it because you're trying to make a baby. As all parents will attest, there's something unforgettably intense about the latter, a sense that all your energy is going to create something significant. The first book Mike delivered after we began to work together, *Memories,* was a hundred million billion times better than anything he'd written before, and won some important awards and got a lot of attention. The critics started writing reviews like "Who is this guy?" and "From a completely unexpected source comes one of the best novels of the year." Part of the phenomenon was McQuay's own discovery of just how good he really was, but part of it, I like to think, came from my whispering "Plan . . . plan . . . plan" into his ear all the time, reminding him that he was working for something Jupiter-size and that there was someone in New York who believed he could do it.

The great goal of your plan should bring great work out of you. Every book must be your absolute best to take you closer to achieving your goal, or it will have the effect of taking you backwards. If you're in the mood to try something goofy, something light, something uncommercial, something dangerous, it would be better to save that for after you've achieved your goals.

What all of this is really about is *building your audience.* Newer writers are cursed by one terrible plague: small readerships, rarely more than six thousand in hardcover, fifty thousand in paperback. Those audiences are too small to make anything happen, to generate the kind of word of mouth you need for a book to become a bestseller. As in atomic physics, these audiences are too small to start a chain reaction—they're beneath critical mass. So you must build your audience, get it to the point where it's big enough to generate word of mouth that will get you an even bigger audience that will generate even bigger word of mouth, and so on. Avoid anything that decreases your audience even for one book, causes it merely to remain steady for one book, or causes it to have only a small rise for one book.

McQuay and I decided that he should stay with his current publisher. As luck would have it, his five previous books had been acquired by Bantam, and his current editor was Lou Aronica (who acquired both science fiction and mainstream fiction). Since we already had precisely the kind of editor we wanted—one who would accept short-term problems and sacrifices if they served a long-term goal—there was no need to think in terms of finding a new home for him.

Momentum is everything. The next part of the plan involved McQuay delivering a new book roughly every nine months. Fortunately, with Aronica and Bantam willing participants in the plan, I anticipated no difficulty in getting sales every nine months. In fact, the first deal I negotiated under the plan was for two books, so that McQuay could begin the second immediately after delivering the first, rather than having to wait for new negotiations, new contracts, etc. After that we did a four-book deal.

Audiences have short memories. They can enjoy a book, buy it in huge numbers, and then, eighteen months later, not even remember the author's name. Nine to twelve months is about the right interval between books; the new book catches an audience that has fond memories of the previous one. This is a very big problem for writers who also hold down full-time jobs, but I'm afraid that if your job prevents you from doing more than one book every two years, there's a much smaller chance you'll ever make enough from your writing to be able to quit that job.

These figures are for paperback originals. It's different with hardcover, because a paperback reprint will appear one year after the hardcover and keep readers' memories of your work alive. I advise most of my hardcover clients to have no more than one new book out every other year.

This involves making each book your very best, with no lapses or detours. And it involves bending every issue to the question of whether it contributes to building your audience. A decision that in any way compromises the goal of building the audience is a mistake, even if it involves a short-term benefit (such as taking a higher advance from a weak publisher that is overpaying in order to build up its list, but that can't distribute its books effectively).

You may also need to make short-term sacrifices in order to further your long-term goals. For example, you might be running low on money when along comes a publisher who needs you to do a quick novel in the Young Nurses in Love series, and he won't let you use a pseudonym. Refuse: Having your name on such a book might make it harder for another publisher to take you seriously. Or you might want to postpone that uncommercial labor of love until later in your career when you can better afford to have your sales figures take a sudden drop. Or you might want to spend some time on a magazine article that won't make you much money but will get your work in front of a new audience, an audience that might then start buying your books. Make your business decisions based on how they affect your master plan.

When you've done all the planning you can do, and laid all the groundwork you can lay, the time has come to go for the Big One. Mike McQuay and I bided our time. Then he came to me one day with an idea for a book that I thought would be a blockbuster. This is the key moment in the master plan. What you have been preparing for all these years—the marketing, selling, writing and publishing of a Big Book.

The problem was that Mike's idea was so much more ambitious and daring than anything he'd ever written that I was afraid no publisher, even his own, would believe he could bring it off. But I knew he was ready, and advised him to write the entire manuscript on spec (that is, without a contract); we would then offer publishers the proven, finished commodity. This involved a spectacular sacrifice for Mike; while working without a contract, his income dried up because he couldn't work simultaneously on his bread-and-butter science fiction projects. Our agency loaned him some money, he took some breaks now and then to work on writer-for-hire projects, and he managed, over a year, to write about 250 pages of the novel plus a 100-page proposal.

This seemed to be sufficient for our purposes and I showed the material to Lou Aronica with a little speech about how our years of working together to bring Mike McQuay along had finally borne fruit. I told him we were going to want $100,000 for it—ten times what McQuay had ever received before. While Aronica didn't say anything, there was that little sound in the throat editors translate as, "You %*$%#%$ agent! Are you out of your *@#%@%* mind?" What a nice sound it is.

Well, Aronica took the material home and read it. He called me, and you know what he said? "You want $100,000 for this book?" And I, getting ready for a fight, said, "That's right, and not a penny less." And he said, "Could I have two for that price?" And that's how Michael McQuay, some fifteen years after becoming a professional writer, became an overnight success with a $200,000 deal.

For the next step in the plan, we go for seven figures.

(Let me be fully accurate here and say for the record that the deal is a complex one in which certain conditions must be fulfilled for the entire $200,000 to be paid. However, the deal still guarantees McQuay a minimum of $150,000.)

IT'S NEVER TOO SOON

I realize that many of you would be happy just to get a sale and may be thinking that it'll be years before you need to worry about any of this stuff, if ever. But even if you're still dreaming about sales, it's not too soon for you to put a plan like this into effect.

There are three reasons.

• Editors look for writers who think this way. Thus, when your chance at that first sale comes, you could easily blow it by answering the editor's questions in the wrong way. If the editor asks "Can you do new books at the rate of one a year?" you must know that the right answer is *Yes.*

• Even at the beginning of your career you're making decisions about what to write, about where to concentrate your resources. You need to make these decisions with your long-term goals in mind because mistakes made at the beginning of a career can take years to undo. If you decide that investigative journalism, for example, is the basket into which you want to put all of your eggs, it's important for you to realize that it's a mistake to begin your career with a romance novel just because you have a shot at an easy sale. You'll be typecast as a romance writer and editors of investigative journalism books may never take your seriously.

• As I'm sure you've already learned, nothing in the world is more discouraging than the early years of a writing career. Having a master plan reminds you that, tough as those first steps might be, they are steps nevertheless; the beginnings of a journey toward a specific destination. The sense that you're working toward something, no matter how distant it may seem, is a hell of a lot more inspiring and exciting than the sense that you're flailing around, collecting random rejection slips. It keeps your eyes on the prize, as the saying goes.

Index

More Great Books for Writers!

1997 Writer's Market: Where & How to Sell What You Write—Get your work into the right buyers' hands and save yourself the frustration of getting manuscripts returned in the mail. You'll find 4,000 listings loaded with submission information, as well as real life interviews on scriptwriting, networking, freelancing and more! *#10457/$27.99/1008 pages*

> **Now Available on CD-ROM!**
> **1997 Writer's Market Electronic Edition**—Customize your marketing research and speed to the listings that fit your needs using this compact, searchable CD-ROM! *#10492/$39.99*
>
> **1997 Writer's Market Combination Package**—For maximum usability, order both the book and CD-ROM in one convenient package! *#45148/$49.99*

Writing for Money—Discover where to look for writing opportunities—and how to make them pay off. You'll learn how to write for magazines, newspapers, radio and TV, newsletters, greeting cards and a dozen other hungry markets! *#10425/$17.99/256 pages*

The Writer's Digest Dictionary of Concise Writing—Make your work leaner, crisper and clearer! Under the guidance of professional editor Robert Hartwell Fiske, you'll learn how to rid your work of common say-nothing phrases while making it tighter and easier to read and understand. *#10482/$19.99/352 pages*

Beginning Writer's Answer Book—This book answers 900 of the most often asked questions about every stage of the writing process. You'll find business advice, tax tips, plus new information about online networks, databases and more. *#10394/$17.99/336 pages*

How to Write Like an Expert About Anything—Find out how to use new technology and traditional research methods to get the information you need, envision new markets and write proposals that sell, find and interview experts on any topic, and much more! *#10449/$17.99/224 pages*

The Writer's Ultimate Research Guide—Save research time and frustration with the help of this guide. 352 information-packed pages will point you straight to the information you need to create better, more accurate fiction and nonfiction. With hundreds of listings of books and databases, each entry reveals how current the information is, what the content and organization is like, and much more! *#10447/$19.99/336 pages*

The Writer's Digest Guide to Manuscript Formats—Don't take chances with your hard work! Learn how to prepare and submit books, poems, scripts, stories and more with professional look editors expect from a good writer. *#10025/$19.99/200 pages*

How to Write Fast (While Writing Well)—Discover what makes a story and what it takes to research and write one. Then learn, step-by-step, how to cut wasted time and effort by planning interviews for maximum results, beating writer's block with effective plotting, getting the most information from traditional library research and online computer bases, and much more! Plus, a complete chapter loaded with tricks and tips for faster writing. *#10473/$15.99/208 pages/paperback*

The Writer's Essential Desk Reference—Get quick, complete, accurate answers to your important writing questions with this companion volume to *Writer's Market*. You'll cover all aspects of the business side of writing—from information on the World Wide Web and other research sites to opportunities with writers workshops and the basics on taxes and health insurance. *#10485/$24.99/384 pages*

Writing and Selling Your Novel—Write publishable fiction from start to finish with expert advice from professional novelist Jack Bickham! You'll learn how to develop effective work habits, refine your fiction writing technique, and revise and tailor your novels for tightly targeted markets. *#10509/$17.99/208 pages*

The 30-Minute Writer—Write short, snappy articles that make editors sit up and take notice. Full-time freelancer Connie Emerson reveals the many types of quickly-written articles you can sell—from miniprofiles and one-pagers to personal essays. You'll also learn how to match your work to the market as you explore methods for expanding from short articles to columns, and even books! *#10489/$14.99/256 pages/paperback*

Writer's Encyclopedia, Third Edition—Rediscover this popular writer's reference—now with information about electronic resources, plus more than 100 new entries. You'll find facts, figures, definitions and examples designed to answer questions about every discipline connected with writing and help you convey a professional image. *#10464/$22.99/560 pages/62 b&w illus.*

The Writer's Digest Sourcebook for Building Believable Characters—Create unforgettable characters as you "attend" a roundtable where six novelists reveal their approaches to characterization. You'll probe your characters' backgrounds, beliefs and desires with a fill-in-the-blanks questionnaire. And a thesaurus of characteristics will help you develop the many other features no character should be without. *#10463/$17.99/288 pages*

The Writer's Legal Guide, Revised Edition—Now the answer to all your legal questions is right at your fingertips! The updated version of this treasured desktop companion contains essential information on business issues, copyright protection and registration, contract negotiation, income taxation, electronic rights and much, much more. *#10478/$19.95/256 pages/paperback*

How to Write Attention-Grabbing Query & Cover Letters—Use the secrets Wood reveals to write queries perfectly tailored, too good to turn down! In this guidebook, you will discover why boldness beats blandness in queries every time, ten basics you must have in your article queries, ten query blunders that can destroy publication chances and much more. *#10462/$17.99/208 pages*

Writing to Sell—You'll discover high-quality writing and marketing counsel in this classic writing guide from well-known agent Scott Meredith. His timeless advice will guide you along the professional writing path as you get help with creating characters, plotting a novel, placing your work, formatting a manuscript, deciphering a publishing contract—even combating a slump! *#10476/$17.99/240 pages*

Discovering the Writer Within: 40 Days to More Imaginative Writing— Uncover the creative individual inside who will, with encouragement, turn secret thoughts and special moments into enduring words. You'll learn how to find something exciting in unremarkable places, write punchy first sentences for imaginary stories, give a voice to inanimate objects and much more! *#10472/$14.99/192 pages/paperback*

Make Your Words Work—Loaded with samples and laced with exercises, this guide will help you clean up your prose, refine your style, strengthen your descriptive powers, bring music to your words and much more! *#10399/$14.99/304 pages/paperback*

The Best Writing on Writing, Volume 2—This year's best collection of memorable essays, book excerpts and lectures on fiction, nonfiction, poetry, screenwriting and the writing life. *#48013/$16.99/224 pages/paperback*

30 Steps to Becoming a Writer and Getting Published—This informational and inspirational guide helps you get started as a writer, develops your skills and style and gets your work ready for submission. *#10367/$16.99/176 pages*

The Wordwatcher's Guide to Good Writing and Grammar—Avoid embarrassing grammar mistakes with this handy volume. Freeman gives hundreds of examples to clarify word usage, meaning, spelling and pronunciation. *#10197/$16.99/320 pages/paperback*

Write Tight: How to Keep Your Prose Sharp, Focused and Concise—Discover how to say exactly what you want with grace and power, using not only the right word, but also the right number of words. Specific instructions and helpful exercises explain and demonstrate the process for you. *#10360/$16.99/192 pages*

Freeing Your Creativity: A Writer's Guide—Discover how to escape the traps that stifle your creativity. You'll tackle techniques for banishing fears and nourishing ideas so you can get your juices flowing again. *#10430/$14.99/176 pages/paperback*
